NOTHING EVER JUST DISAPPEARS

NOTHING EVER JUST DISAPPEARS

SEVEN HIDDEN QUEER HISTORIES

DIARMUID HESTER

PEGASUS BOOKS

NEW YORK LONDON

NOTHING EVER JUST DISAPPEARS

Pegasus Books, Ltd.
148 West 37th Street, 13th Floor
New York, NY 10018

First Pegasus Books cloth edition February 2024

ISBN: 978-1-63936-555-5

10 9 8 7 6 5 4 3 2 1

Printed in the United States of America
Distributed by Simon & Schuster
www.pegasusbooks.com

For Josh Schneiderman

Contents

Introduction   3

1. Egress: E. M. Forster in Cambridge   25

2. Invert: London's Queer Suffragettes   61

3. Excess: Josephine Baker and Paris   107

4. Neither: Claude Cahun's Jersey   145

5. Exile: James Baldwin between America and France   187

6. Utopia: Jack Smith and New York   227

7. Niche: Kevin Killian's San Francisco   269

Epilogue: Sanctuary   309

Notes   317

Acknowledgements   339

Index   343

Front view of Prospect Cottage, Dungeness, 1991, by Howard Sooley.

Introduction

Every room looks queer in a convex mirror – this one de-
cidedly so. The wood-panelled walls on either side are bent
and bowed. The furniture bulges absurdly. Straight lines are
curved and twisted. In its etymology, the word 'queer' is related to 'twist', and similar words like 'contort' and 'distort'.
Objects in this mirror may be queerer than you think.

All of the artefacts in the room – the grandfather clock,
the string of hag stones on the wall, the crucifixes arranged on
the sideboard – seem to congregate around a vortex, albeit an
inverted one. Here, at the centre of everything, is a chunky oak-
wood chair pulled up to a desk, underneath a large window.
The pale light of an overcast afternoon falls onto a single sheet
of paper left on the desk, lines written in a long, elegant hand.
It feels as if the writer has just stepped out.

In his poem 'Self-Portrait in a Convex Mirror', John Ashbery writes of all that is reflected in a surface such as this: 'it
is life englobed'.[1] But the mirror in this room and the room
mirrored in it aren't so much a portrait of me (or indeed of
Ashbery) as they are of the former occupant of this englobed
place: the artist, filmmaker and AIDS activist Derek Jarman.

I have come to Prospect Cottage, this small clapboard
house that clings to a spit of land on the south-east coast of
England, to begin a journey. From here, I will wind my way
through the queer spaces of the twentieth century, the homes

and haunts that have been central to subcultural art, writing and performance over the past 125 years. Few places have been as central or as beloved as this one, so where better to start my wanderings.

Jarman found this small Victorian fisherman's hut in the spring of 1986, while driving around the Kent coast scouting locations for a new film. By that point he had made a name for himself as an auteur of unapologetically queer cinema. Trained as a painter, he fell in with a crowd of London creatives during the 1960s who were much more messy and multidisciplinary in their approach; with their goading he began to stretch himself, turning to costume design, sculpture and finally filmmaking. His films like *Sebastiane* (1976) and *Caravaggio* (1986) are sumptuously over-the-top masterpieces made on a shoestring with the participation of actor and artist friends like Tilda Swinton, Sean Bean, Duggie Fields and Lindsay Kemp.

When he discovered it, Prospect Cottage was a simple, four-room building with a shower and a toilet out the back. It was one of only a few residences located in the arid, inconceivably flat expanse of shingle known as Dungeness, which was also home to two nuclear power stations and a miniature railway visible from the kitchen window. The cottage and its environs lit up Jarman's imagination. Even its name seemed auspicious to him, implying as it did unwritten futures and wide-open vistas, while also connoting comfortable domesticity. He bought the place for £32,000 and moved in soon after.

It was his home for the final eight years of his life, until he died of complications resulting from AIDS on 19 February 1994. In that time, the house and its setting had a huge influence on his style, and inspired films like *The Garden* (1990) and *Blue* (1993), his two volumes of collected journals *Modern*

Nature (1991) and *Smiling in Slow Motion* (2000), and numerous other artistic experiments, including, most notably, gardening. Jarman was a devoted gardener when he was young, and here, in his forties, he rediscovered a passion for horticulture, patiently coaxing bushes and delicate blossoms out of the inhospitable earth. The resulting garden fulfilled his desire to create a place, he said, 'where poor wayward humanity is capable of being swayed by emotions which make for peace and beauty'.[2]

It is peaceful at the cottage on this summer afternoon – beautiful too. The window of Jarman's writing room looks out onto the garden at the front of the house. Bright poppies in orange and yellow have burst forth from the shingle, shivering in the breeze. Bumblebees wind round the red-hot pokers, and blunder about clumps of sea kale clustered here and there. Purple foxgloves spring up on the borders of the makeshift rockeries between the house and the road. A band of grey tarmac with my small, baby-blue car parked by the side of it separates Jarman's well-kept garden from the coast and the wide wild sea beyond. I confess I know next to nothing about gardening, but it's obvious to anyone what an achievement it is to have created such a gorgeous, green refuge in this shingle desert.

I pour myself a cup of tea and, as it cools, wander slowly from room to room, wooden floorboards creaking with each step. Jarman's small studio, its walls lined with books, still smells faintly of oil paint. In the kitchen his iconic blue overalls are hanging casually on the back of the door. His bedroom reminds me of a monk's cell in its austerity – sparsely furnished with a bed and a chair made in the same style as the one in his writing room.

I recognize much of the furniture in the house as the work of Andy the Furniture Maker, a sometime rent boy from Essex with an uncanny eye for proportion whom Jarman took under his wing. I'd known Andy's story and admired his pieces for a long time, but until now I hadn't realized just how intimate he and Jarman were, or how much Jarman wanted to have Andy near him always. Here in the cottage, I understand better than ever the artist's practice and his personality, his interests and motivations (the abundance of crucifixes is a surprise), but, more than that, I've also been able to reflect on my own attachment to the place, what I want from it . . .

The sight of a visitor outside the bedroom window disturbs my reveries. Someone dressed in a denim jacket and khaki trousers walks across the pebbles and between the flower beds. I watch them run a hand over the pieces of driftwood in the garden, and ponder their arrangement. Both of our visits today, mine and theirs, have been made possible by a recent crowdfunding effort to 'save' Prospect Cottage.

After Jarman's death, his partner, Keith Collins, maintained the house and garden for many years, lovingly keeping it as a memorial, exactly as Jarman had left it. When Collins died in January 2020, however, the cottage went up for sale. Jarman's friends and fans worried that if it ended up in the hands of a private owner, it would cease to be what it has been for so long – a place of solidarity and inspiration to many. A kind of secular shrine. The fear was that it would be enclosed, as the commons were enclosed, and that it would vanish from the public map. So a crowdfunding campaign to acquire house and lands for public ownership was launched. Backed by celebrities including Swinton, Tacita Dean and Isaac Julien, the campaign raised £3.5 million within three months to buy the place and maintain it in perpetuity. Prospect Cottage was saved.

It is now managed by a local arts group called Creative Folkestone, who let me into the house earlier today. Visiting Prospect Cottage was part of a larger project I had in mind, which would examine the importance of queer places in the history of arts and culture. It would explore their impact on queer identity and investigate why they seem to disappear so easily. Going deeper, I also wanted to reflect on the special relationship LGBTQ+ people have to space, and the ways in which places have been *queered*, their meanings distorted and appropriated. Underneath it all, I was looking for proof that queerness has a place in a world that has often seemed so inhospitable to it.

Lately, it seems like much of the conversation about queer spaces has been concerned with their disappearance, and rightly so. In 2017, the Urban Lab at University College London revealed the extent to which LGBTQ+ night venues are under threat. Over the course of a decade, researchers found that 58 per cent of London's queer venues closed down: in 2006 there were 125 venues, but by 2017 this number had fallen to just 53.[3] One can only imagine the state of things now, in 2023.

When I've talked with friends and the topic comes up, we tend to agree that *the internet* must be the problem. Forums, social media and hook-up apps like Grindr and Scruff have cut out the need for people to get to know each other in physical spaces; fewer people are going to bars and clubs, so fewer businesses are able to turn a profit. Except that's not actually the case, according to the research. Viability of businesses (i.e. their ability to make money, how popular they are) accounts for only 5 per cent of closures. The biggest factor is actually development: 38 per cent of venues were forced to shut when they were priced out of an area by gentrification and urban redevelopment.[4]

The need for queer spaces hasn't gone away – far from it. One of my friends is a drag king named Orlando, who channels the spirit of the shape-shifting protagonist of Virginia Woolf's experimental novel *Orlando* (1928) with a dandified, androgynous act that was born on the London stage five years ago. When I asked them about their experience, they said that they bitterly lamented the demise of places like the Chateau in Camberwell and Her Upstairs and Them Downstairs in Camden, which had been personally and creatively transformative for them. Venues like these had empowered them and many others to experiment lavishly with gender and sexuality in a safe space, in front of eager and supportive audiences. LGBTQ+ people surveyed as part of the UCL study said similar things, describing such places as essential to a sense of belonging, community, education and history. Their loss threatened to erase or invalidate queer heritage. As one respondent put it: 'Venues shift and change over time, but if they disappear entirely, the LGBTQI community is poorer for it.'[5]

The book you're now reading started out as an attempt to retrieve and reconstruct these places, especially the bars, clubs and performance spaces that have been key to the emergence of LGBTQ+ communities and modern queer identities. But in fact it didn't start out as a book at all. Its roots lie instead in an audio trail (a kind of recorded walking tour) I created of my adopted home town of Cambridge. I'd moved to the city in 2017 after I received my doctorate, to work on a post-doc research project based at Cambridge University. I was supposed to be writing a cultural history of waste, but it was never finished because almost as soon as I arrived, I became fascinated by queer spaces and turned all my attention to them.

What happened was this: I looked around the city and was surprised to discover that there was not a single queer bar under a bridge or a café down a side street, and, as far as I could tell, only one infrequent club night. This couldn't have always been the case, I thought. Hadn't Cambridge once been home to the likes of E. M. Forster, Edward Carpenter and Ali Smith – some of the most familiar names in queer British writing? How could somewhere be so straight in the streets and yet so queer in the sheets? (Of paper, I mean.)

I set myself the task of exploring the queer spaces of Cambridge's past, drawing on the literature created here and conversations I had with older members of the LGBTQ+ community. Piecing together these recollections and fictional fragments, and mapping them along a route through the city, I found that I could conjure up the places I had discovered: the gay disco next to the river; the lesbian-only nightclub by the football grounds; the gay pub in the centre of town with the jovial barman everyone called 'Mother' . . . Using audio recordings of interviews and drawing on literary extracts, I tried to unearth the substrate of the city that persisted beneath the Cambridge that most people would recognize, and make it visible, *navigable*. In reference to Forster's remark that queer past is 'a great unrecorded history', I named it 'A Great Recorded History'.[6]

As part of my research, I spent hours interviewing older queer people in their homes. Sharing a pot of tea in suntrap gardens or in floral living rooms with overstuffed armchairs, they told me anecdotes about this or that place, which was now no more. These interviews helped to broaden the scope of my interests beyond the social spaces that were the subject of the audio trail. While we talked, my attention would sometimes stray a little, and I'd start to think how funny it was that we were chatting so intently about queer spaces in general without acknowledging the ones in which our conversations were taking place – domestic spaces that often went unremarked upon. It seemed to me that these were at least as important as more public spaces.

Our discussions also showed me how important personal stories were, and how vital it was to attend to them closely: the throwaway details, the idiosyncratic jokes, the juicy bits of gossip, the laughter. Better than any overarching theory, these ostensibly trivial elements helped me to understand – and, more importantly, to feel – the elusive interconnections between queer sexuality and certain places. And if the stories of the people I interviewed were important, I came to realize that my story was too. After all, my desire to explore the queer spaces of Cambridge's past wasn't entirely a disinterested, academic one. It was inextricable from my status as a queer Irish immigrant who has lived almost half his life outside the country of his birth.

I grew up in a green and pleasant but rather sedate part of rural Ireland. After school, I moved to Dublin to go to university, then I quickly emigrated – to France first, then Britain, with extended stopovers in the United States and Mauritius. Some debate exists about the best way to interpret my surname, which is usually translated in the Irish language as 'Mac an Aistir', but the most widely accepted one is 'son of the journeyman'. While there is no reason that the son of a journeyman should himself turn out to be a journeyman, bearing all this moving around in mind, I think it's safe to say that I have inherited an itinerant nature.

Travelling through different countries and encountering different cultures, I've had the opportunity to observe the peculiarities of different places (and the peculiarities of my homeland have likewise stood out to me whenever I return). An immigrant disposition is, in some ways, the very source and matter of this book; if I'd never left Ireland, who knows if I'd want to explore natural and built environments, and emplace them in words. As I've travelled, I've also observed who I am in relation to these places, and how I've changed in response to them. Not simply in how I've presented myself, but in the variety of ways my queerness has come across.

I lived for more than a decade in Brighton, for instance – an unquestionably liberated place that vies with Manchester for the title of England's gayest town. During that time, I had relationships with both men and women, and thought of myself as queer, but I rarely felt the need to declare it loud and proud. Brighton Pride was just a massive corporate orgy as far as I was concerned, and I think I only ended up going twice. With my friends, in bars, walking down the street, I didn't feel like I had to throw my weight behind a particular identity. In Brighton, it didn't seem necessary.

But then I arrived in Cambridge. As soon as I did, I felt the city exert a pressure on me I hadn't felt before. Something about the rigorous, conservative division of urban space and the exclusions it represented encouraged me to think about my sexuality and my own experience – my queerness, my Irishness. People who know me say I have a strong transgressive streak: I am wilful and push back hard when I feel I'm being told what to do. Considering how I reacted to the constraints of Cambridge, they're absolutely correct. More and more I defined myself as queer (or even the more quaint-sounding bisexual); I looked for ways to become involved in the LGBTQ+ community; I made the audio trail; I set up a queer club with my friends to create a provisional queer space in the city. Pretty quickly, I went from being someone who just had queer feelings to being a card-carrying queer activist.

Social scientists call this 'place responsiveness': certain environments shape such fundamental aspects of ourselves as our characters, our self-understanding and our relationships with other people. Human beings are more sensitive to a sense of place than we may once have thought, and recent research attests to the central role it plays in the lives of LGBTQ+ people in particular.[7] Where it comes to sexual identity and real estate, it seems, it's all about location. Factors such as where you live, what kinds of queer spaces are available, what the demographic is – all have an enormous impact on how you inhabit and express your sexuality. You may feel more comfortable being butch in Manchester than in Doncaster, for example, or you can be properly effeminate in Philadelphia more than in Pittsburgh. On the other hand, in some towns you hide any signs of difference or you don't do public displays of affection at all. Some can be wonderfully freeing and some can be terribly restrictive but, whatever the case, *places make us.*

This book considers the stories of seven different artists and writers, and delves into their relationship with the places they occupied; following their stories, I trace a new history of queer culture and identity over the past 125 years. The book's origins lie in Cambridge, so we set out from there, exploring the university city and how its cloistered spaces influenced the life and work of the much-loved queer novelist E. M. Forster. Although most of his time was spent in the conservative environs of Cambridge, Forster was fascinated by the places he couldn't occupy – fantastical, sexually liberated spaces far removed from the disappointments of the present. As we'll see, his experience was not unique, and like many men educated at Oxford or Cambridge at the time, he yearned for the imagined homoerotic spaces of ancient Greece. Following Forster through Cambridge and through the lines of his fiction, we explore his conflicted commitment to a closeted double life.

Taking the train a little way south to London, we next turn our attention to the world of the suffragette movement before the First World War. Skirting the Bloomsbury Group, who are much better known but by no means the entirety of queer London in this period, we linger awhile with the forgotten women of Theatreland. Vera 'Jack' Holme, Cicely Hamilton, Edith Craig and her partners Christopher St John and Clare 'Tony' Atwood were part of a community of queer women whose work underpinned the arts and culture of the movement. Their lives and their radical feminist theatre show how desiring differently gave them a particular advantage in the suffragette struggle over the public and private spaces of London.

Next we cross the Channel to France, and spend some time in smoky Parisian cabarets in the company of the black bisexual entertainer Josephine Baker. Shortly after she exploded onto the stage of the Théâtre des Champs-Élysées in 1925, Baker became the face of interwar Paris. She and the Jazz Age city she adopted as her own were both characterized by unbridled extravagance that cast inhibitions aside and transcended all limitations, moral and physical. The story of

Baker's life has been recounted by many and read by many more, but few have thought about where her bisexuality fits into it. Stepping through the streets of Paris with a bisexual Baker allows us to observe the characteristics she and her beloved city shared: their wildness, their freedoms, their *excesses*.

Leaving the bright lights of the city for a more rural setting on the shores of Jersey, we wash up on the island home of surrealist Claude Cahun, whose gender-bending art echoes Jersey's status in between England and France. Long before either performance art or photography were accepted art forms, Cahun used the body as a prop and a costume, gleefully parodying gender stereotypes and capturing the results on camera. Urban areas, with their promise of freedom and anonymity, have played an important role in shaping queer sexuality in the twentieth century; Cahun's story allows us to consider gender variance beyond the city. Her performances and photographs raise the question of how we think about rural areas, and nature itself, in relation to queer and transgender identity.

Then to America (and back again) with James Baldwin. Born and raised in a Christian household in Harlem, Baldwin fled to Paris in 1948 at the age of twenty-four, seeking the kind of sexual freedom and racial tolerance enjoyed in the years before the Second World War by the likes of Josephine Baker. Turning the pages of his novels, we trace his movements between America and Europe, and pay a visit to the small town in France where he spent the last sixteen years of his life. Baldwin wasn't so different from many homosexual men who came of age before gay liberation and pursued impossible love affairs with ostensibly straight men. Searching for Baldwin where he is no longer remembered, we gradually uncover the complicated and tragic portrait of a writer who carried the shame of his upbringing with him wherever he went.

Our next stop is Lower Manhattan, sashaying through the historic neighbourhoods of the city in the footsteps of the flamboyant underground filmmaker Jack Smith. Beloved by the likes of Andy Warhol and John Waters, Smith was catapulted to fame in 1963 with the scandal of his first film, *Flaming Creatures*, a fever-dream of camp exoticism that was put on trial for obscenity. Smith's art and New York were inextricable: not only were his outrageous films and glitzy durational theatre pieces made *in* Downtown, they were made *from* Downtown – out of all the rubbish and discarded objects he retrieved from the streets around his apartment. Smith and the movement for gay liberation were both invested in utopian thinking and the creation of alternative queer spaces but, as will become apparent, only one of them remained steadfast in their ideals.

Finally, San Francisco – hitting the hilly streets with the ghost of my friend the prolific gay poet, novelist and American Book Award-winning editor Kevin Killian, taking in the history of the city's radical queer spaces from the 1960s through the AIDS epidemic to the present day. Following the life and work of one of the city's pre-eminent queer writers, we witness through Kevin's eyes the accelerated disappearance of these spaces. As tech start-ups and behemoths alike headquarter themselves in and around San Francisco, and their affluent workers descend on the city in search of a liberal sourdough dream, gentrification ramps up. Those on moderate incomes, who have made San Francisco what it is, can't afford to stay, and queer spaces and their communities have little option but to leave the city entirely – or move online. Kevin's story is a hopeful one, however, and his tireless creation of online spaces and communities exemplify the kind of resourcefulness queer culture needs, as the world lurches to the right and LGBTQ+ rights come increasingly under threat.

The majority of this book was researched and written during a global pandemic. Although I had been thinking about queer spaces for years beforehand, almost as soon as I put pen to paper in the spring of 2020, Covid-19 turned the world upside down. Suddenly there was nowhere to go. As catastrophe swept through all the countries of the world, health services scrambled and death rates soared, we clung on as best we could.

Days turned into weeks, into months, with little change in our circumstances, each day bringing more of the same. Weddings: cancelled. Christmas: cancelled. Socializing: cancelled (except for 10 Downing Street, where staff and politicians toasted each other as the rest of us buried our dead – or watched them being buried on Zoom). Travel was cancelled or greatly restricted. My plans for archival visits and international research trips were postponed, sometimes on several occasions. The research skills I'd honed over the years were severely tested, as I tried every trick I knew to get a glimpse of the books and articles I needed.

From time to time, I'd think about 'The Good-Morrow', a poem by John Donne taught to me by my father, whom I'd end up not seeing for two years. 'For love, all love of other sights controules, / And makes one little roome an every where.'[8] My partner and I were in love, thankfully, and our small terraced cottage in the south of Cambridge did become an everywhere, although perhaps not in the way that Donne had in mind. It was our office, our library, our gym; our pub, our club, our cinema. Everyone seemed to have the same experience. Domestic space warped and shifted. Overlapping with public space, its meaning became progressively ambiguous and uncertain. Public space, too, took on different meanings, inflected by our terror of the virus and terror of others. With face masks and hand sanitizer, we navigated the world outside our homes with a fear and trepidation that many of us haven't lost.

The spaces we occupy have always been open to recoding and repurposing, as the stories of London's queer suffragettes will so vividly show. But never in the history of humankind have public and private spaces been so dramatically and traumatically recoded, with such speed and for so many people, as during the Covid-19 pandemic. As we enter into a post-pandemic era, emerging out of crisis and trying to return to some semblance of normality, I find myself wondering: what is its legacy in terms of how we relate to the world, inside and out?

Certainly there is now more flexibility than ever before about workspaces. Many employers allow and even encourage working from home – to the relief of the disability-rights activists who had been campaigning for home-working for years with little success. Queer social venues, like many commercial establishments, have struggled to make ends meet, and anecdotally it would seem that there are fewer queer venues as a result of the pandemic. The new space race seems also to have intensified. Having depleted the world's natural resources making themselves rich, multibillionaires have stepped up their efforts to escape a plagued Earth, on the hunt for new places to colonize – in space.

But these are just a few of the most observable, immediate effects of the pandemic. The true legacy of its traumatic recoding will take some time to materialize. Commentators are fond of saying that the pandemic 'changed everything'; the actual extent of that change may not be known for many years. I am reluctant to prognosticate about the impact of Covid-19 on our experience, but in the pages that follow, the pandemic is like the weather – read between the lines, and you'll find it there, always.

A short story by Sam D'Allesandro, first published in 1984, called 'Nothing Ever Just Disappears' gives this book its title. Sam was Kevin Killian's friend and one of a group of experimental, San Francisco-based writers we will meet in the final chapter. By all accounts, he was also drop-dead gorgeous, and everyone who met him fell under his spell. He passed away due to AIDS-related complications in 1988 at the age of thirty-one.

The story starts out as a simple tale of falling in love and into a relationship. The narrator, whom we take to be Sam, meets a guy at the cigarette store, and they start seeing each other. To begin with, there's a certain distance, a strangeness between them that Sam enjoys, but in time, inevitably, they start to learn about each other, and learn from each other. They start to dream and make plans. Then it all changes.

When his boyfriend dies, Sam says:

> I don't remember driving home. I unlocked the door and closed all the windows. I took a bath. I sat. I listened to the phone ring. I went to bed. It was day again and then it wasn't . . . Sometimes I'd reach out as if to touch his face in the dark so I'd know I wasn't alone.[9]

These simple lines, describing domestic acts performed automatically in the wake of a loved one's death, convey the brutality and overwhelming sense of loss of a sudden bereavement. Crushed by grief, Sam's home is his only protection and comfort. A cocoon. A carapace.

When I read this story now, decades since it was written, in the aftermath of the worst devastations of AIDS, it seems as much a public statement about the role of queer domestic spaces during the crisis as an intimate record of loss. That is reason enough to take the story's title as my own – but there are other reasons too.

Few people have heard of Sam D'Allesandro. Talented though he was, he didn't publish much, and posthumous collections of his writing edited by his friends are now long out of print. His name may be destined to pass out of memory altogether, along with the names of thousands of other people who died from AIDS. Kevin made Sam a character in his last novel in an effort to push back against his cultural obliteration. By adopting the title of Sam's story, I'm attempting something similar. Kevin put Sam into his book; I've put him onto the cover of mine – in his memory, and in memory of others like him who died. *Nothing Ever Just Disappears*. You might call it a performative utterance.

My preference for Sam and his tale is a personal one. Avowedly so: in any grand narrative of LGBTQ+ culture in the twentieth century, it's hard to see him making the cut. How could he? He died before he could make any impact. The selection of people and places that make up this history of queer culture is similarly personal. Here you will find writers, performers, photographers and filmmakers, all of whom I feel an affinity with. Some figures are relatively well known, even canonical; others are as obscure as Sam is, but all the more interesting for their marginality, which casts the terrain of history in a different light. Taken together, this group also represents the spectrum of ways that LGBTQ+ people relate to the world. Whether they have cleaved to it (Forster) or struggled against it (the London suffragettes), grown intertwined with it (Baker) or tried to ignore it (Baldwin), as my journey from Dungeness to San Francisco shows, queer people have responded to it in a range of distinctive, creative ways.

When I refer to queer places and queer histories, I use *queer* in a broad sense to mean a range of orientations and identifications distinct from those of the heterosexual majority and those who identify with the gender they were assigned at birth. The word is especially practical when we talk about same-sex desire or gender nonconformity in times and places where behaviours and identities weren't defined in the same way as they are now. Its capaciousness allows us to talk about people's lives and loves in the past without falling into anachronism and without reducing their experience to our own; without calling someone a lesbian, for example, when that label hadn't yet acquired its current range of meanings. I am aware, however, that the term has a history, and that some may feel its connotations are quite specific, even unwelcome.

For many of us, *queer* originates as an insult, which may have first been heard in a schoolyard or on a city street after closing time, hurled before a punch or a kick or another violent, humiliating attack. When activist groups reclaimed the word in the 1980s and 1990s, it was precisely this sense of powerlessness and humiliation they sought to turn inside out. Inspired equally by Black Power and the queer punk movement's embrace of the lowly and derided as an alternative to a creeping gay and lesbian conservatism, organizations like Queer Nation made a rallying cry out of what was once a shameful label. As the slogan they roared out at AIDS demonstrations famously ran: 'We're here, we're queer, get used to it!'

As *queer* became a topic of conversation in university courses and academic journals in the 1990s, it also became institutionalized and lost much of its radical, transgressive frisson, emerging into the mainstream of the 2000s newly laundered and mostly respectable. Nowadays, it's most often used as an umbrella term under which a contemporary LGBTQ+ minority may be grouped together – for better and for worse. It can, for instance, draw on the sense of oppression shared by sexual and gender dissidents, and evoke an imagined sense of political solidarity. But it can just as easily obscure the very real differences between people in terms of life experience and how well a particular society accommodates them. Ultimately, how and where the word is used is key; I've tried to be attentive to this throughout the book.

Another couple of terms that will come up and may require a little explanation are *space* and *place*. Simply put, *space* refers to the area around everything that exists, while *place* is a part of space or a modification of it. Space is general, place is specific. These basic definitions underpin the various interpretations of both over the centuries by philosophers, scientists and geographers, from Aristotle to Albert Einstein, who each tend to show a preference for one term over the other. Where appropriate, I touch on their ideas but I'm mindful that they can sometimes be confusing or contradictory, and discussions in these fields are often insular and wearyingly academic.

For most of the twentieth century, the tendency among critics on the right and the left was to regard place with some suspicion. It represented the local and specific, and was therefore either an antiquated impediment on the path towards a modern (global) society, or a fetishistic attachment that hampered a critique of the more profound process of class struggle. Of late, however, people have started to reconsider the role of place in human life. Geographers especially have argued for its importance in a globalized world increasingly dominated by connections and flows.

Such a world is afflicted by an alienating sameness, especially in cities and megacities, where the phenomenon of what the French philosopher Marc Augé called the 'non-place' proliferates – shopping malls and high streets and airports that look and feel identical whether you're in Dublin or Dubai.[10] The march of economic and technological progress has demanded the loss of place, a *placelessness*, to which London's LGBTQ+ venues, for example, have been too readily sacrificed. But if we turn our attention back to such places, if we really look at them and try to connect with their stories, we can start to see how vital they are to the lives of individuals and societies, to history and culture, to identity and community. We can also see how devastating their loss can be. Understanding their importance, we may be less willing to allow them to slip away so easily.

This book is thus part of a wider attempt to emphasize the significance of place. It tries to reorient our thinking by taking a situated approach to queer history. My account of queer culture in the twentieth century isn't comprehensive, but I hope it is provocative. It issues a challenge: to conceive of history more in terms of place than time. Traditional approaches are preoccupied with dates and timelines (*then* homosexuality was decriminalized, *then* the Stonewall riots happened, *then* gay marriage . . .), which gives the whole endeavour a comforting feeling of progress but rather misrepresents the forms of queerness that were available at different times *in different places*. Taking the locations that follow as our guiding thread, we can shift the emphasis from timelines to places and, in so doing, gain access to a new, broader, more diverse perspective.

In his journal in February 1989, Jarman wrote: 'Time is scattered, the past and the future, the future past and present.' As the storm raged outside and the winds battered Prospect Cottage, his home, a sanctuary that would endure long after his death, he noted: 'I have not moved for many hours.'[11]

E. M. Forster in a window seat at King's College, Cambridge, 1955.
Photo by Edward Leigh. Courtesy of King's College Archive Centre.

Egress: E. M. Forster in Cambridge

In the distance, a row of ornate spires looms ominously in the pre-dawn dark. The sky appears bluish, almost lilac, through the clouds. The details of each spire are clearly discernible – the delicately wrought ribbing of stone tapering to a point and marked with a cross. It's hard to say if this is a church or a castle; religious and defensive connotations are all intermingled. It's old, though, no doubt about that.

A clock on one of the spires reads twenty to five. Oxidized shapes lean and loiter at the base of a monument in the foreground. A figure standing immobile on top of it holds in his hand the shadow of an open scroll. It's all so still and seems so timeless. How many other eyes have gazed on this scene – over how many centuries? A tawny owl cries out, its hoot echoing across the courtyard: *Whoo!*

The next shot, as if in answer, reveals a young man dozing on a narrow bed, buried under a mountain of blankets. A bedside lamp in an art nouveau style throws light across his handsome face, the smooth complexion of his skin, his floppy brown hair parted in curtains on his brow. The boy stirs in his sleep as the owl, implacable, calls out again. *Whoo?* The bird is looking for someone else.

And suddenly, here he is: a head of blond hair outside a darkened window. His hand appears and reaches up, prying the window open. The dark draperies on either side lightly flutter with the inrushing breeze as, breathing hard, the young man pulls himself up and squeezes his lanky frame through the narrow space. He crosses the room swiftly, making for the light by the bed. His cheeks are flushed, his eyes all aglow, agitated, intent.

'Maurice?' the floppy-haired boy croaks from the bed, before embracing the intruder. 'I love you,' he says, arms wrapped around him. The blond Maurice pulls back momentarily and replies, 'I love you,' before kissing him full on the lips. His kiss is fervent yet brief; the culmination of some long-pent-up emotion but also as if he's settling something – between the two boys or for himself, it's not yet apparent.

Then, just as suddenly, he's gone. Out of the window again, his blond hair tousled by the wind as he descends, leaving the other with his mouth agape, struggling with his bedclothes and wondering what the hell just happened.

'It is generally assumed that whatever exists, exists *somewhere* (that is to say, *in some place*),' writes Aristotle in his fourth-century BC treatise *The Physics*. 'In contrast to things which are *nowhere* because they are non-existent.'[1] In this chapter, and the chapters that follow, I'm interested in *how* the artists and writers we will meet existed in some place – their manner of being, the different ways that different places influenced them, and how they influenced these places in turn. What impact do places have on the kinds of people we become? Can we understand someone's life according to the spaces they have occupied? More specifically, can we map our sexuality onto where we grow up, where we live, where we find ourselves?

Needless to say, these questions aren't addressed by

Aristotle – not least because he didn't have a relational concept of space. For the great Greek philosopher, *topos* is that which contains and surrounds. Akin to a vessel whose purpose is to hold something without interacting with it, space defines the limits of things and to a degree constitutes them as things just as they constitute it as a space. Beyond that there isn't much of a relation between the two.

Aristotle, Plato, Socrates, the thought of ancient Greece, its long-lost culture: all of it goes by the name of Hellenism, and was intimately familiar to the writer E. M. (Edward Morgan) Forster, well-known author of novels such as *A Room with a View* (1908), *Howards End* (1910) and the queer classic *Maurice* (1971). He and his Victorian and Edwardian fellow countrymen were immersed in Hellenic culture and ideas – never more so than during their time at the colleges of Oxford and Cambridge. Fearful of the coming of mass democracy and the dreaded feminization of the Empire's subjects, the English in this period looked back to the Greeks for a model of a masculine, military culture and tried to propagate it through their educational strongholds. This proliferation of Greek thought in England during the late nineteenth and early twentieth centuries came with attendant ideas of homosexual 'Greek love' between men, which had a profound impact on the lives of many, including, most famously, Oscar Wilde, of whom more in a moment.

In his student rooms at King's College, Cambridge, with the River Cam flowing gently underneath his window, Forster pored over Greek texts including Aristotle's *Physics*. Even as he ruminated on the theory of space as a container or vessel, however, Forster's life in the actually existing spaces of Cambridge seemed to prove otherwise: that space and the bodies

that move through it are in fact mutually dependent and inter-
active. Forster's Cambridge, which he came to know as an
undergraduate and later as a life fellow of King's, and the fictional spaces of his novels and stories were incompatible with
the Aristotelian ideas he had learned as a teenager. Yet, as we
will see, the principles of ancient Greece couldn't be applied to
the English society of Forster's time without producing some
very interesting contradictions.

I first watched James Ivory and Ismail Merchant's film *Maurice*,
an adaptation of Forster's novel, in 2006 while sitting on my
bed in a dingy university hall of residence that looked out on
Brighton's seafront. The flashing fairground lights of Brighton
Pier intermittently lit up my bedroom walls at night, and I fell
asleep to the sound of waves pounding and fizzing up the peb-
bled shore. In summer, through the open window, the breeze
would carry in the seaside smell of fried fish and chips.

I was doing a master's degree in queer studies at a university just outside the city. In our seminar the next day, we
were supposed to talk about Forster's book and its place in a
canon of queer writing. Brighton is a party town with no end
of charming distractions that make time management next to
impossible; I hadn't read the book, so I had to cheat and borrow
the Merchant Ivory film from the university library.

Made in 1987, the film – and the book it's based upon –
is the story of a young man's sexual awakening in Edwardian
England in the years before the First World War. Watching it
on my wheezing laptop was my first introduction to Forster,
whose work I would read and come to love later on. It was also
my first introduction to Cambridge, a place I'd only ever heard
about in passing. The city, along with the university that shapes

the look and feel of the place, plays an important role in how the story unfolds.

We follow Maurice Hall (played by newcomer James Wilby), a dull, snobbish lad, from his days at university in 1909 to his entry into the world of work. From the outset, his struggles with his sexuality are a constant. At Cambridge it slowly dawns on him that he's attracted to his classmate, the Greece-obsessed Clive Durham (played by a young Hugh Grant, pre-*Four Weddings and a Funeral*). In the beginning, Maurice rebuffs Clive's attentions cruelly. When Clive declares his love, Maurice says: 'Durham, you're an Englishman. I'm another. Don't talk nonsense.' But in time he comes to acknowledge his true feelings – which lead him to scale the walls of King's College in the early hours of the morning, burst in through his sleeping friend's window and declare his love for him.

The relationship between the two friends blossoms in Cambridge and they ease into a blissful – if chaste – intimacy, which is only ruptured when Maurice leaves to work in London. Soon the very real possibility that they could be locked up for carrying on together becomes too much for Clive. He calls it off and gets engaged to a young lady of some standing. This sends Maurice into a horrible downward spiral, hell-bent on finding a cure for his 'disease'. Trousers around his ankles, he confesses to his doctor, 'I'm an unspeakable of the Oscar Wilde sort!' – before buttoning up and heading off to try a hypnotherapist (played by the sepulchral Ben Kingsley).

Maurice finally finds love and reciprocal affection in the most unlikely of places with the most unlikely of people. One stormy night while he's visiting the now-married Clive at his enormous country estate, the gamekeeper, Alec Scudder, (Rupert Graves) comes through the window of Maurice's room and they sleep together. Their first time mirrors the scene in Cambridge years earlier, but significant details have shifted and changed. Scudder is from a lower class, for one thing. He's also much less inhibited than Clive and more ready to say what he wants. 'Sleep the night with me,' he says to Maurice, after he follows him to London. 'I know a place.' Maurice falls in love with this 'flesh and blood' man, to the dismay of an appalled Clive. Ultimately Maurice and Alec turn their backs on English society and its homophobic laws and customs, and set out for a new life far from the constraints of civilization.

When the movie came out, the American film critic Roger Ebert was delighted with its aesthetic, writing that it was 'so handsome to look at . . . that it is worth seeing just to regard the production'. He wasn't so impressed with how it ended, however; this love affair between a toff and a game-keeper wasn't realistic, he said, and 'no matter how deep their love, I suspect that within a few weeks or months the British class system would have driven them apart'.[2] Lytton Strachey said something similar when he was shown the manuscript of *Maurice* by Forster in 1915. The flamboyant Bloomsbury biographer and Forster's on-again, off-again friend declared: 'I should have prophecied a rupture after 6 months – chiefly as a result of lack of common interests owing to class differences.'[3]

But the writer of *Maurice* always insisted that Maurice and Alec *should* live happily ever after, regardless of how unlikely it may have been. 'A happy ending was imperative,' Forster wrote in a note pinned to the manuscript of the novel. 'I shouldn't have bothered to write otherwise. I was determined that in fiction anyway two men should fall in love and remain in it for the ever and ever that fiction allows.'[4]

When the novel was conceived in 1913, publishing a book with queer protagonists – especially ones who ended up together *and happy* – was a radical idea. Forster had no real precedents he could look to in English and, apart from one or two pioneering works like André Gide's *The Immoralist* (1902), the more filthy-minded French weren't much help either. The book was way ahead of its time. Radclyffe Hall's lesbian downer *The Well of Loneliness* (1928) was banned for obscenity when it came out almost a decade and a half later, and even that, as we'll see, was a miserable portrait of the homosexual 'invert' who submits to a life of sadness and solitude. Convinced that same-sex desire was a disease, both Hall and her characters internalized the same fears that first troubled Forster's Maurice, before he woke up in Alec's arms and realized that what they'd done together wasn't unnatural at all.

In the end, a queer novel proved too radical even for Forster himself. Throughout his life he was plagued by the question of 'whether I am conventional or not'.[5] Strachey certainly believed he was. When they met in Cambridge, he nicknamed Forster 'the taupe' – French for 'mole' – for being so shy and retiring, and was forever needling him about his lack of sexual experience. Forster was always worried about upsetting his mother (he was an only child and his father died when he was a baby), so he kept his relationships secret from her. When a friend encouraged him to be more forthcoming about his sexuality and urged him to think of the openly gay Gide, whose work Forster loved, Forster replied: 'But Gide hasn't got a mother!'[6]

Maurice seems to have been the ultimate test of whether Forster was conventional or not. He was, as it turned out. Although the book was written at the dawn of the twentieth century and circulated for decades among friends like Strachey and Christopher Isherwood, Forster allowed it to be published only after his death. It finally appeared in 1971.

Gay liberation was in full swing by that point. In 1967 homosexuality was partially decriminalized in Britain. Two years later, on 28 June 1969 in Greenwich Village, New York, a bungled police raid on a Mafia-run gay bar erupted into violence. Patrons at the Stonewall Inn, including sex workers, transgender women and 'stone butch' lesbians, struck back against police harassment, kicking off a weekend of riots, and further catalysing the movement for gay liberation. By 1970 the Gay Liberation Front (GLF) had spread around the world, with a group in Forster's native England that would include prominent gay campaigners like Peter Tatchell. To the out and proud gay reader, *Maurice* could have looked like a stuffy old relic from a distant past. The suburban public schoolboy Maurice would have been an unlikely figure at a GLF rally, among those calling for gay rights and the abolition of the patri-archal family. But in fact there were many, very enthusiastic readers of *Maurice* among the crowds of newly liberated gays.

Straight critics hated the novel when it first came out, of course, and their assessments of it were marked by heterosexism – the presumption that any orientation other than heterosexuality is abnormal and unnatural. They called it weak and fanciful and worried that it might tarnish the distinguished reputation of an author who had written such important, quint-essentially English novels as *A Room with a View* and *Howards End*. One review in *The Times Literary Supplement* said, 'it adds nothing to [Forster's] achievement as a novelist, and little to his reckoning as a man',[7] while another called it 'an infantile book'.[8] But Forster's queer readers were far more forgiving of the novel's faults, and it soon became essential reading for every gay and bisexual man – and not a few lesbians too.

Why did they like it so much? Well, to tell the truth, at that point there wasn't much else to choose from. Lists of gay and lesbian novels included only a handful of important books: Hall's *Well of Loneliness*, Gore Vidal's *The City and the Pillar* (1948), James Baldwin's *Giovanni's Room* (1956), John Rechy's *City of Night* (1963); and others like Truman Capote's *Other Voices, Other Rooms* (1948) and Mary Renault's *The Charioteer* (1953).

In all of these books, unhappiness was a common factor – hundreds of pages of gays ashamed (Rechy), turning into drunks (Vidal), losing their mind (Capote), renouncing happiness (Baldwin, Hall, Renault) . . . Forster offered something different. What his gay readership treasured in his book was its positive take on love between men, even men from different class backgrounds. It didn't much matter how improbable it was. *Maurice* imagined a place where such relationships could be conducted without shame and without secrecy – a queer kind of utopia.

The Greenwood

I finally got around to reading Forster later that year, on a budget flight to Dublin with my head full of images of the Ireland where I grew up: roadsides lined with grey pebbledash bungalows; a green monotony of endless pastures; a small, dilapidated castle on a hill. What impressed me wasn't so much the realism that people often praised in Forster's books. I was more interested in how he incorporated delicate, often unsettling fantastical settings into his otherwise realistic tales. This is especially true of short stories like 'The Other Side of the Hedge', which was published in 1911, a couple of years before Forster sat down to write *Maurice*.

At the beginning of the story, the narrator stops for a moment by the side of the road, taking a break in the middle of a very long walk. Sitting on a milestone, he considers his journey and the arid, endless route he's been following: 'dust under foot and brown crackling hedges on either side, ever since I could remember'.[9] The road stretches off into metaphor in front and behind, and we feel an existential crisis in the offing.

Suddenly, from the direction of the hedge there comes a refreshing little puff of air. Diving into the thorny bush in pursuit of its source, the narrator conveys us to an otherworldly realm far from the road. We soon emerge into a lush and lovely landscape.

> I had never been in so large a space, nor seen such grass and sunshine. The blue sky was no longer a strip, and beneath it the earth had risen grandly into hills – clean, bare buttresses, with beech trees in their folds, and meadows and clear pools at their feet. But the hills were not high, and there was in the landscape a sense of human occupation – so that one might have called it a park, or garden, if the words did not imply a certain triviality and constraint.[10]

Accompanied by a jovial middle-aged stranger with a youthful voice, the narrator explores the countryside and meets cheerful men and women occupied with gardening or making hay. A young man streaks past, jumps a fence and plunges suddenly into a lake. We infer that he's not wearing any clothes. Everyone might be naked here, in fact: they seem to have thrown off all the other trappings of civilization like progress and competition, so why not also clothes? On the other side of the hedge is a place the narrator has only ever dreamed about; down the rabbit hole, there's beauty and simplicity waiting for this weary, middle-aged Alice.

Alec and Maurice similarly swerve from the beaten track in *Maurice*. Like the narrator in 'The Other Side of the Hedge', they also find themselves a long way from the modern world and, although the novel only hints at it, Forster himself imagined the destination of his two lovers as somewhere he called 'the Greenwood'. When they disappeared off the pages of his book, he said, they'd settle down in a wild, premodern idyll beyond the reach of buttoned-down, mechanical modernity.[11]

The Greenwood is synonymous in the popular imagination with Robin Hood's Sherwood Forest, as a mythical place beyond the reach of society and its rules. A natural refuge for outcasts and outlaws, it has endured in fantasy and folktale as civilization has pushed the wild places from the map. Little wonder, then, that the Greenwood has a special place in Maurice's imagination. Early on in the novel, when he's reflecting on his hidden homosexual feelings, he imagines himself as 'an outlaw in disguise'. Yearning for somewhere he might be free to explore these feelings with another man, he thinks: 'Perhaps among those who took to the Greenwood in old time there had been two men like himself – two. At times he entertained the dream. Two men can defy the world.'[12] At the end of the novel, Forster makes Maurice's dream come true.

Where did Forster's idea of the Greenwood come from? Same-sex desire has been associated with outlawry in fact and fiction for a long time, of course, and secret groups of sexual renegades peer out at us from the pages of the historical record, yet Forster's notion of off-the-grid gayness seems to have been inspired by a much less sensational source.

Maurice was written after a visit to the home of Edward Carpenter and his partner, George Merrill, near Sheffield in the autumn of 1912. Carpenter was a well-known supporter of such radical causes as women's suffrage and prison reform, but he is perhaps best remembered as a pioneering sex reformer and champion of homosexual love. For Forster, who deeply admired the openly homosexual Carpenter, the trip to his house and garden in the tiny Derbyshire village of Millthorpe was something of a pilgrimage. He referred to the house as a 'shrine'.[13]

Born into an affluent middle-class family from Brighton on 29 August 1844, Carpenter spent his childhood in a large, fashionable house on Brunswick Square, on Brighton's border with Hove – then, as now, a much-sought-after place to live. I visited it once – my own kind of pilgrimage, I suppose – and was startled by the grandeur of the house onto which they'd stuck Carpenter's memorial blue plaque. Neoclassical columns and the ornate cornicing of the facade trumpeted wealth and privilege. The terrace of elegant four-storey buildings surrounded a tidy little park set back from the seafront, which would keep the kind of noise and drama that played out beneath my bedroom window on a Saturday night at arm's length. Was *this* where the sandal-wearing queer anarchist guru grew up?

Carpenter had hated the house, however, which was always full of other children – and the city of Brighton and Hove, which represented an upper-class Victorian respectability that he would spend his life trying to tear down. In his memoir, *My Days and Dreams* (1916), he says: 'at home I never felt really at home'.[14] It would be some time until he found a place he could truly call home in his utopia of the north.

Carpenter credited his sexual awakening to an encounter with the poetry of Walt Whitman while he was at Cambridge (he had attended Trinity Hall, next door to King's, thirty years before Forster). A friend came by his rooms and loaned him a book of Whitman's poems. As he read it, he had a marvellous realization – along with a creeping sense of being totally out of place in Cambridge with all its connotations of wealth and heterosexist tradition.

> From that time forward a profound change set in within me. I remember the long and beautiful summer nights, sometimes in the College garden by the riverside, sometimes sitting at my own window which itself overlooked a little old-fashioned garden enclosed by grey and crumbling walls; sometimes watching the silent and untroubled dawn; and feeling all the time that my life deep down was flowing out and away from the surroundings and traditions amid which I lived . . . [15]

Whitman's vision of democratic comradeship across class lines, shot through with homoerotic attachment, came to define how Carpenter would live and love in the years that followed. Soon afterwards, he resigned his fellowship at the college and set off for the north of England. In Sheffield he met Merrill, who was almost twenty-three years younger than him and had grown up in the city's working-class slums. They moved in together in 1898 and would spend the rest of their lives at Millthorpe, in the countryside outside Sheffield, writing books and cultivating a peaceful little garden together.

During his visit to their home, Forster remembers that Merrill 'touched my backside – gently and just above the buttocks. I believe he touched most people's.' The sensation was strange for him: he was a slow starter and wouldn't have sex for the first time until four years later, at the age of thirty-seven. Creatively speaking, it seems to have jolted him to life and the idea for *Maurice* came to him, I'm inclined to say, like a bolt from the arse: 'It seemed to go straight through the small of my back into my ideas, without involving my thoughts.'[16]

Really, it was the combined impact of Merrill and Carpenter, and their relationship, that prompted the conception of *Maurice* – and the happy ending that would set the tale apart. According to Forster's biographer Wendy Moffat, 'only in the isolated example of George Merrill and Edward Carpenter had Morgan [Forster] seen even an inkling of the domestic life for gay men that he had glimpsed in Whitman's poems, that he believed in and desired'.[17] Their blissful domestic partnership and their life together away from civilization was Forster's model and was what he had in mind when he sent Alec and Maurice off to the mythic Greenwood.

Forster penned his note insisting on the imperative of *Maurice*'s happy ending in September 1960. By that stage, the Greenwood was already a thing of the past: Carpenter had died in 1929 and with him, it seemed, had gone any chance of queer love outside civilization. Forster's great tale of same-sex passion, its author said, 'belongs to the last moment of the Greenwood . . . There is no forest or fell to escape to today, no cave in which to curl up, no deserted valley for those who wish neither to reform nor corrupt society but to be left alone.' Only images of the Greenwood remained, which offered a mere semblance of freedom. 'People do still escape, one can see them any night at it in the films,' he wrote.[18] There is, in this last remark, a note of disappointment or derision – that the fantasy of the Greenwood offered nightly by moving pictures is a rather hollow one. Perhaps escape shouldn't be so easy, or happen with such frequency. You get the feeling he might have been more than a little ambivalent about the adaptation of his book by Merchant and Ivory.

Nonetheless, readers and scholars alike have been preoccupied by the enigmatic Greenwood since *Maurice* first appeared. What does this kind of utopian space signify? What does it mean for Forster and queer identity? If utopia literally means 'no place', then why pin one's hopes for future happiness on somewhere that doesn't even exist?

'One of the most curious aspects of *Maurice* – especially for contemporary readers,' writes the novelist David Leavitt, 'is the extent to which it privileges the rural over the urban as the locus of freedom for homosexual men.'[19] Modern queer coming-out stories have tended to plot the sexual awakening of their characters along a path that runs from repression to liberation, rural to urban. Edmund White's narrator in *A Boy's Own Story* (1982), for example, idealizes the spaces of New York; he imagines that once he gets there, he'll find others like him and be able to assume a more authentic sexual self. In most of these stories, the friends of Dorothy find themselves and their community only on the way to the Emerald City. By orienting his heroes towards the Greenwood, Forster's book flips that familiar trajectory.

The space of Forster's Greenwood is vitally important, then, both in terms of the story of *Maurice* and a broader history of LGBTQ+ literature and its readers. But focusing too much on it has meant that over the years the other places in Forster's work have been a bit neglected. With its cobbled streets and ancient stone buildings, its shimmering parks and languid waterways – in other words, *with all its contradictions* – Cambridge is one such place.

Cambridge

I arrived in Cambridge in the winter of 2017. Apart from brief, ill-advised sojourns in such far-flung places as Mauritius and Norwich, I'd been in Brighton for more than a decade. In that time the city had changed, utterly: drastically expensive, unbelievably gentrified and, with one or two exceptions, devoid of the kind of underground culture I loved. A couple of my closest friends, two queer women, had recently moved, finally pushed out by skyrocketing rent prices. With Carpenter's ghost watching over them, they ended up in Sheffield, where they made their own queer utopia – girl-style. It was time for me to leave the seaside for the Fens.

Cambridge was so different from Brighton that it might as well have been the moon. Growing up in rural Ireland and spending my childhood surrounded by nothing but green fields, cities are always strange to me. It's an exciting kind of strangeness – I take pleasure in observing how urban spaces are laid out, how the look and feel of built-up areas change as one moves from one part of town to another. I'd loved walking down Western Road from Brighton to Hove, watching the organic, spontaneous arrangement of buildings, higgledy-piggledy, give way to wide-open boulevards and sumptuous middle-class houses of the type Carpenter hated. Walking through Cambridge was something else entirely.

The first thing I noticed was the careful planning of

the place. The improvised feel of a city like Brighton was very hard to come by. Everything felt very static and very administered, and you got the sense that even the most inconsequential outhouse was built only after endless deliberation at meetings attended by old white men in mahogany-panelled rooms.

Public space in the city also felt very hemmed in, *restrained* by the private institutions of the colleges. Everywhere you looked there was a big stone wall or a building topped with ornate battlements bearing the crest of such-and-such a college built in seventeen-whenever that reminded you that you were here only under sufferance. Sometimes this was quite literally the case: lots of the parks and greens you're allowed to walk through as a member of the public are in fact owned by colleges, which graciously submit to their use by the hoi polloi. And those were the spaces you *could* access. Behind the colleges' enormous wooden gates firmly closed to outsiders stretched acres of beautifully maintained gardens, shaded woodland paths, secret streams and swimming pools all open only to members.

College and city, private and public, inside and outside; I came to know Cambridge as a space of carefully managed dichotomies. This seemed to be Forster's experience too. In her biography of Forster, Moffat argues that Cambridge's geography became a kind of 'psychic landscape' for him, 'alternately claustrophobic and liberating'. The city centre he walked or cycled through was full of narrow cobbled alleyways and shadowy lanes, which would suddenly give way to bright, welcoming vistas. The lush green expanses of Parker's Piece and Midsummer Common. The clear-flowing waterways of the Cam. The cattle-grazed meadows of 'the Backs' behind King's College.[20]

Reading Forster again after I arrived in Cambridge and in light of my growing familiarity with the city, I began to understand how the place affected the author; how his experience of the space resonated in his writing, his sexuality, his constant negotiation between feelings of constraint and freedom, reticence and candour. His double life.

Forster was intimately acquainted with the city. He spent his formative years here as a student, returned in middle age and finished his days as a fellow of King's College. From start to finish, the physical environment of Cambridge shaped Forster's daily life. Yet if it features at all in comments upon *Maurice* by readers of the book, the university city is cast only as the villain in the tale – the evil twin of the Greenwood. If one is all imposing ramparts and still stone halls, the other is nature, movement and life. If one is social or religious authority, then the other is rebellion and outlawry. If Cambridge connotes heterosexist tradition, the Greenwood stands for queer liberation.

This neat definition doesn't exactly hold, however, and the truth of Cambridge's relationship to queerness in the novel is much more complicated. After all, it's while Maurice is living in Cambridge that he starts to come to terms with his homosexual feelings. It's in the rooms of his college that he begins to explore those feelings, and in the fields dotted around the city that he finds out what it means to love another man, lying out in the grass with Clive, kissing him and whispering to him sweetly. Cambridge is in fact the cradle of queerness in the novel and although it may require a little gymnastics to fit his burgeoning queer self through the old structures it represents, to an extent Maurice has Cambridge to thank for awakening his queer desires. This was as much the case for the author himself as it was for his protagonist.

Forster came here in the autumn of 1897 at the age of eighteen. He had been accepted to King's College to study classics – a significant choice of subject, as we'll soon see. King's was once little more than a playground for posh boys who had been to Eton, but by the end of the nineteenth century it had evolved into one of the more progressive colleges in the University of Cambridge system. Old restrictions on entry were eased, students from a much wider range of backgrounds were admitted, and young men were prepared for entry into the professions rather than a life of affluence. One of the beneficiaries of this transformation was Forster, an unremarkable freshman from the suburbs who had attended an unremarkable public school in Kent. On entering the college, he found himself part of a cohort of lively, intellectual young men who would go on to become doctors or lawyers or swell the ranks of the civil service at home and abroad.

Late-Victorian England was not a good place for a boy with homosexual desires. Just a couple of months before Forster arrived in Cambridge, Oscar Wilde was released from Reading Gaol; for the crime of gross indecency, he had been sentenced to two years' hard labour. Wilde's trial in 1895 caused a sensation in British society – not least because there were three of them.

In the first, Wilde sued the Marquess of Queensberry for libel when the latter left a calling card at Wilde's club that read: 'For Oscar Wilde, posing somdomite [sic]'. Queensberry was the father of Wilde's lover, Lord Alfred Douglas, or 'Bosie', a profligate, self-centred young man with no talent and less discretion, who was adored by Wilde. The indignity of being named a sodomite by someone who couldn't even spell the word was presumably too much for Wilde. Goaded by Bosie and others, he sued Queensberry for falsely accusing him of sodomy, but when it became clear that Queensberry had embarrassing evidence that could back up his claim, Wilde dropped the case.

In the second trial, based on evidence unearthed at the first, Wilde was charged with gross indecency with another male. During that trial, Wilde made his famous defence of 'the love that dare not speak its name'. It's the love one finds openly expressed in earlier eras, he said; the kind of love that inspired the sonnets of Michelangelo and Shakespeare, and 'such as Plato made the very basis of his philosophy'.

> It is beautiful, it is fine, it is the noblest form of affection. There is nothing unnatural about it. It is intellectual, and it repeatedly exists between an older and a younger man, when the older man has intellect and the younger man has all the joy, hope and glamour of life before him. That it should be so, the world does not understand. The world mocks at it, and sometimes puts one in the pillory for it.[21]

Wilde was one of the most successful writers in England at the time, and a gifted orator too. When he finished speaking, the courtroom erupted into spontaneous applause, so moved were his listeners by his impassioned defence. He must have also moved the jury because, when the trial ended, they were unable to reach a verdict.

There was some talk about aborting his retrial, but it was impossible: the matter had simply attracted too much attention and nobody in a position of power was willing to stick their neck out for him. So, with a kind of rhetorical injustice, Wilde was finally found guilty in the third trial. In the epic letter he wrote to Bosie from his cell in Reading Gaol, later published as *De Profundis* (1905), he reflects on the shame his crime brought on his family name. 'I had made it a low byword among low people. I had dragged it through the very mire,' he says. 'I had given it to brutes that they might make it brutal, and to foes that they might turn it into a synonym for folly.'[22]

From this point on, Oscar Wilde would forever be associated with the vice of homosexuality – his name standing in for the love one daren't speak about. An interesting upshot of this is that many of Wilde's attributes, such as effeminacy, immorality, decadence and wit – attributes that previously had no direct connection to same-sex desire – suddenly coalesced into the figure of the queer. The notoriety of Wilde, as the queer scholar Alan Sinfield writes in *The Wilde Century* (1994), 'afforded a simple stereotype as a peg for behaviour and feelings that were otherwise incoherent or unspeakable'. What's more, because of the silence on matters of sexuality after the trials, few models apart from this one were available to homosexuals, so that 'between 1900 and 1960, a dandified manner afforded by far the most plausible queer identity'.[23] You could say the quintessential modern queer identity was forged in a cell in Reading Gaol.

Forster was sixteen and still at school when Wilde was sent to prison. There's no record of how he felt about seeing this colourful and celebrated writer brought low for having the same feelings he had, but its impact is obvious in the way that a disgusted Maurice calls himself 'an unspeakable of the Oscar Wilde sort'. Wendy Moffat goes so far as to claim that Forster wore the effects of the Wilde trials on his very person. His 'mousy self-presentation was no accident', she says. 'Naturally quite shy, he consciously inverted Wilde's boldly effeminate persona.'[24]

But if the author of *Maurice* came of age in a repressive and homophobic England, at King's College in Cambridge a more tolerant attitude prevailed. Its halls and sitting rooms were something of a refuge from the conservatism of the world outside. For one thing, students had a certain amount of freedom when it came to practising religion. From 1871, unlike at other colleges, if you matriculated as a student at King's you weren't required to take a compulsory religious test to prove your attachment to the Church of England. This meant that you could be Catholic or Jewish (or, in Forster's case, increasingly agnostic), and you could still take your place.

Relaxing requirements like this laid the foundation for a liberal, questioning kind of atmosphere among the students of King's, and Kingsmen thus felt empowered to challenge many popular ideas and attitudes. While he was there, Forster's two atheist friends John Maynard Keynes and Hugh Owen Meredith protested about the college's support of a religious organization that worked with the poor of London; their protest ensured that King's worked with secular groups from then on.

The lively intellectual environment at King's was also an all-male one. Whatever its progressive pedigree with regard to religion, sexism nonetheless reigned at the college and women were not admitted as students until 1972. This kind of misogyny could be found across the University of Cambridge, which has the dubious honour of being the last university in Britain to allow women to take full degrees, in 1947. Women had their own colleges of course, such as Girton and Newnham (still staunchly women-only), but they were refused entry to older colleges like King's until the latter part of the twentieth century.

Forster's college was therefore a strictly homosocial space – one of exclusively same-sex relationships. Like most colleges at the universities of Cambridge and Oxford, the student body was exclusively male and so were all the fellows. From the moment he woke up to when he went to bed at night, Forster was surrounded only by men: he ate breakfast with them, went to class with them, and took instruction from them. If he didn't sleep *with* them, he certainly slept *near* them. Students of the colleges were usually housed together in halls of residence that bore more than a passing resemblance to the boarding schools where many of them had started their male-only education.

Cambridge's homosociality was fertile ground for the growth of ancient Greek ideas, which praised bonds between men as central to society and politics. As the Oxford graduate Oscar Wilde had declared from the dock, love of other men was 'such as Plato made the very basis of his philosophy', and the study of the ancient Greeks found a niche at King's and many other colleges at Cambridge and Oxford at the end of the nineteenth century. Hellenism, as it was known, not only permitted the discussion of male love, it made it into an ideal.

Ancient Greece

'The Greeks, or most of them, were that way inclined.' The scene is sumptuously filmed in the 1987 adaption. Clive, Maurice and their flamboyant friend Risley (played by Mark Tandy) glide down the River Cam in a punt, one of those long, flat-bottomed boats that throng the waterways of Cambridge in

the summertime. Clive is holding forth again about the customs of the ancient Greeks, which he says have been grossly
misrepresented in their translation seminar that morning.

As one of the students read his translation from the
Greek aloud, their tutor, in a toneless voice, had interrupted:
'Omit: reference to the unspeakable vice of the Greeks.' The
hypocrisy! Afterwards, with the characteristic intensity of the
intellectual young man, Clive announces to his friends that 'to
omit it is to omit the mainstay of Athenian society'. It's all there
in Plato's *Symposium*, he says, before turning slyly to Maurice
and asking: 'You've read the *Symposium*?'[25]

Hellenism was a homosexual code in the Victorian era –
and for a long time afterwards. Even now, every so often you'll
hear someone say that the Greeks invented gayness. The roots
of these ideas lie in Oxford, where university reforms in the
mid 1800s changed how students were taught and what they
learned, and the impact of these changes were felt throughout
the British education system and in the colleges of Cambridge
especially. The reformers first brought back the tutorial – a
one-to-one 'meeting of the minds' between the student and
a more experienced fellow – as the keystone of college teach-
ing. This platonic model of education fitted well with the study
of ancient Greek culture, which was then introduced into the
Oxford curriculum in the following decades.

The turn to Greek studies from the mid 1800s came as a
direct response to changes in the Victorian era. The coming of
mass democracy and the impending erosion of the class system
spelled crisis for the upper echelons of British society. With a
wearying predictability, the reaction to this took a misogynistic
form. In public and in print, liberal intellectuals worried about
the feminization of British men. 'The age is an effeminate one,'

blustered the social reformer Charles Kingsley – and he wasn't alone in his fears about the emasculation of Britain.[26]

Greece offered a solution. Looking backwards to the masculine, military culture of the ancient Greeks could reinvigorate British culture, and the future of the nation and the Empire would be assured. The idea was that young British men would be indoctrinated into a masculinist ideology at university, and this would then radiate outwards into the world and to the very edges of the British Empire. It worked, to a degree: notable British imperialists like Cecil Rhodes, George Curzon and Alfred Milner were all classics scholars, educated at Oxford.

One thing the reformers didn't expect, however, was that with the embrace of the ancient Greeks came a very visible model of same-sex relationships. Where previously men with homosexual desires had to search high and low to find any kind of representation they could identify with, now they had a very public, very respectable treatment of homosexuality – one that showed it was not an abnormality. Love between men was justified by its association with the ancient Greeks. The great irony of the liberal Victorian project was that it used Hellenism to save British culture from degeneration but, in doing so, it offered homosexual apologists a way of legitimating their erotic desires.

The English poet and literary critic John Addington Symonds was one such apologist. A distinguished Oxford don who is credited with first introducing 'homosexual' into the English language, Symonds was interested in the role homosexuality played in the spiritual and social life of ancient Greece. More importantly, he was interested in how a careful history of same-sex relations in Greece could be used to make homosexuality palatable for a nineteenth-century audience.

A Problem in Greek Ethics, Symonds' most famous book, was written in 1873 but like Forster's *Maurice* circulated privately for years before it became publicly available. It opens with a plea of sorts. He asks that scientists and psychologists take a good look at the phenomenon of Greek love. 'Here alone in history,' he says, 'have we the example of a great and highly-developed race not only tolerating homosexual passions, but deeming them of spiritual value, and attempting to utilise them for the benefit of society.'[27] If a civilization as great and powerful as ancient Greece could accept homosexuality, shouldn't modern Britain do the same?

In terms that Wilde would echo years later, Symonds describes Greek love, or *paiderastia*, as a relationship between a young man and an older man. It was, according to him, 'a passionate and enthusiastic attachment subsisting between man and youth, recognised by society and protected by opinion, which though it was not free from sensuality did not degenerate into mere licentiousness'.[28] Greek love was also a masculine love: a 'hardy', noble attachment that 'implied no effeminacy'.[29]

This sounds a little sexist and Symonds obviously wanted to appeal to other eminent Victorians for tolerance of homosexuality based on what they seemed to like most, i.e. hard, manly men. But before we throw him into the same category as Charles Kingsley and the rest of Britain's terrified imperialists, it's important to note how sympathetic he was towards the plight of women in Greek history. The Greek idealization of love between men, he says, came about in tandem with their denigration of women. 'To talk familiarly with free women on the deepest subjects, to treat them as intellectual companions, or to choose them as associates in undertakings of political moment, seems never to have entered the mind of an Athenian,' Symonds says, and this strikes him as a 'defect' of Greek culture.[30]

If Greek love was a macho, 'masc4masc' kind of affair, it was also a chaste one. Symonds portrays it as the union of two souls on a spiritual level with as little carnal activity and 'licentiousness' as possible. In other words, Greek love was an ideal and something that sat uncomfortably with physical reality. The asexuality of same-sex attachments *à la grecque* was central to how it was interpreted by readers like Symonds, who for years practised what he preached – although he had extramarital affairs with men, he never consummated these relationships. (Later, he would reject celibacy, move to Switzerland and take up with a string of lovers.)

Forster was fascinated by Symonds' work, which can be seen in *Maurice* as the basis for Clive's outlook on homosexuality. For Clive, as for Symonds, chastity is key to how he interprets Greek models of same-sex love and it affects how he relates to Maurice in turn. Clive's image of love between men can't bear fleshiness, eroticism, lust or anything like a physical yearning. This is one of the reasons he reacts so violently when Maurice tells him that he and Alec have slept together.

'I have shared with Alec,' he said after a deep thought.

'Shared what?'

'All that I have. Which includes my body.'

Clive sprang up with a whimper of disgust. He wanted to smite the monster, and flee, but he was civilized, and wanted it feebly. After all, they were Cambridge men . . . pillars of society both; he must not show violence.

Clive is jealous here, of course, but he's also angry that his image of how respectable homosexuals should conduct themselves has been shattered, as the physical body intrudes upon his ideal. 'But surely – the sole excuse for any relationship between men is that it remain purely platonic,' he bleats.[31]

The sudden appearance of Cambridge in the middle of all this ('they were Cambridge men') suggests that, in Clive's mind at least, the place is indistinguishable from how he envisages love between men. Cambridge is as idealized and unassailable to him as the forms of same-sex attachment he read about in the *Symposium*. As an old man, alone with his nostalgia, he wistfully imagines: 'Out of some eternal Cambridge his friend began beckoning to him, clothed in the sun, and shaking out the scents and sounds of the May Term.'[32]

The male homosociality of long-lost ancient Greece was something that the university reformers of Oxford and Cambridge sought to rescue from the mists of time. As the nineteenth century neared its end and the New Woman started to assert herself in the public spaces of Victorian England, often astride a bicycle, they sought it with increased intensity. Between ancient Athens and Forster's Cambridge, therefore, there were many real and imagined associations – although the climate certainly wasn't one of them. Plato would have been unpleasantly surprised by the icy north wind that blows unimpeded across the Fens in wintertime.

At times it must have seemed to the young Forster as though he was living in two very different places at once. His tall, lanky form could most often be found in his rooms at King's, which consisted of a top-floor bedroom and a sitting room, the windows of which offered a panorama of the flat green Cambridgeshire countryside. Bisecting this view was the slowly flowing river, punts bobbing past full of passengers all stretched out, enjoying this delicious slice of English country life.

In his head, however, Forster was elsewhere, spending day after day immersed in ancient Greek language and culture in the company of vigorous, smart young men with whom he cultivated intimate friendships for the very first time in his life. Physically he was in Cambridge, but mentally he was a couple of thousand miles away and a couple of thousand years in the past.

Forster's fiction shows a sensitivity to the strangeness of all of this. In his first novel, *The Longest Journey* (1907), a large part of which takes place in Cambridge, his protagonist, Rickie Elliot, spies some elm trees from the window of his rooms in King's College (a lightly fictionalized version of Forster's own). We're told that the elms 'were motionless and seemed still in the glory of midsummer', yet as Rickie gazes out the window, they transform in his mind into the tree-nymphs of Greek mythology: 'Those elms were Dryads – so Rickie believed or pretended, and the line between the two is subtler than we admit.'[33]

The line between Edwardian England and ancient Greece is often portrayed in Forster's work as very subtle indeed, and had to be cautiously monitored, in case the one would break through into the other and cause all kinds of confusion, sexual and otherwise. His short stories especially get to the heart of the matter: how British culture at the start of the twentieth century was saturated by Hellenic ideas that were in fact incompatible with it from the point of view of homosexuality. For a time, the ancient Greeks were central to the rejuvenation of Britain, but they were employed only on condition that any reference to their 'unspeakable vice' was omitted, at least in polite society.

In 'Albergo Empedocle', a story published in 1903, a couple of years after Forster finished his studies at Cambridge, a pleasant young Englishman named Harold is visiting Sicily with his fiancée, Mildred, and his future in-laws. A strange tiredness overcomes him and he disappears into the ruins of a Greek temple for a nap. When he finally awakes, he is much changed. 'I've lived here before,' he says.[34] He can't remember many details but he may have been a Greek from Sicily in perhaps the fifth century BC. One thing is clear to him, however: 'I loved very differently.' Did he love better? Mildred asks. 'One of the thorns scratched him on the hand. "Yes, I loved better too," he continued, watching the little drops of blood swell out.'[35] The blatant homoeroticism of the thorn that pricks and blood that 'swells' implies of course that Harold's Greek life included love of the Symonds' variety.

The cruel disjunction between past and present finally becomes too much for Harold, however ('I'll have no queerness in a son-in-law,' Mildred's father harrumphs), and by the end of the story we find him in an asylum, talking to himself.[36] His tale is narrated by a close male friend, who concludes that Harold has retreated to an imaginary life among the Greeks, 'among friends of two thousand years ago, whose names we have never heard'.[37] In this story, Forster is keen to imagine Greek love breaking through the membrane between here and now, then and there, but he's also pessimistic about the chances of that happening and concerned about the backlash that might ensue if it did.

Forster's position didn't change that much over the years. In his 1960 note on *Maurice*, he declared that, since the writing of the book, 'there has been a change in the public attitude here: the change from ignorance and terror to familiarity and contempt'. The public still loathed homosexuality, he said, and correctly predicted that 'police prosecutions will continue . . . Clive on the bench will continue to sentence Alec in the dock. Maurice may get off.'[38]

In the face of such deep-seated public contempt for homosexuality, the only possible option for Forster seemed to be desire's careful management – an activity that must have felt natural to one who had spent so long in the city of Cambridge. Refusing to publish *Maurice* while he lived, Forster was committed to a strict compartmentalization of his experience into public and private, open and secret; tracing lines across his life like a map.

Forster's Room

Setting off early, as I pedal down the lane on my bike, pebbles scatter on either side and a memory of Brighton beach surfaces briefly in my mind. The crunch and clatter of stones underfoot. The screams of seagulls on the air. A luminous carousel, horses spinning past. Here, the terrace is still, and the sound of my leaving echoes all around.

Flying up Trumpington Road on my way to the centre of Cambridge, a gentle summer breeze brings my brain to life. A pigeon clatters out of the trees and into a cloudless sky. The bicycle clicks a metronomic rhythm. On Trumpington Street, I pass the great grand edifice of the Fitzwilliam Museum on my left, its entrance marked with huge, towering columns (in the Greek style, naturally). Forster walked this way for decades. From 1947 to the week of his death in 1970, he went back and forth each day from his accommodation on Trumpington Street to his room at King's – which is where I'm headed. My friend David Hillman is a fellow of the college and I persuaded him to get me in and let me have a look around. (He didn't take too much convincing; Shakespeare scholars are usually up for anything.) For a moment I think I see Forster's reflection in the window of the old dispensing chemist. He isn't there, of course; not many people are at this time of day.

Soon enough, the view up ahead narrows and I come to where the colleges congregate. The sheer walls of Peterhouse and Pembroke and Corpus Christi press in on both sides, squeezing the road in between. At the gatehouses of these places, old white men, faces lined and sagging like a bulldog's, eye each visitor with suspicion. And then, an opening: the concourse of King's College. The old city's bustling heart to which the tourists will soon throng, gathered together in groups, wielding selfie sticks. Chaining my bike to a nearby lamp post, I think about how quiet it is, except for the sound of my footsteps on the paving stones. In front of me is another gatehouse and another enormous oak door just like the others, barring entry and belying the apparent welcome of the forecourt.

A small door in the large one creaks open and David's head appears; his beard is grizzled and his eyes have the tired, impatient look of a new parent running on adrenaline. He beckons to me and I step swiftly through the opening; once we're inside, the lawns of the college spread out before us. In the centre of the front court stands the oxidized statue I'd seen long ago in the film of *Maurice*. Real and cinematic worlds collide.

We make quickly for the Wilkins Building over to the

left, great Gothic windows cut into its limestone walls like empty eye-sockets. In one of them, I see what looks like a figure, balding and with wire-rimmed glasses, bent over a desk. 'I hope it's worth it,' David mumbles jovially. When I look back the figure is gone, replaced by an antique globe.

Through the door of the building, up the stairs, and soon enough, there we are. Without ceremony, David opens the door to Forster's old room and the lights come on in a flash: unflattering fluorescent glare revealing an unremarkable room with municipal white walls. I remember Vivien Leigh as Blanche DuBois in *A Streetcar Named Desire* (1951), flinging herself around desperately, exclaiming: 'I can't stand a naked bulb any more than I can a rude remark or a vulgar action.' Under this stark light, neither nostalgia nor Blanche's beloved magic could survive.

Looking around, I can see that little remains of Forster's sitting room, which is now the home of the college's graduate society – if 'home' is the right word for so dull and anonymous a place as this. Instead of the writer's well-loved objects and furniture, such as his aunt's nursery table, there is a football table, a TV and a bookshelf filled with out-of-date travel books. I count four sagging grey Ikea sofas, and a matching armchair slouching in the corner, none of it owned by anyone. It's hard to believe that this is once the room that was so important to Forster, who'd come here almost every day to meet students and write his letters. In photos and films I'd found of his time in Cambridge, it seemed like such an intimate space. I remember one photo in particular from 1947, taken in this room by Bill Brandt with Forster seated over there by the mantelpiece . . .

'The mantelpiece is Forster's,' David says with a yawn,

as if he had guessed what I was thinking. 'The only thing left here that is.'

So it is: the imposing oak mantelpiece that almost fills one wall. Designed and made by Forster's father in 1876, and carted from one of his mother's houses to another, it finally ended up here. A massive, ugly thing from another time, painted the dark brown that children get when they mix all the colours together indiscriminately. I suppose it should give me some comfort – here is something of Forster's that survived, an object that he loved that still lingered on in his room. But in the midst of all this blandness and flat-pack Swedish furniture, it looks embarrassingly out of place. I flop down onto one of those terrible sofas, overwhelmed by disappointment and feelings of loss.

I'd watched a BBC documentary about Forster once, a black-and-white film made in 1958 in which he was shown walking around this very room, reading in an armchair, writing at a table. Sitting in front of his mantelpiece, he'd spoken frankly about his work, why he'd written so few novels, and why it'd been so long since his last one (*A Passage to India* came out in 1924). 'One of the reasons I stopped writing novels is that the social aspect of the world changed so very much,' he said. 'I'd been accustomed to write about the old, vanished world, with its homes and its family life and its comparative peace. All that went . . .' With the Great War and the social upheaval it unleashed, the old Edwardian world Forster knew so well vanished, and with it went the subject of his novels. He wouldn't publish another one in his lifetime.

For Forster, the vanishing of the old order was insurmountable. It blocked his creativity and caused him to give up writing novels altogether. But as I sit there, in that garishly lit thoroughfare of a room, and in spite of the inauspicious surroundings (or maybe because of them), an idea starts to grow in my mind. It follows me as I retrace my steps down the stairs and out through the gates of the college, thanking David for his kindness as I go.

Out on the street again, I find myself wandering through Cambridge's lanes and alleyways holding onto this. What if the vanishing demanded by the forward march of progress wasn't an obstacle to imagination or a barrier to thought, as it was for Forster? What if, instead of simply a cause for sorrow, disappearance inspired us to write and create?

To turn things around this way would be to take vanishing and disappearance not as the exhaustion of thinking, but as its starting point; to approach disappearance as a provocation that calls on us to ask *why did it happen* and *what were its effects*; to bear witness to what was lost. From a queer perspective, this kind of approach would counteract what Forster himself referred to as the 'great unrecorded history' of the queer past. What and who were unrecorded? Was it neglect or negligence that caused their omission? What now remains that allows us to set the record straight? The answers to these questions would form the basis of a new history, the one that you're now reading: a counter-history of queer people and places.

Vera Holme with unknown woman, London, 1910.
Photographer unknown. Courtesy of LSE Library.

2.

Invert: London's Queer Suffragettes

The tremendous roar of the thing! Rattling the windows of the cab, making the mechanisms of the dashboard shudder. A deep rumbling din that fills the air and makes the human body tremble. Juddering vibrations felt keenly in the bones, in the belly, between the legs. What it must be like to master this gigantic metal beast. To hold all its power in one's fists and then – to unleash it.

Moving up the gears with a tremendous inhuman whine. First gear to second: an extraordinary momentum building, shoving the machine forward. Third gear: passing an omnibus on the left, still drawn by horses. Passengers on the top deck craning their necks, trying to catch a glimpse of who it is that zooms by in this loud luxury automobile. A shining Austin 18/24 Landaulet painted purple, green and white, driven by a woman in a peaked cap. *AROOGAH!* The horn blares out, acknowledging their interest.

Across the view sweeps a flurry of pigeons – and there it is: the chaotic spectacle of London traffic circa 1909. How exhilarating it is to be part of it, at one with the flow that circulates through the Empire's beating heart. Horse-drawn carriages, cars, tricycles; more buses converging, moving arrhythmically forward in spurts, plastered with advertisements for Dewar's Whisky and Seeger's Hair Dye. The sight overpowers the senses. The smell too: a thick, pervasive aroma of sour horse-dung and belching drains. Dense black smoke that pours, billowing, from the backs of automobiles, smearing the windows of buildings on either side, blackening the bell tower of St Clement's Church rising up to the right.

'Oranges and lemons, say the bells of St Clement's . . .'

On to the Strand, now, thundering past Somerset House and on into Theatreland. All in a sparkling rush come the famous theatres of the West End. The Lyceum, over to the right in grand Rococo style, home of melodrama and sophisticated adaptations of the Bard for an elegant crowd. Up on the left, the Savoy, beloved by fans of comic-opera, of Gilbert and Sullivan, and the headquarters of the famous D'Oyly Carte Opera Company. Now on the right, the Vaudeville, followed by its sister, the Adelphi, hosting comedies and musical revues mostly – gussied-up music halls, the pair of them, with artistic pretensions.

Up ahead, pedestrians swarm the pavements and roadways. Men dressed in suits and bowler hats, and sporting great big moustaches. In and around the oncoming traffic they weave like determined ants. Moving between the vehicles impulsively with little order or caution, reckless in their efforts to get to the other side. All of them going somewhere terribly important.

All except this one: a delivery boy dawdling on a traffic island with his mind on other matters, picking his nose as he watches the human comedy unfold. He spots the car and arrests his investigations in slack-jawed wonder. 'A woman chauffeur?' he mouths, his words swallowed up by the cacophony of the street. He gawps as the car speeds by, mouth open, catching flies. Regaining his senses suddenly, he shouts: 'Votes for Women!'

A great roar of laughter bursts forth from the driver. A powerfully built twenty-eight-year-old northern woman with big teeth and an abundant sense of humour. Vera Holme: actress, singer and newly appointed chauffeur to Emmeline Pankhurst, the charismatic leader of the suffragettes. The only female chauffeur in Britain when she got the job in August 1909. 'Anybody who has seen Miss Holme starting up, changing gear, and steering in and out of traffic, will freely acknowledge her right to call herself a chauffeur,' noted a reporter for *The Chauffeur* magazine in June 1911. But this pioneering queer suffragette would never have sought a male reader's acknowledgement for anything – least of all her right to occupy the streets. Jubilantly, she hits the horn again. *AROOGAH!*

In 1967, the French thinker Michel Foucault declared that 'the present epoch will perhaps be above all the epoch of space'. If earlier epochs were defined by a preoccupation with time, this one would be centrally concerned with the spaces around us, the ones we inhabit, the ones we move through. According to Foucault, the built environment in particular 'appears to form the horizon of our concerns, our theory, our systems'.[1] The women who fought for the right to vote in the early decades of the twentieth century might well have agreed with him. They arguably laid the foundation for the epoch he belatedly identified.

The struggle for women's enfranchisement was inseparable from a struggle over space. At the turn of the century, patriarchal power was maintained by keeping control over who was able to use particular places, who was able to occupy them – and when. The world was strictly divided into public and private spheres, and on that basis gendered either male or female. The militant suffragettes implicitly understood that, in order to change society, the meaning attributed to certain spaces like the street and the home also needed to change; by occupying them differently and using them differently, they might be recoded in people's minds.

Queer suffragettes (who were many, in spite of scant reference to them in the history books) were especially well placed to undertake the necessary recoding of spaces. Their sexual orientation situated them curiously. Outside the heterosexual norm, but neither banned by law nor yet pathologized by science, they had an ambiguous position that afforded them a unique perspective on how society worked. It also helped them to see how social prejudices were maintained and reproduced by the careful management of the physical environment, and how they could be subverted. Vera Holme's spectacular invasion of London's streets by both car and horse; Cicely Hamilton's dramatic intervention into the argument for separate, gendered spheres; Edith Craig and her lovers' vigorous subversion of domesticity: space was a battleground in the suffragettes' fight against a misogynistic culture, and on the front lines were the epoch-making queer women we will meet in this chapter.

A couple of miles north of the Strand, but a world away from its sights and sounds and rhythms of life, is Tavistock Square. A light, airy, beautifully tended park in the heart of Bloomsbury. Relatively small, perhaps, it nonetheless feels roomy and breathable. Buildings around it maintain a respectable distance, standing a good way back from its wrought-iron railings, letting in the sky. Above, a pale-blue expanse is rent by a couple of gossamer contrails.

The park's giant sycamore trees reach up into the sky,

grasping the sun's warmth eagerly. Everything is peaceful and serene. On the benches that line the dusty gravel paths, couples lounge, canoodling. Tourists chat quietly to each other, face masks trailing from their fingers, gazing at their phones. A middle-aged man in a suit is stretched out, taking his ease. Here, traffic noises sound like a sigh – a vague memory of somewhere else. I think to myself: what writer wouldn't love to live in a tranquil place like this?

I'm standing in the sunlit south-western corner of the square, facing a bust of the modernist writer Virginia Woolf, whose name is synonymous with this area of London. Woolf moved to Bloomsbury in 1904 with her sister, the artist Vanessa Bell, and stayed in various flats around here as her career as a novelist and critic took off. This monument to her was erected in 2004 in recognition of her importance to the history of Bloomsbury – and how inextricable her reputation is from the place.

I'm sorry to say, she's seen better days. In this rendition by a contemporary, the sculptor Stephen Tomlin, Woolf is frankly hideous. An inhumanly long face; a mouth opened in what appears to be a low moan; two bronze eyes, blank and unseeing: she looks like a zombie. Today, to complete the effect, the bust is covered with pigeon shit that trickles down in dirty white rivulets like melted ice cream down a screaming toddler's fist.

But I suppose it doesn't really matter that Woolf's monument is so irretrievably bad. The whole of Bloomsbury is, in fact, a kind of vast monument to her and the group of artists and writers who also lived here, with whom she was intimately connected. I take a short walk next door to Gordon Square, and it's speckled with blue and brown plaques none-too-subtly informing passers-by that members of the Bloomsbury Group lived in this or that building. Woolf and Bell cohabited with their brothers at number 46; when they moved out, the economist John Maynard Keynes moved in. Lytton Strachey arrived at number 51 after the Great War. Bell later lived with her husband, Clive, and the artist Duncan Grant at number 39. Peering into the windows of some of these houses, I see they've all been converted into offices and university seminar rooms. Like the King's College room of E. M. Forster (who was an intimate of the Bloomsbury set), these spaces are now vacant and anonymous.

As Dorothy Parker is rumoured to have said, the Bloomsbury Set 'lived in squares, painted in circles, and loved in triangles',[2] and over the years Woolf, Bell, Strachey and Co. have attracted as much attention for their unconventional love lives as they have for their work. Woolf's affair with the writer Vita Sackville-West and the Bells' open marriage have been the focus of much dreamy speculation; perhaps a little less well known is Keynes's stunning transition from homosexuality to a happy heterosexual marriage with the Russian ballerina Lydia Lopokova, or Strachey's sadomasochistic crucifixion fantasy. In any case, for the best part of a century Bloomsbury biographies have been strip-mined for salacious details such that, by this point, everyone must surely know about these queer pioneers and their London.

In terms of queer spaces, the peaceful, sunlit squares of Bloomsbury have many delights to offer – as indeed do the other places connected with the group, like Charleston House in rural Sussex. But I'm after less obvious pleasures, less monumental figures. There's more to London than this handful of residential squares, and there's much more to queer London than the Bloomsbury Group – especially in the opening decades of the twentieth century.

This was when the movement for women's suffrage began in earnest. After decades of small-scale agitation and a seismic shift in women's fortunes in Britain, the 1890s saw the emergence of the New Woman – a newly educated, newly independent, largely middle-class woman who chafed at her perceived inferiority to men in most walks of life. Following closely on her heels, the campaign for women's votes erupted into the public consciousness with the power of an epiphany, and reached fever pitch in the years before war broke out in 1914. Women's suffrage was passionately debated (or assiduously ignored) in the streets and homes of London, as Emmeline Pankhurst and militant suffragettes like her staged one demonstration after another to keep the public's eye fixed on their cause.

For queer women, the chance to associate freely at meetings and demonstrations, out of reach of a draconian patriarchy, came with other benefits – namely the opportunity to meet like-minded women. Women who loved women mingled together at meetings, and public demonstrations, and suffrage fairs like the Women's Exhibition of 1909. The shared activity of selling newspapers or sewing banners for the cause gave them unprecedented opportunities to strike up a conversation or go for an intimate cup of tea with any of their sisters-in-arms. In this way, according to the lesbian historian Emily Hamer, the suffrage movement created the conditions for the emergence of 'a positive lesbian environment'.[3]

Yet hardly anyone seems to know about the homosexual undercurrents of women's suffrage. They weren't recognized at the time, and this hasn't been corrected in the intervening years. Everything I know (and everything you're going to read here) has been pieced together from an assortment of fragments: a couple of incomplete archives, essays in books long out of print, glancing references in the major studies of the movement. Sometimes the evidence just isn't there – same-sex desires between women were often left unarticulated in print, and private letters were frequently destroyed out of fear. More often, it's simply been ignored. But as we'll see in this chapter, queer women played essential roles in the struggle for women's suffrage in Britain, and their influence had a special impact on the arts and culture of the movement. Down in Theatreland especially, queer actresses, playwrights and theatre producers all made enormous contributions to the cause.

On Queer Street

Vera Holme, mischief-making mounted suffragette, chauffeur to the Pankhursts and male impersonator extraordinaire, was born on 29 August 1881 in Birkdale, an unremarkable village near Liverpool. Her family was relatively well off (her father was a timber merchant), so when she was a teenager, she was sent abroad to be educated at a convent school for girls in Belgium. In a black-and-white photograph taken during her time there, she's seated beneath some trees with three of her classmates. All four of them wear the sober convent uniform of a dark dress with a white clerical collar clasped around the throat. Turned towards the camera, the faces of the others display boredom or indifference, while Holme's expression is eager and happy.

I wonder about the source of her incongruous happiness. Maybe it's the friend who's sitting beside her, a dark-haired girl with sad, deep-set eyes and a crucifix dangling from her neck. They might have been lovers. In Holme's archive at the London School of Economics Library there are in fact two copies of this photograph. In the other one, Holme has cut the other girls out so that only she and this sad-eyed brunette remain. Together for ever in the sepia-toned shelter of a tree. Or maybe what made Holme so happy was simply being immersed in a community of women, far from the reach of men – such women-only spaces were rare enough in 1900. When Holme joined the suffrage movement sometime later, she would find that community once more.

At the convent school, huge emphasis was placed on music, singing and other subjects that would enable young, middle-class women to attract and entertain wealthy young men. This would secure their future (it was hoped), with marriage, a husband and, God willing, a family. But Holme had other ideas. From around 1902 this Lancashire lass put her musical skills to much better use by supporting herself as an actress and singer on the Edwardian stage. It was a rather unusual choice of career; then again, Holme was a rather unusual woman.

She started out working with small theatre companies that toured the provinces, performing in pantomimes and revivals of popular plays in the theatres of places like Sunderland and Edinburgh. Within a couple of years, her career was more established and she was at least making enough money to settle in London. 'Trouser roles' seem to have been her speciality – the kinds of parts that required cross-dressing. Publicity photographs from the early 1900s show she had carved out something of a niche for herself as a male impersonator, and around this time people started calling her Jack. In one photograph, she stands dressed in a police uniform, her hair arranged into a man's crop. With a broad, cheeky smile on her face, she looks like she's enjoying every minute of it.

A handful of photographs show her performing in other male roles. As an eighteenth-century aristocrat in breeches and an embroidered knee-length coat. As a working-class Victorian man pleading with his comically irate spouse. Joking with another male impersonator, both of them dressed in top hat and tails. Looking at this last photo, I can't help but think of Sarah Waters' *Tipping the Velvet* (1998), a gloriously queer, cross-dressing romp of a novel set against the backdrop of the Victorian music hall.

The narrator of Waters' book is an oyster girl from Whitstable named Nan King, who falls in love with Kitty Butler, a male impersonator who's touring the local music halls. Nan is bewitched by Kitty's gender-bending performances, but it's the clothes as much as the woman inside them that capture our young heroine's imagination. Breathlessly, she describes Kitty's dapper outfit:

> She wore a suit – a handsome gentleman's suit, cut to her size, and lined at the cuffs and the flaps with flashing silk. There was a rose in her lapel, and lavender gloves at her pocket.[4]

Before long, Kitty and Nan have run off to London together, and they end up sharing a room in a boarding house in Brixton. Apologizing for the cramped conditions, the landlady says: 'You'll be quite on top of each other in here, I'm afraid.' Sure enough, we soon find Nan and Kitty on top of each other, making trembling love in a narrow bed. In Nan's feverish account,

> At last she was naked, all except for the pearl and chain about her neck; she turned in my hands, stiff and pimpled with cold, and I felt the brush of her nipples, and of the hair between her thighs. Then she moved away, and the bedsprings creaked; and at that, I didn't wait to pull the rest of my own clothes off but followed her to the bed and found her shivering there, beneath the sheets.[5]

Although Waters' novel is set a decade or so before Holme would tread the boards in London (and written almost a century afterwards), the stories of Nan King and Vera Holme overlap and interconnect in interesting ways. For one thing, Holme's primary romantic relationship in the early 1900s was also with a woman who shared her room and her bed in a boarding house in London. In her diary of 1903, she frequently writes about her friend 'Aggie', who was most likely another actress. Tiny details of their life together surface in the curling script of Holme's fountain pen: they spend Sunday morning together in bed, reading and smoking; they take care of each other when they're ill; they fight, say 'vile' things in the heat of the moment, and eventually make up . . . We don't know for sure if their relationship was a sexual one – the diary is no help on that score. It falls to writers like Waters to imagine the erotic lives of intimate female friends such as these; to infuse the historical record with sensual pleasures that were rarely committed to paper at the time.

Like Nan, Holme also enjoyed wearing men's clothes even when she wasn't performing. In Waters' novel, Nan follows Kitty's lead and becomes a male impersonator. Thrilled by the independence and freedom of movement that men's clothing allows, she takes her act off the stage – and into the streets. London! she exclaims. 'To walk freely about it at last – to walk as a boy, as a handsome boy in a well-sewn suit, whom the people stared after only to envy, never to mock – well, it had a brittle kind of glamour to it, and that was all I knew, just then, of satisfaction.'[6] Holme was a big, butch woman who loved putting on a shirt and tie, and would later gravitate towards professions in which she would be allowed to wear them every day – dressed as a chauffeur as she drove the suffragettes' leader around, or going into the battlefields of Serbia in the uniform of a Scottish Women's Hospital unit.

It's tempting to read Holme as something of a prototype of the mannish lesbian, that iconic butch woman dressed in men's clothing who is by now a well-known cultural figure. Given that she lived her life as a queer woman, it might seem to twenty-first-century eyes that she chose to declare her sexual preference in how she dressed – that she wore men's fashions *because* she was a lesbian. But things would have looked slightly different to a spectator in the early 1900s. At that time, women wearing men's clothing didn't necessarily connote queerness. The mannish lesbian was in fact a later invention, a figure that emerged out of the censorship of *The Well of Loneliness* in 1928 and the infamy surrounding Radclyffe Hall, who would become friends with Holme in the 1930s. We will delve into the murky depths of *The Well* and its trial in the next chapter.

Of course, that's not to say that a woman walking around in a shirt and tie didn't raise eyebrows, but the intended effect wasn't so much about announcing one's sexuality. It was more about asserting one's presence – one's right to exist – in spaces dominated by men, using styles that were familiar to them. As the historian of sexuality Deborah Cohler points out, forms of female masculinity in the period 'were not primarily coded references to female homosexuality, but rather signals of women's efforts to gain subjectivity, enfranchisement, and access to the public sphere'.[7] Holme's choice of clothing was just one of the ways she asserted her right to occupy traditionally male spheres.

Irrespective of what they wore, the category of the lesbian or the queer woman was itself relatively undefined at this point in time. Although the male homosexual was becoming infamous by the early 1900s as the repercussions of the Wilde trial were felt throughout Britain, culturally, scientifically and legally the female homosexual had a much more ambiguous status. Same-sex desire between women rarely appeared in nineteenth-century literature; where it did, the authors were generally men, and the representations weren't flattering. Likewise, sexology, the scientific study of human sexuality founded by Havelock Ellis that had advanced so many claims about homosexual men, had surprisingly little to say about women. Pioneering scientists like the German sexologist Magnus Hirschfeld limited themselves to figuring out whether or not such women actually existed. In England, Ellis dedicated more space to queer women in the second volume of his *Studies in the Psychology of Sex*, which was published in 1900, but his work didn't receive much attention beyond the scientific community until much later.

Meanwhile, according to British law, same-sex relations between women were not a crime and the subject was rarely raised. Whenever it did come up, as in a famous libel case in 1918, it caused nothing but confusion. In what was called the 'Trial of the Century', the actress Maud Allan sued a homophobic MP named Noel Pemberton Billing for claiming that she was at the centre of a homosexual conspiracy, which he called the 'Cult of the Clitoris' (the faithful presumably worshipped on their knees). During the trial, the topic of lesbianism and the term 'clitoris' as homosexual code were both discussed at length by such notable witnesses as Lord Alfred Douglas, who was recently reborn as a Catholic and repudiating Wilde and homosexuality to anyone who'd listen. At its conclusion, however, the judge instructed the jury to disregard any mention of lesbianism they'd heard. Unsurprisingly, the befuddled jury returned a verdict of not guilty.

Regarding this widespread – and often wilful – ignorance about female homosexuality, the sociologist Jeffrey Weeks writes: 'The truth is that if male homosexuals were the "twilight men" of early twentieth-century history, lesbians were by and large the "invisible women".'[8] Yet the illegitimacy of women's queer desire in the eyes of the majority, and the inability to even conceive of erotic or romantic love between women, may not have been as limiting as we might expect. The ambiguity of female homosexuality in fact offered queer women advantages and opportunities that would have been denied their male counterparts.

Given that society considered sexuality in purely heterosexual terms, a woman who only had sex with another woman could honestly claim to be a virgin. Likewise with monogamy: because an erotic relationship with another woman wasn't considered a true sexual relationship, a married woman might have sex with all the women she wanted and still consider herself faithful. Without labels or guidelines or culturally dominant reference points, some queer women were remarkably free about how they chose to conduct themselves in their relationships. As we'll see later on in the case of Edith Craig and her 'Boys', they were also free to decide what forms those relationships would take.

By December 1906, Holme was on stage at London's Savoy Theatre, performing in the ladies' chorus of the D'Oyly Carte Opera Company's repertory season of works by W. S. Gilbert and Arthur Sullivan. Gilbert himself was nominally in charge of the series that year, which included revivals of classic Savoy operas like *Patience, The Yeomen of the Guard* and *The Gondoliers*. When Holme returned for the second repertory season in 1907, the run also included *The Mikado*, Gilbert and Sullivan's most popular opera.

Holme was earning £2 a week as a contralto chorister at the Savoy, which meant she could give up all her side hustles and focus exclusively on the theatre. But soon the movement for women's suffrage came calling; it arrived on her doorstep, in fact. Emmeline Pankhurst and her daughter Christabel set up the militant Women's Social and Political Union (WSPU) in Manchester in 1903, but to better press their case with the government, the headquarters of the organization moved to Clement's Inn, London, in 1906. This, as it turned out, was a short, ten-minute walk down the road from the Savoy Theatre. In February 1907, the constitutional National Union of Women's Suffrage Societies (NUWSS) organized the United Procession of Women, which was attended by upwards of three thousand women – at the time the largest-ever demonstration for women's votes. The procession paraded from Hyde Park Corner to the Strand, ending up directly across the street from the Savoy. Holme's day job was right at the heart of militant and constitutional movements for women's suffrage, and it wasn't long before she'd throw herself into the fray with her usual enthusiasm. Sylvia Pankhurst remembered her as 'a noisy and explosive young person, frequently rebuked by her elders for lack of dignity'.[9]

In 1909 she joined the Actresses' Franchise League (AFL), an organization founded in 1908 as 'a bond of union between all women in the theatrical profession who are in sympathy with the Woman's Franchise Movement'.[10] The AFL counted among its members the well-known theatre producer Edith Craig, writer Christopher St John and playwright Cicely Hamilton – all queer women with whom Holme became lifelong friends, as we'll soon see.

She also signed up to the WSPU, whose militant tactics appealed to her. The WSPU was a direct-action group, whose motto was 'Deeds not Words'. Such deeds were initially limited to harassing MPs on the street, interrupting public meetings and demonstrating outside parliament in order to draw attention to the issue of women's suffrage. When their calls for enfranchisement were ignored, however, the campaign escalated to more violent activities, like breaking the windows of politicians' houses, setting fire to postboxes and, when they were imprisoned, going on hunger strike. Most notoriously, the WSPU's Emily Davison also ran onto the racecourse during the Derby on 4 June 1913 and was trampled to death by King George V's horse.

Although Holme was committed to the cause (she was sentenced to a short spell in Holloway prison for her part in a demonstration in 1911), her style of militancy was more mischievous. In 1909, she took the train to Bristol with a few other suffragettes. Their idea was to interrupt a speech by the Liberal MP Augustine Birrell at Colston Hall. Women weren't allowed into the meeting, so Holme and her comrade Elsie Howey came up with a plan. To attend a concert in the hall beforehand, then hide themselves inside the organ until the time came for the speeches. In her colossal history of the suffrage movement, *Rise Up, Women!* (2018), Diane Atkinson describes the hilarious scene that ensued:

> Vera and Elsie waited until Birrell launched into his speech and when he reached his 'most telling sentences', a disembodied voice shouted: 'Votes for Women! Give women their political freedom.' The stewards 'scampered here, there, and everywhere' while the suffragettes looked down into the hall from their secret eyrie through the slivers of light between the pipes. No one could find them and Birrell carried on. When he started to talk about liberty one of the women shouted: 'Why don't you give women liberty?'[11]

After a chase – which must have had something of a comedy sketch about it – the stewards finally caught up with the suffragettes and succeeded in kicking them out. Holme's witty poem about the incident later appeared in the WSPU's newspaper *Votes for Women*.

Our voices rang out from the twilight,
But nowhere could we be found;
They looked from the floor to the ceiling –

Then stewards came searching round.
We asked for votes for women,
And that justice should be done;
But Birrell he could not answer,
And the audience made such fun.[12]

Through her involvement with the WSPU, Holme also met Lady Evelina Haverfield, who became the great love of her life. Rich and married, the daughter of a baron and fourteen years older, Haverfield might seem on the face of it to have been an unlikely match for the boisterous, 'explosive' Holme, but they were in fact very well suited. Both were passionate about women's suffrage, of course, and Haverfield was especially ready to fight for the WSPU. At a protest held in front of 10 Downing Street in November 1910, she was arrested for punching a policeman in the mouth. As she hit him, it was later reported, she said: 'That is not quite hard enough. Next time I come, I will bring a revolver and shoot you.'[13]

Holme and Haverfield were also drawn to masculine styles of dress, and each was an excellent horsewoman. None of their letters to each other remains, but one especially tender artefact that survives in Holme's archive – an acrostic poem written by her on a sheet of notepaper – reveals something of their intimacy, which is woven through with a shared love of horses and the freedom they felt galloping across an open field.

<u>E</u>arly the morn, list! the song bird sings sweet
<u>V</u>aried the pleasures I meet on my ride
<u>E</u>very gift nature has falls at my feet
<u>H</u>orse – thou my good friend, through time and tide

<u>A</u>way thou and I, from life's maddening throng
<u>V</u>alliant [sic] old fellow, just gallops along
<u>E</u>ager to do my desire? aye, I know
<u>R</u>esolute boy, yes I know you can go!
<u>F</u>ield it is ours – you are leading the way
<u>I</u>ncline or hill, ne'er to slow you they tend
<u>E</u>ven the fields left behind us look grey
'<u>L</u>eader', well named, you have carried your friend
<u>D</u>ear.

I imagine Holme musing over these lines as she and her lover lay together, morning sunlight rippling across the eiderdown of their big wooden bed – the one with their initials, 'E.H. & V.H.', carved into it. On a yellowing piece of paper in Holme's archive, the bed is listed as part of an inventory of items contained in Peace Cottage, Haverfield's small stone house nestled in a corner of Exmoor National Park in Devon, where the two stayed when they weren't campaigning for the vote. The inventory also says that the curtains were styled in the WSPU colours of white with a purple-and-green trim. These women evidently took their work home with them.

Both Holme and Haverfield put their horse-riding skills at the service of the movement, signing up to become part of the WSPU's cavalry regiment and accompanying the organization on various marches through London. Suffragettes on horseback gave protection to women on the ground, and lent the marches themselves a certain status and ceremony. If Holme was a big, tall, noticeable presence on the ground, astride a horse trotting through London, she was unmistakable. Syliva Pankhurst remembers her riding valiantly ahead of a WSPU delegation to the House of Commons on 29 June 1909. Emmeline Pankhurst and others were due to present a petition to Prime Minister Herbert Asquith and

> Miss Vera Holme was dispatched on horseback with an advance letter announcing that the deputation was about to appear. With all possible speed she rode on, forging her way through the masses of people, until, close to the House itself, she was met by a body of mounted police, who demanded her business. She handed the letter for Mr. Asquith to the Inspector but he merely flung it on the ground where it was lost to sight amongst the crowd.[14]

Holme's embrace of her role as a mounted suffragette hints at how essential the street is to her story. Taken together with her appointment later that year as the WSPU chauffeur, and her work selling *Votes for Women* newspapers on London street corners, it's clear how much the street was part of her identity. Or rather, how much it meant to her to be able to assert her presence in a space that was ordinarily presided over by men.

In this regard, Holme's various occupations were of a piece with the larger aims of the movement, which fought for greater participation in public life for women. If women got the vote, they could have an impact outside the home – perhaps even in the streets.

It might not seem as if they were asking for much, but to conservatives at the time this amounted to nothing less than an attack on the natural order. The latter subscribed to the idea of 'separate spheres': God (or Nature, if you like) had divided the world into two different sexes, and each sex was given its own, separate space or sphere of influence. Women were in charge of the home and domestic matters, while men were responsible for everything else: the public sphere, politics, national and international affairs . . . For those who opposed women's suffrage (the 'Antis', as they were called), the resistance of the women's suffrage movement to the natural way of things showed how crazy they were – hysterical, even.

This abstract argument about women's access to male spheres quickly spilled over into a struggle over actually existing spaces of the city. The WSPU's campaign of window-smashing, which targeted the physical barriers that separated women from political spaces like 10 Downing Street, catapulted their attack on the ideology of separate spheres into the physical world. One of the most contested places in this struggle was the street. The WSPU sent its members out onto the street corners and traffic islands to sell their newspapers; suffragettes chalked 'Votes for Women' on the paving stones; they even rained down pamphlets from hot-air balloons floating in the sky: underfoot and overhead, incursions were constantly being made into this male-occupied territory.

Unsurprisingly, the Antis, who were fanatically attached to the distinction between this and that, outside and inside, male and female spaces, violently repelled suffragette intrusions. Feminist historian Martha Vicinus writes that women on the streets, who were attending demonstrations or at their newspaper pitch,

> could be repeatedly pinched, punched in the breasts, fondled under their skirts, and spit [sic] at in the face, have their hats pulled off, have rotten fruit thrown at them, and suffer other indignities . . . When middle-class women did

not do as they were supposed to, or stay where they were supposed to be, the public assumed they were fair game.[15]

Holme wasn't the only suffragette who occupied the street, therefore, or who did so as an act of defiance. On many occasions, at demonstrations and protests, she was joined by her sisters-in-arms. But there's something distinctive about the way she did it: her confidence; her flagrant disregard for custom. On foot, on a horse, behind the wheel of a car, whatever the mode of conveyance, Holme navigated her way through this male-dominated zone with ease and vigour. She seems to have been as comfortable moving back and forth between male and female spaces as she was scrambling the gendered sartorial codes of the day in a shirt and tie.

It's in the street where Holme's queerness made its mark. Her sexual life and its cultural ambiguity equipped her for the roles she would take on in the suffrage movement, and allowed her to make such a remarkable impact. As we have seen, before 1928 and the trial over *The Well of Loneliness*, female homosexuality had a pretty undefined status: socially and legally speaking, it didn't conform to existing rules or language. Queer women in this period knew what it was to have sexual desires for which there was no official terminology, and those like Holme, who pursued such unnamed desires, were true pioneers. Not only were they breaking with convention, they were blazing a trail through it without any idea of what they'd find on the other side.

In short, by the time she became a suffragette, Holme understood transgression intimately – *existentially* – which made transgressing borderlines between separate spheres a breeze for her. Precisely because her status as a queer woman was so ambiguous (and so filled with possibility as a result), she was able to move with conviction between differently gendered spaces, recoding them as she went. If E. M. Forster, ensconced in Cambridge, cleaved to the strict division of the physical world around him, mapping it onto his emotional life and his closeted passions, Vera Holme turned the inside out, rushing into the spaces of London and transforming them with a disposition born of uncodified queer desire.

Holme's involvement with the 'Votes for Women' campaign came at the expense of her burgeoning career and she no longer worked professionally in theatre after 1909. But if her commitment to the cause left her little time for acting, it didn't mean she was short of opportunities to perform. Theatre was, in fact, a vital part of the movement and its efforts to rally supporters. At the time, plays and pageants were the most important form of popular entertainment, and feminist performance was key to engaging audiences. Here, as in the case of her horse-riding, Holme was eager to use her skills to support the movement. Her most notable role was in a 1911 performance of *A Pageant of Great Women*. Unsurprisingly, she appeared in a 'trouser role', playing the part of Hannah Snell, an eighteenth-century Englishwoman who impersonated a man in order to join the army.

A Pageant of Great Women was a triumph of suffragette theatre. Written by Cicely Hamilton and first produced by Edith Craig at the Scala Theatre in London in 1909, the concept for the piece was simple. By parading a large number of heroic women from history across the stage, it unequivocally showed how much women had achieved in spite of their social disadvantage, and how ready they were to wield the vote. Set out like a court case, the play had one act and three main speaking

Edith Craig (left) with Cicely Hamilton, London, 1909.
Photo by Lena Connell. Courtesy of LSE Library.

parts: the symbolic figures of Woman, who pleads for freedom and enfranchisement; Justice, who hears her request; and
Prejudice, who argues against her.

Women are silly, vain creatures, unfit for freedom,
Prejudice says. If they are, Woman replies, then Prejudice has
made them so. It's Prejudice that has 'prized a dimple far
beyond a brain', and marriage above all else. Woman declares:

Oh, think you well
What you have done to make it hard for her
To dream, to write, to paint, to build, to learn –
Oh, think you well! And wonder at the line
Of those who knew that life was more than love
And fought their way to achievement and to fame![16]

She then welcomes onto the stage, one by one, an enormous procession of famous women from all walks of life – from
Hypatia to Jane Austen, Marie Curie to Florence Nightingale.
Suffragette icon Joan of Arc was included, of course, and, given
that the piece was written by a queer woman, it also featured
sexually dissident figures like Sappho, the artist Rosa Bonheur
and the cross-dressing soldiers Christian Davies and Hannah
Snell. Woman calls forth one remarkable figure after another
until forty-four great women fill the stage. Overwhelmed with
evidence of woman's intelligence and ingenuity, Prejudice
slinks away, and Woman's request is granted. 'Go forth,' Justice says. 'The world is thine.'[17]

Hamilton, who was born on 15 June 1872, was already
a well-known figure when she composed *A Pageant of Great
Women*. A witty, energetic writer with a shock of reddish-gold
hair and pale, greenish-grey eyes, her breakthrough play, *Diana

of Dobson's, was a massive success when it premiered at the Kingsway Theatre in London in 1908. Combining melodrama and comedy, it was also a serious comment on the status of working women, which would presage the themes of her later work. She joined the WSPU in the same year, although she had some reservations about the organization from the start. As a feminist who prized independent thinking over everything else, she was concerned about the unquestioned leadership of Pankhurst, whom she later called a demagogue and compared to Hitler and Lenin.

She was also critical of the WSPU's stance on members' dress, which unofficially insisted on a 'feminine note'. This obedience to traditional gendered ideas made no sense to her, committed as she was to overturning the stereotype of what she called 'the "normal woman" with her "destiny" of marriage and motherhood and housekeeping'. To her, this aversion to masculine dress showed that the WSPU wasn't as radical as it first seemed. Winning the vote for women meant only cosmetic change if society's ideas and attitudes weren't also fundamentally transformed. 'My personal revolt was feminist rather than suffragist,' she wrote in her 1935 memoir, *Life Errant.* 'What I rebelled at chiefly was the dependence implied in the idea of "destined" marriage, "destined" motherhood – the identification of success with marriage, of failure with spinsterhood, the artificial concentration of the hopes of girlhood on sexual attraction and maternity.'[18]

Hamilton left the WSPU after only a few months, but she continued to work with organizations like the Women Writers' Suffrage League (WWSL) and the AFL in support of the cause. She became an important part of a community of queer suffragettes whose work underpinned the art and culture of the movement. This included fellow suffragettes in the performing arts, like Vera Holme, and women from a range of other fields, like the artist Pamela Colman Smith, co-creator of the famous Waite–Smith tarot deck, who illustrated posters and leaflets for the Suffrage Atelier, and the composer Dame Ethel Smyth, who collaborated with Hamilton on the official suffragette anthem, 'The March of the Women', in 1911.

The power couple of this creative queer network was Edith Craig (whom everyone called Edy) and Christopher St John. Their principal involvement with the movement centred on their home in Bedford Street on the Strand, which became a base of operations for radical suffragette activity and powered their creative work like a dynamo. As two queer, cohabiting artists, they had a critical take on traditional ideas of the home and domestic space, and could see how it dominated the mindset of many Britons at the time – a mindset that the suffrage campaign endeavoured to change. If Holme's queer ambiguity allowed her to occupy the street with confidence, turning the inside out, Craig and St John's domestic arrangement queered the physical and social form of the home, bringing the outside in.

At Home

As the only daughter of Dame Ellen Terry, the most celebrated actress of Victorian and Edwardian times, Craig was theatrical royalty from the day she was born, on 9 December 1869. She spent her twenties performing at Henry Irving's Lyceum Theatre, where Terry was the lead actress and the manager was one Bram Stoker of *Dracula* (1897) fame. However, as her mother's friend George Bernard Shaw is said to have remarked,

Craig was too clever for acting. Her strengths seemed to lie more in costume design and direction, and it was as a theatre producer that she would make her greatest impact on the suffrage movement.

According to Hamilton, *A Pageant of Great Women* was Craig's idea. She had attended many of the huge suffragist demonstrations and parades in London and noted the appetite for grand spectacle among the crowds. 'Edy came to me one day full of the idea of a pageant of great women which she would stage and which, she suggested, I should write for her. "Suggested" perhaps is the wrong word to use; if I remember aright her suggestion was more like an order.'[19]

As Hamilton affectionately implies, Craig could be kind of bossy, and not everyone appreciated her manner. Virginia Woolf in particular seems to have disliked Craig, and took the opportunity to ridicule her in *Between the Acts* (1941). In the novel, she is the theatre director Madame La Trobe, who strides around the fields in a smock frock planning the pageant at the heart of the story. The narrator remarks on 'her abrupt manner and stocky figure; her thick ankles and sturdy shoes; her rapid decisions barked out in guttural accents'.[20] But Woolf was hardly an impartial observer of Craig – or indeed of Craig's partner St John, who dared to rival Woolf for the affections of Sackville-West. Woolf called St John 'a mule-faced harridan'.[21]

Born Christabel Marshall on 24 October 1871, St John changed her name to honour St John the Baptist when she converted to Catholicism in 1912. She read history at Somerville College, Oxford, and after her studies moved to London, where for a time she worked as a secretary for Lady Randolph Churchill and her son Winston Churchill. Although she occasionally acted, she was first and foremost a writer – and a prolific one

Christopher St John, Smallhythe, 1910.
Photo by Vera Holme. Courtesy of LSE Library.

at that. Her first novel, *The Crimson Weed*, about a passionate love affair between an opera singer and a young bank clerk, was published in 1900. This was followed by a slew of articles and books, including another novel, *Hungerheart: The Story of a Soul* (1915), many plays, and biographies of prominent figures like Ellen Terry and her friend Ethel Smyth.

St John was a reserved, bookish woman, who nonetheless possessed intense, dramatic passions that surfaced suddenly with unexpected violence. Few images of her survive; with her hooked nose and cleft palate, perhaps she didn't feel comfortable sitting for a photographic portrait, as many of her suffragette friends had done. But Holme took a rare, candid snapshot during one of her many visits – catching St John in a private moment, poring over a book. With her brow and prominent nose cast in daylight against an inky background, the chiaroscuro quality of the photograph is well suited to this woman of stark contrasts. In the words of Sackville-West: 'It is as easy to imagine her raging, battle-axe in hand, against false idols, as to imagine her in a medieval monastery, scrupulously bent over the illuminated capitals of a manuscript; for she combines, in a way to provoke a smile from those who love her, extreme lustihood with extreme delicacy.'[22]

Craig and St John set up home together in London in 1899, having met through St John's pursuit of Ellen Terry. Like many young women, St John was a Terry fangirl. She'd managed to get backstage after a show at the Grand Theatre in Fulham, and, intending to find the famous actress, instead she discovered her brusque daughter. St John remembers that Craig was sewing at the time and didn't put her work to one side before shaking hands. 'I was pricked by her needle,' she wrote. 'Cupid's dart, for I loved Edy from that moment.'[23]

Although she was reticent about ever discussing her sexuality, Craig seems to have been bisexual; she had relationships with men before she started seeing St John – and afterwards too. But St John could be a volatile lover. Craig's affair with a young musician named Martin Shaw came to an abrupt end when St John attempted suicide by swallowing a bottle of cocaine lotion.

For her part, St John was quite open about her sexuality, and in *Hungerheart*, a roman-à-clef that fictionalized her life story, she implied that she was congenitally queer – framing her desires in the language of ancient Greece. St John had studied at Oxford, which was ground zero for English Hellenism, as we know, so naturally she described same-sex attachments in terms of noble, spiritual, platonic friendships – the kind of friendships John Addington Symonds would have approved of (before he fell into the lusty arms of his lower-class lovers). Writing about her relationship with Craig, she says:

> We fought sometimes, but we loved – that was the great point. Even our fights were interesting, and our reconciliations bound us together more closely . . . We were as happy as a newly-married pair, perhaps happier; and we certainly disproved the tradition that women were incapable of friendship.[24]

By 1909, Craig and St John had been together for ten years, and were at that point deeply involved in the suffrage movement. As Craig recalled, in notes for a memoir that she dictated to Holme but never finished, she'd been born into a family that was headed by a strong, independent woman, so it came as a surprise when she grew up and saw that women were so devalued in society. 'I did not realise that women were under any disabilities, because in our family the women always seemed to be the ones who did the things . . . they seemed much more brave and capable than men.'[25]

Craig worked with the WSPU and the breakaway Women's Freedom League, as well as the WWSL and the AFL, planning events and coordinating processions for each organization. Like many other suffragettes, she also went out into the street to sell the *Votes for Women* newspaper. 'I love it,' she said to an interviewer at the time. 'But I'm always getting moved on.'[26] St John seems to have been more militant, taking part in many of the WSPU demonstrations and deputations to the House of Commons; she was arrested a couple of times, first for grabbing a police horse's bridle at a protest, and later for setting fire to a pillar box.

According to Craig's biographer Katharine Cockin, 'the women's suffrage movement gave Craig a formal meaning to her individually unconventional life and allowed her to attach this to a movement, giving her some creative space and freedom to do what she wanted'.[27] The same could be said of St John, and both women revelled in the creative space opened up by the cause and the artistic opportunities it afforded. They seemed to enjoy collaborating with Hamilton especially; even before the success of *A Pageant of Great Women*, St John and Hamilton wrote *How the Vote Was Won*, probably the best known of the many suffrage plays, and Craig produced it at the Royalty Theatre, London, in April 1909.

The piece is a one-act farce that takes place in a mean little house in Brixton belonging to a mean little man named Horace Cole. According to the stage directions, it's a spring day 'in any year in the future', and the curtain rises on a 'modest, and quite unpleasing' sitting room. Cole's mousy wife, Ethel, is listening to her vivacious suffragette of a sister, Winifred, who is holding forth about the impending women's strike. 'At this very minute,' she declares, 'working women of every grade in every part of England are ceasing work, and going to demand support and the necessities of life from their nearest male relatives.'[28] Men like Horace have made the absurd claim that women don't need the vote because they're supported by men; let's see what happens when they actually do have to provide for their women relatives!

Soon enough, Horace's relatives start to pour into his home. His sister Agatha, who's given up her job as a governess; his first cousin Maudie, an actress and self-proclaimed 'Queen of Comediennes'; his niece Molly, a 'scandalous novelist', who arrives with only a nightgown and a set of golf clubs . . . 'I will be master in my own house!' he swears helplessly, as an endless parade of great women traipse into his living room demanding lodgings.[29] When his Aunt Lizzie arrives leading a fat spaniel and carrying a birdcage with a parrot in it, he has a sudden realization. 'The Government are narrow-minded idiots!' he announces, and heads off to petition Westminster with a crowd of other men who are newly converted to the cause. 'When you want a thing done, get a man to do it! Votes for Women!'[30]

Audiences loved the play, and so did the critics – one of them wrote that 'the story is funny enough, but the way in which it is told is funnier still'.[31] On one level, the piece quite simply skewers the arguments against suffrage that were going around at the time, while ridiculing the blinkered narcissism of the Antis – and who doesn't like to see a pompous, empty-headed man bested by a group of women.

More importantly, it's about the idea of home and

the struggle over its different meanings. For Horace, and old-fashioned, heterosexual men like him, the home was a woman's sphere. It was also a private, domestic space that was safely closed off from the outside world. The arrival of all these radical women in his house overturns that idea. As space invaders, trooping ceaselessly through the front door, their presence redefines the idea of home as something far more porous and social.

What terrifies Horace, then, is not just the prospect of having to support all these women on his meagre salary; it's the fact that his home is mutating before his very eyes from an insular, private residence into an open, communal one – a domestic space unfurling into a strange hinterland. Alarmed by the subversion – or inversion – of his world by the suffragette strike, he comments: 'Every industry in this country is paralyzed and every Englishman's home turned into a howling wilderness.'[32]

In its mischievous approach to the notion of domestic space, *How the Vote was Won* was part of a broader effort made by suffragettes to recode and redefine the home. Just as they had subverted entrenched ideas about public spaces, and who was allowed to occupy them, with demonstrations in the streets, so suffragettes would also subvert ideas about private spaces. Here, too, dismantling the ideology of separate spheres was key.

In response to the traditional logic that tried to keep politics out of the private sphere, the movement tried to politicize the latter. 'At Home' meetings pioneered by the WSPU, for instance, brought politics into hundreds of homes around Britain. Part branch meeting, part public assembly, they were hosted each week by women volunteers who would throw open the doors of their houses to welcome in suffragettes and members of the public alike; over refreshments, attendees could listen to invited speakers, discuss their views on the campaign and recruit new members to the cause.

For conservatives, reimagining the home in this way was a veritable assault on the status quo, and anti-suffrage propaganda vividly shows how livid they were about it. In one famous example called 'A Suffragette's Home', a 'Votes for Women' poster hangs on the back wall of a dingy room with a note pinned to it that reads: 'Back in an hour or so'. The woman of the house has obviously gone out in support of the cause, and abandoned her children – illustrated by two ill-kempt piles of rags sobbing in the foreground. A working-class husband looks out from the picture with consternation. 'After a hard day's work!' reads the caption. This is what happens when politics invades the home. A man might have to console his own children – or make his own dinner!

Given that St John was the co-author of *How the Vote was Won* and Craig was its director, it's not surprising that the play was so deeply invested in pulling apart traditional definitions of domestic space. One of the best examples of a home that was politicized and made porous by the suffrage movement was their apartment at 31 Bedford Street.

It's located just up from the Strand: a four-storey, red-brick building on a busy side street. The ground floor is now an overpriced pasta restaurant. Unlike Bloomsbury's Gordon Square, it has no commemorative plaques that might draw your attention to it as a one-time hub of queer radicalism. I come upon it almost by accident, having wound my way through the lanes that empty into Covent Garden. Craig and

St John lived on the third floor. Peering up, there isn't much to see, save the ornate wrought-iron railings in a whimsical daisy design painted white. They bring to mind the drawings of Pamela Colman Smith, especially the stylized, art nouveau-esque patterns of her tarot designs, and for a moment I wonder if she had a hand in creating them.

In pubs and restaurants all around me, people are eating forkfuls of something delicious, drinking from glasses glowing with the early-evening sun, laughing, with expensive sunglasses on. In the air: constant chatter and the scent of perfume, intoxicating, with notes of sweet vanilla and jasmine. I'm struck by the sensuality around me – teeming with bodies, doing the things bodies do, performing for the passer-by.

So much has changed in the intervening years, but in this regard at least – in the *feel* of the place – I wonder how different it was in Craig and St John's days. The flashing lights on theatre marquees on the Strand still dazzle and entice, as they ever have, promising ephemeral thrills. Was it the hubbub that had drawn these two theatrical women here? The sense of bodily excitement coming off the city's crowds, out for a night's entertainment, urging the observer to join in: to laugh, to gesticulate, to indulge one's appetites. To put one's body on the line and act, not think. To trade in 'deeds not words'.

Away from the street, inside Craig and St John's apartment, according to the American actress Florence Locke, it was 'lovely'. There was a 'hushed beauty' about it, she said, with 'soft lights glinting on lovely oriental objects'.[33] But don't be fooled by her description; it was also a resolutely bohemian – and rather messy – place. Another friend who visited the flat remembered that 'the atmosphere was quite undomestic'. She continued: 'The telephone rang incessantly, Edy and Chris shouted commands from different headquarters, and all the things that I had been brought up to believe should be done first, bed-making, dusting and washing-up, were done last or, quite likely, not done at all. It was a revelation to me, born and bred in suburban propriety.'[34]

The untidiness of Craig and St John's flat seems less like laziness and more like a political choice, if we consider the degree to which radicalism had permeated their space. Located just up the road from the Women's Freedom League headquarters at 3 Bedford Street and a ten-minute walk to the WSPU headquarters in Clement's Inn, like Vera Holme, they were right at the heart of things, and their home soon became a centre of suffragette activity. The International Suffrage Shop started there in 1910, when the actress Sime Seruya began selling feminist books and 'Votes for Women' collectables out of one of Craig and St John's rooms. More sensationally, 31 Bedford Street was also a suffragette safe house during the days of the so-called Cat and Mouse Act of 1913. This allowed the government to let suffragettes who were on hunger strike out of prison and arrest them again as soon as they had recovered. But many wily women evaded capture by the police by hiding out in places like the Bedford Street safe house. As a neighbour recalled: 'Some of the most determined of the "militants" would take refuge with them, either before they set out on some mission, or after they were released from prison.'[35]

Cicely Hamilton once wrote: 'It was natural that Edith Craig should be a good feminist . . . Had she not taken it for granted since childhood that a woman's interests could reach beyond the home, since her mother was artist and breadwinner?'[36] But a home is more than just the four walls and a roof that Hamilton is talking about here. It's also the people that occupy the space and the bonds between them, and Craig and St John took as unconventional an approach to their domestic relationship as they did to physical space.

As cohabiting queer women, from the outset they dissented from the presumptive heterosexuality of the home – even if two women living together wasn't that uncommon at the time and rarely aroused much suspicion (for the general public and the legal establishment alike, lesbians were somewhat mythic creatures, like unicorns). But in 1916 Craig and St John also opened up their relationship, and invited a third woman in to share their intimacy and their home.

By that point, the First World War had been under way for a couple of years and the suffragette campaign was called off. In a confusing reversal, Emmeline Pankhurst urged WSPU members to put down their window-smashing hammers and support the very government of men they had all railed against for more than a decade. St John and Craig had no interest in Pankhurst's nationalism; with their radical theatre group, the Pioneer Players, they continued to produce feminist plays throughout the war that broached taboo topics like pregnancy out of wedlock. During one of these performances, Craig met Clare Atwood, an artist who was working on the set design, and asked her to move in.

Atwood was born on 14 May 1866. A quiet, gentle woman everyone called Tony, she was educated at the Slade School of Art, and exhibited her work at both the Royal Academy and the more progressive New English Art Club, of which she became a member in 1912. Although she could ably paint portraits and landscapes, she excelled at depicting interior scenes; critics praised her ability to capture the play of sunlight across the wall of a room, and the sense of spaciousness her canvases evoked.

Sackville-West described Atwood as a 'peacemaker' whose presence was 'a soothing influence'.[37] Her interiors communicate something of that peace, yet her choice of subjects also suggests that she was compelled, not by peace per se, but by calm places that had just been or would soon be the setting for great excitement: Drury Lane theatre in deep shades of red painted during a rehearsal; the empty, light-filled dressing room of John Gielgud composed while the great actor was on stage; even the Royal Army Clothing Depot, cavernous and filled with bales of fabrics waiting to be shipped out to the front. Such places appealed to Atwood, perhaps, as containers of grand passions and intense activity. I imagine that she saw something of herself in them, or at least something of her polyamorous relationship, which peaceably held herself, the bustling Craig and the mercurial St John in an inimitable ménage à trois.

Craig had some concerns about St John's legendary jealous streak, and before Atwood moved in, she told her: 'I must warn you that if Chris does not like your being here, and feels you are interfering with our friendship, out you go!'[38] St John soon warmed to Atwood, however, and later even confessed that 'the bond between Edy and me was strengthened, not weakened, by Tony's association with us'. The throuple would live together for the next three decades, splitting their time between the flat in London and a cottage in Kent that Ellen Terry had bought for Craig, which shared a garden with Terry's own house next door.

It's known as Smallhythe Place, and one bright day in early September I decide to pay it a visit, snaking through the narrow, rain-washed roads of the south east of England for an hour or so, flanked on both sides by acreage in burnt gold. Soon, up ahead through the trees, Terry's rambling sixteenth-century home appears: black-and-white-striped, half-timbered, looking quintessentially Tudor, with a red roof that sags endearingly at the edges. I feel a little giddy with anticipation as I approach the front door, which is bordered with pink climbing roses. The peak of the pandemic isn't so far in the past, and the pleasure of visiting somewhere I've never been before returns all in a rush.

Smallhythe is conserved and maintained by the National Trust, and this afternoon it's in the care of my friend Nicci Obholzer, a heritage professional I met online while enthusing about Craig. She opens the door with a knowing smile, and welcomes me into the dark, cool interior. Floorboards groan and snap underfoot as we make our way through the house, remarking on Terry's sumptuous costumes, the furniture, photographs, props and personal effects. I'm thrilled by the place. It's the kind of beautiful, affectionately maintained museum I love: a bit chaotic, with every square inch of wall and floor space filled with paraphernalia. Here, a hairpin feels as important as an oil painting. In other words, it's warm and personal. Craig wanted the house to be turned into a museum, and her love for her mother is tangible in the care and attention paid to even the most commonplace of Terry's belongings.

In the years following the Great War, Craig, St John and Atwood would spend more and more time at home in Small-hythe. Not many examples of their correspondence survive, and none offer anything like a candid description of the dynamics of their relationship. Nonetheless, St John did leave a single, moving portrait of their communal home. 'Such discords as there were in our communal life were always quickly resolved,' she wrote.

> The fine point of our pleasure in being together was not blunted by excess of it. It always had the flavour of a treat, whatever its source, a meal in common, going to the theatre, cinema, concerts or picture-galleries, playing Majong, or Bezique, listening in, discussing books we had read, talking about all sorts of people and things, exchanging reminiscences, chaffing, teasing, joking, quarrelling. Different as were our antecedents, our characters, our temperaments, our talents, we belonged to the same world, the artist's world. That established a camaraderie which was perfectly easy, unguarded and spontaneous.[39]

One of Craig's young relatives fondly recalled visiting the older woman and her partners when she was a child. It was 'a new and enchanted world', she said, 'where grown-ups wore sandals on bare feet, drove about the dusty lanes in a coster cart, dressed in smocks, were gay and laughing and unconventional'.[40] There are echoes of sandal-wearing Edward Carpenter and his queer utopia in Smallhythe and this lesbian trio's countryside encampment. Sackville-West remembered it as an almost dreamlike place where the world was viewed askew:

> Was it a place in a fairy story? It certainly had the quality which makes things and places both more real and more unreal. Whenever you went there, you wondered whether you were living in the world you normally knew, or had

walked through into a world more poetical, a world more romantic, a world where values were different.[41]

The caretakers of Smallhythe have always been very open about the alternative, queer values of its former residents, Nicci says, as she leads us across the garden to a huge thatched barn that Craig converted into a theatre in 1929. There we find a large visitor information board that describes the ménage à trois, noting that 'they had many creative lesbian and homo-sexual friends from the literary and theatrical world who were afforded a freedom of thought and dress when visiting Edy'. These friends descended on the Barn Theatre every year for the annual Ellen Terry memorial celebrations, when a perfor-mance would be staged here in her honour. Looking around the rustic space of the barn, its oak beams gently lit by daylight streaming in through an open doorway, I imagine its rows of wooden chairs filled with figures from the past. Cicely Ham-ilton on the left, turning her head to talk to Pamela Colman Smith, who's dressed in vibrant patterns; Vera Holme, laughing uproariously, perhaps drawing a disdainful glance from Ethel Smyth . . .

Like Carpenter's home in Sheffield, Smallhythe also became a place of pilgrimage for younger queer people – women especially. Sackville-West visited regularly (enflaming St John's largely unrequited passions whenever she came by), as did Virginia Woolf, looking down her nose at the eccen-tric habits of the three women. The most frequent visitors were Radclyffe Hall and her partner, Una Troubridge, who had settled in the nearby town of Rye. They all met in 1930, and became lifelong friends; when Holme came down from Scot-land, she was welcomed into the group too. Troubridge named the Smallhythe set 'Edy and the Boys', and remarked on the 'great consolation and gratification' she felt 'in the company of these friends who like us and want to be with us because they know us for what we are'.[42]

By that point, *The Well of Loneliness* had been prosecuted for obscenity and banned. The novel and its trial drew the British public's attention to the queer women in their midst, and popularized the idea of the female sexual invert – a term that only sexologists had used up to then. According to Havelock Ellis, 'the commonest characteristic of the sexually inverted woman is a certain degree of masculinity or boyishness'; she was also hairier than other women and had 'a decided taste and toleration for cigars'.[43]

Leaving Nicci behind in the barn, I head outside to explore the garden, which is full of blackbirds twittering, and song thrushes peeping, and wood pigeons being insistent. I wander around the orchard, with its plum trees, crab apple and pear, the soft white blossoms of Queen Anne's lace proliferating beneath their boughs. A couple of inquisitive Friesians from the adjoining field amble over to the garden fence, and from the reedy edge of a pond comes the sound of frogs, croaking away contentedly to themselves. An aeroplane drones overhead. At the side of the house, underneath an awning where wicker chairs are gathered around an old table, I find shelter from the sun.

It strikes me that, despite the many problems associated with the term, and how it was used to describe the experiences of cigar-chomping queer women, *inversion* is an excellent way to describe how the queer women we've met in this chapter related to the spaces of London before the First World War. Turning the inside out, and bringing the outside in, Holme and the Bedford Street ménage inverted traditional ideas of the street and the home, dismantling the reigning ideology of separate spheres in the process.

These inversions correspond to what the French historian and philosopher Michel de Certeau would call 'spatial practices'.[44] According to de Certeau, the world is made up of places and spaces. On the one hand there are given locations and destinations created with a fixed purpose by planners and authorities, which he calls places; on the other, there is the use of these locations, the human navigation of them, which he refers to as space. 'Space is a practised place,' he writes. Viewed differently, place could be a word on a page, and 'space is like the word when it is spoken, that is, when it is caught in the ambiguity of an actualization'.[45]

For de Certeau, place is top-down and space is bottom-up, and meaning is created when space is practised or 'enunciated'. When this happens, the two cease to coincide: the intended uses and meanings of the places we occupy are added to, subverted or simply ignored. New and different meanings accumulate: 'another spatiality' is formed, distinct from one envisaged by those in power.[46] In the work of London's queer suffragettes, in their respective inversions, we find them practising another spatiality – a feminist and queer one.

Their practice contrasts sharply with that of Forster's in Cambridge. His closeted, mousy character seemed to adopt and adapt itself to the compartmentalization of the city; Holme and her friends, on the other hand, refused to accommodate a misogynistic management of space, and sought to overturn the seemingly immoveable dichotomy of public and private. 'Places make us', as the sociologists would have it; these women and their radical approach to the worlds they occupied show that the inverse is also the case – *we make places*. This is obviously true in a literal sense – we build roads and erect houses – but we also imbue them with significance, define their limits and give them ideological weight. Just as we make these places, however, so too can we unmake them: scramble their coding, prise them apart, invert their meanings.

Josephine Baker in the *Ziegfeld Follies*, New York, 1936.
Photo by Gilles Petard. © Getty Images.

3.

Excess: Josephine Baker and Paris

The gendarmes gave her special permission to park her car on the pier. Its magnificent chrome headlamps glinted in the morning light and the wave-like swoop of its fenders flashed silver as the vehicle rolled to a stop. A door was thrown open, and onto the dark asphalt alighted a pair of brilliant white stilettos, from which extended the most famous legs in all of Europe.

Josephine Baker stepped out of her Delage D8 luxury sports car into the October sun. She was dressed sumptuously, all in white, her ivory cloche hat and the snowy fur collar that erupted around her neck accentuating the coppery colour of her skin. As she raised a hand to shade her eyes, an expression somewhere between apprehension and exhaustion passed quickly across her face. Then, her features set, she turned her celebrated smile on the assembled onlookers and well-wishers shouting her name.

'Joséphine! Joséphine!' Above the noise of the crowd, reporters flung questions at her in French. How did she feel about returning to the United States? Did she think segregation would affect her performance? Was she intending to come back to France? She tactfully put them off with one of those lines *à la Baker* they loved so much, in charmingly muddled English and French. 'Très sweet, le public, and it's grâce à les journalistes that I have a life aussi agréable, understand?'[1]

The group hustled down the pier and into the shadow of the enormous ship that would bear her across the Atlantic, back to America where it all began. Rising up out of the oily black waters of Le Havre's Gare Maritime, the SS *Normandie*: the greatest and most opulent of all ocean liners. Extravagantly art deco, arrayed in scarlet and gold, she was the first ship to carry a movie theatre and had the largest on-board swimming pool. In her one-of-a-kind enclosed winter garden, budgies flitted among jade lily leaves and pink hydrangeas fashioned from Lalique glass. The dining room alone was three decks high and bigger than the Hall of Mirrors at Versailles.

Historians would deem the *Normandie* 'unrealistic, impractical, uneconomical, and magnificent'.[2] They could easily have been describing the ship's most famous passenger on that bright day in October 1935 – the dazzling black woman whom the captain welcomed aboard with a massive bouquet of flowers. Ascending the gangplank on his arm, she turned over her shoulder to give the crowd one last smile. Photographers' bulbs flashed and popped, fixing forever her hand, gloved in white, waving *adieu* to her adoring fans as they cheered for her and begged her not to forget them.

In four days, she would arrive in New York. Time enough for her to reflect on where she was headed and how far she had come. How much had changed between then and now. How implausible it was that this black superstar with the adulation of a French crowd still ringing in her ears had been born less than thirty years before, on 3 June 1906, in a St Louis slum.

The luxury accommodation of the *Normandie* was so far removed from the homes of her childhood, it must have made her head spin to think about it. Growing up, she had lived in a succession of run-down, two-room tenement apartments where thin mattresses teemed with bedbugs and tin cans were nailed to the floor to stop rats from scrabbling up through the rotten floorboards. The heating never worked. Later, she would claim that she started dancing simply to keep warm. 'Why did I become a dancer? Because I was born in a cold city; because my childhood was a cold one,' she said.[3]

She needed a way out – and fast. In 1920, the manager of a local theatre offered her an audition after he found her dancing and singing ragtime tunes in the street. She seized her chance and, at the age of thirteen, found herself part of the chorus. From the wings of the Booker T. Washington Theater, she saw some of the finest, soon-to-be-famous black entertainers ply their trade; watching them closely, she studied their performances and learned their moves by heart.

The theatre gave her a first glimpse of freedom – if not perhaps from racial oppression in a country so bitterly segregated as the United States, then at least from misery, from poverty, from the cold. It also presented her with a certain amount of sexual freedom, and she had her first fling with a woman in the dressing rooms of the theatre. Clara Smith, a twenty-six-year-old blues singer, was the show's leading lady. Baker loved to watch her out on stage, wrapped in a blue boa, singing in that light, sweet voice of hers: 'she had a magnificent voice that sent shivers down your spine', she remembered.[4] Smith noticed the rapt attention of her young admirer, and took a shine to Baker too. As one of their friends later recalled, the relationship became ambiguously intimate: she was Smith's 'lady lover'.[5] Soon, according to Baker's own account, the singer was 'monopolizing' her time and she would spend hours alone with Smith in her dressing room.[6]

Previously, Baker had only been involved with men.

She'd even been married to a man named Willie Wells – if just
for a couple of months. But her time with Smith seemed to
unlock something queer in her; as her career took off, sending her to places like Chicago, Philadelphia and ultimately to
New York and the heart of the Harlem Renaissance, relationships with both men and women would follow. According to
her son Jean-Claude Baker:

> In Josephine's scheme of things, men were more import-
> ant, or at least more necessary, than women. Not so
> much for sex as for power. Men had the money, they ran
> the banks and wrote the contracts. Still, once in a while –
> starting with Clara Smith – there would be a lady lover in
> Josephine's life.[7]

When she left Smith and joined the cast of *Shuffle Along*,
an all-black revue that had taken New York by storm, the new
focus of her adoration was a doe-eyed young woman from the
chorus named Evelyn Sheppard. Through *Shuffle Along* she also
got to know Bessie Allison, an entertainer who, in 1954, would
become the first black woman in history to occupy a position in
the New York State Legislature. The two women began a relationship while treading the boards that would endure for the
rest of their lives. In 1923, Baker signed up with a show called
Plantation Days, and she soon fell for one of the cast: violinist
and dancer Mildred Smallwood, who was the first black woman
to appear in *Dance Magazine*. According to one of Baker's con-
fidantes, such same-sex relationships among the women of a
theatre company weren't that unusual – even if nobody talked
about them: 'I guess we were bisexual, is what you would call
it today.'[8]

As women like Vera Holme had discovered in London two decades earlier, the theatre offered queer women the chance to explore their unconventional desires. But if Baker's bisexual passions were kindled in the dressing rooms of American theatres and music halls, Paris, to which she travelled in 1925, fanned them to a blaze. The city and its racial and sexual freedoms created a territory that was uniquely conducive to her self-expression. Not only was it somewhere she could explore her bisexuality without fear of condemnation, it was also a place where a bisexual disposition, one unconstrained by an either/or mentality, could find its corollary in a city that embraced a life without limits.

By 1935, she had wowed the audiences and critics of Paris for a decade, and hopes were high for her trip to New York. In just a couple of months, she would be the first black woman ever to perform in the *Ziegfeld Follies*, a world-famous, over-the-top Broadway variety show. Singer Fanny Brice and comedian Bob Hope were her co-stars, Vincente Minnelli was creating her costumes, and George Balanchine was doing the choreography. 'I'm so excited,' she exclaimed. 'I'm all puffed up like a frog!'[9] Paris had made her into a star and now it seemed as if it was giving her back to the United States, as the people of France had once given them Lady Liberty: a magnificent symbol – of freedom, progress and all that might be achieved if a person could only be permitted to live without experiencing prejudice.

The last time Baker had seen the Statue of Liberty, she hated it. A decade before, she had sailed out of New York harbour, bound for France with two dozen other black entertainers, who were part of a new, all-black music and dance show called *La Revue nègre*. Their ship, like the rest of America, was segregated and they were only allowed to occupy certain parts of it.

'What was the good of having the statue without the liberty, the freedom to go where one chose, if one was held back by one's color?' Baker acidly remarked.[10] It represented the hypocrisy of the American experiment, and she felt free, she said, only when the statue disappeared from view. But as it appeared to her again now, its silhouette coming over the horizon as she stood out by the polished brass railing on the prow of the *Normandie*, perhaps she felt something else – that, in spite of everything, the Mother of Exiles would finally welcome her home.

La Revue nègre

Ten years earlier, almost to the day, 22 September 1925 was a grey morning in Paris. The cast of *La Revue nègre* stepped off the train from Cherbourg with the rain falling pitter-patter on the roofs of the taxis and buses idling outside Gare Saint-Lazare. But they were radiant, this high-spirited troupe of Harlem's finest. I imagine them pouring from the station, joking, laughing together brightly, full of excited anticipation and ease, with their arms around each other – the City of Light welcoming them as her own.

While the company took their seats aboard the open-top tour bus, an ebullient Baker made her way upstairs, paying little mind to the rain that was now coming down in sheets. She'd later say it was a good omen if you arrived in a city for the first time and it was raining: rainfall brought happiness and prosperity. It must have been falling at a particularly auspicious slant on Baker's first day in Paris, given the life-changing successes that would shortly follow.

From the station, through the streets, the bus chugged its way towards the Théâtre des Champs-Élysées, down near the river on avenue Montaigne. Baker savoured her first glimpses of this strange old city: grey buildings with ornate facades; bistros and boulangeries; department stores opening up for the day, arcades twinkling, cafés on corners. Haussmann might have plunged his grand boulevards through the heart of Paris half a century earlier, sending the poor running for the outer boroughs, but to Baker it all seemed so . . . small. 'Oh! it was so funny,' she recalled. 'Small houses, tiny streets, narrow pavements . . . I thought: I'll never be able to dance here, everything's far too small. Where are all the large straight lines of New York?'[11] But she would soon find out that Paris offered much more to a woman of her colour and ambition than New York ever had. Its small streets spelled freedom, not restraint – but she would have to learn to read them first.

The France that Baker discovered in 1925 was still reeling from what was at the time the greatest war the world had ever seen. In the aftermath of 1918, the country was traumatized and almost destitute. The north was a wasteland: town and country pitted by artillery fire and ruined by bomb blast; the landscape littered with the rusting evidence of murder on a mass scale. Facing overwhelming war debts and with the value of the French franc in free fall, the economy was also on its knees. Only later would the full human cost come to light: 1.4 million French dead on the battlefield and 3 million more wounded, sent back broken and shell-shocked from the front to their homes in Bordeaux or Reims or somewhere in Normandy.

In a few short years, however, Paris (if not the rest of the country, perhaps) had recovered, and with the beginning of the 1920s a bold new era dawned in the city. After the war and its quagmire of privation and death, Parisians were gripped by a desperate, almost reckless yearning for gaiety, freedom, excess;

for life, really. They called it *l'esprit nouveau*, a new mindset – one with an insatiable appetite for the new. These were *les Années folles*: the crazy years of cocktails and jazz, the Charleston and Chanel No. 5. No single figure represented this time and place better than Baker, whom Ernest Hemingway once called 'the most sensational woman anyone ever saw. Or ever will.'[12]

Much of the city's cultural and economic comeback could be credited to the arrival into Paris of unprecedented numbers of American tourists like Hemingway. The strength of the dollar compared to the franc meant that Americans could holiday there cheaply. Tourists could also drink alcohol in France, while back in the United States lawmakers had decided to ban the stuff. This was the era of Prohibition: Americans looking for good cheap fun went elsewhere, and came to Paris in their droves. In just one week in July 1924, 12,000 Americans disembarked from transatlantic ocean liners, flooding into France and heading to Parisian bars like the Dingo and the Dôme for a *demi* of this or a *ballon* of that.

Many also stayed. By 1923 there were 32,000 Americans living in Paris, compared to 8,000 in 1920 – a fourfold increase in three years. For Gertrude Stein, the quintessential American expatriate writer who landed in France in 1902 and lived there for the rest of her life, 'Paris was where the twentieth century was.'[13] Later, she would be joined by other American writers who would form what she called the 'Lost Generation' – Hemingway, F. Scott Fitzgerald, Ezra Pound, Djuna Barnes and others.

Among these Americans abroad were many black Americans – drawn, like whites, to the affordability of the city, its culture and its cuisine. But they also sought something else: freedom from the injustice and daily humiliations of segregation. Paris appealed enormously to those black Americans who wanted to live free of the racial prejudice that had blighted their upbringing. The city wasn't entirely free from discrimination, of course, as the Algerians who lived there could attest, but black Americans in Europe were treated differently; according to a journalist writing in the black Chicago newspaper *The Defender*, they had 'no bars to beat against; they have disappeared as if by magic'.[14] African Americans flocked to Parisian neighbourhoods like Montmartre and Montparnasse – hubs of a thriving black émigré culture centred on jazz.

Clubs were full of well-known black jazz musicians and singers fresh off the boat from Harlem: Sidney Bechet, Buddy Gilmore, Florence Emery ('Embry') Jones, Crickett Smith . . . From the kitchen of Le Grand Duc, a well-known Montmartre club where he worked as a pot wash, the young Langston Hughes heard them all. His 1924 poem 'Jazz Band in a Parisian Cabaret' shows how universally loved jazz was among Parisians from all walks of life. 'Play that thing' it begins; lords and ladies, sex workers and school teachers, they all go wild for 'that tune / that laughs and cries'.[15]

Performers like Ada Smith even owned their own clubs. Known as Bricktop because of the shock of red hair she inherited from her Irish father, Smith arrived in Paris in 1923 to sing at Le Grand Duc, and before long opened a place called Bricktop's on a side street in Montmartre. There, she'd teach Cole Porter and his wife the Charleston, and become the confidante of a newly arrived Baker. Bricktop and Baker's lifelong friendship was a fraught, sisterly kind of affair that nonetheless carried the suggestion of a more romantic involvement. Baker's story is full of these kinds of passionate, half-beheld liaisons with other women.

Paris in this period might be called a *heterotopia*. From *heteros* meaning 'other', heterotopias are places that are wildly different from the norm, where the conventional rules of behaviour are suspended and normative relations are subverted (if perhaps only temporarily). An influential coinage of Michel Foucault, the concept of a heterotopia resonates with the Russian philosopher Mikhail Bakhtin's idea of the carnivalesque. This refers to those periods in medieval society when everything went topsy-turvy: when physicality, the body and its functions were celebrated not debased; when individuals from different classes could freely associate; when cultural hierarchies failed to obtain, confusing the sacred and profane, high and low. Bakhtin's concept related to time, however; Foucault's related to space. Heterotopias, he said, are 'outside of all places, even though it may be possible to indicate their location in reality'.[16] Transgressive and excessive, like 1920s Paris, they defy categorization, much like the excessive, bisexual (and excessively bisexual) Baker.

She and the heterotopia of Paris, as we will see, formed an unprecedented coincidence of habitus (one's disposition, in sociological terms) and habitat (one's domain). The relationship between person and place here was neither one-directional, as in the case of Cambridge and the Forster it produced, nor antagonistic, as in the case of the queer suffragettes in London. Baker and the city she loved were instead mutually constitutive – each couldn't have become what it was without the other; they were inextricable. *Symbiotic.*

Fitzgerald called it the Jazz Age. The music, the singing, the dancing, the smoky clubs and after-hour bars: Parisians were crazy about it all – white Parisians especially, whose infatuation with jazz was inseparable from their fascination with the black Americans who played it. At a time when difference and newness were especially desirable qualities, Europeans yearned desperately for new cultural forms. Art historian Petrine Archer-Straw named it 'negrophilia' – a love of all things black that flattened the many differences between black cultures.[17]

Negrophilia is a form of love some of us may be familiar with, where, instead of being taken on their own terms, the beloved is a space of projections, a receptacle for the lover's wants and needs. Thus, for white Parisians, jazz signalled life, power and creativity because these things seemed to them to have been drained out of the world of post-war Europe. Black wasn't just beautiful, it was everything that white European culture wasn't, and couldn't be. Against a background like this, a show like *La Revue nègre* would clean up.

It premiered on 2 October 1925 at the Théâtre des Champs-Élysées in an auditorium that was packed to the rafters. All two thousand seats for the evening performance were sold out. Excitement zipped and crackled through the crowd – a show hadn't been so eagerly anticipated since the heyday of Sergei Diaghilev's Ballets Russes. His *Rite of Spring*, which had outraged pre-war audiences with its cacophonous score and strange, angular choreography, was first staged in this exact spot in 1913. It was so transgressive, so divisive, at the premiere there were reports of punch-ups in the aisles. People wondered if *La Revue nègre* would be just as shocking – so of course everybody wanted a ticket.

When the audience finally settled down, eight members of an all-black orchestra filed onto the stage, taking their places in front of a curtain bearing a trippy black-and-white-chessboard design. They started up and snappy jazz melodies soon filled the expansive auditorium: a lively, teasing conversation between piano and sax, backed by trombone and tuba, and adjudicated by a snare drum.

The curtain rose and behind the band appeared a backdrop painted with Mississippi steamboats. On stage: a simulacrum of a sunny quayside with piles of cargo strewn about, waiting to be loaded onto large painted ships. Here and there, black men dressed incongruously in vibrant plaid suits lounged on bales of cotton, ostentatiously taking their ease. Next, a group of young black women entered, decked out in eye-catching feathers and colourful ribbons. One of them began to sing, and the others sprang to their feet. Soon, the entire cast was dancing, stomping around smilingly to the amazement of the audience. Never before had so many black performers appeared on the same Parisian stage at once. It felt extraordinary, exotic, almost indecent.

Other surprises were in store – none more than Josephine Baker herself, who now emerged from the wings. In her later incarnations, 'La Baker' would stride onto the stages of Paris, the consummate diva, commanding the audience's attention arrayed in lavish, sparkling costumes and colossal headdresses. But for this, her first appearance in Europe, she skittered onto the stage on all fours, clowning. Head down, ass up, dressed in an old shirt and cut-offs, she scampered about, jumped around, did the splits. She twisted and bended, pulled faces, crossed her eyes. Uproarious laughter greeted her japes – the audience couldn't get enough.

Baker had been hired to inject some humour into the show, and it was clear to anyone watching that she was a genius of physical comedy. It was like nothing they had ever seen. Yes, there was a soupçon of slapstick about her performance, and some picked up on echoes of the vaudeville comedy circuit where she began her career, but it also seemed like something entirely new and bizarrely different.

So much exaggerated movement, and such a variety of it, gave one the impression that she had pushed beyond the limits of what a human body could do. She was a shape-shifter. Theatre critics later compared her to a boxing kangaroo, a giraffe, a tropical bird, a snake . . . 'Is this a man? Is this a woman?' one awestruck reviewer wrote. 'Her lips are painted black, her skin is the colour of a banana, her hair, already short, is stuck to her head as if made of caviar . . . Is she horrible? Is she ravishing? Is she black? Is she white?'[18] For many, her lithe ambiguity was fascinating and hilarious; for a few, it was monstrous. 'Stop!' one woman screamed. 'We didn't come to see this ugliness!'[19]

The show's finale offered the audience something even more astonishing. The backdrop changed to that of a Harlem nightclub – the setting for what the director called the 'danse de sauvage', the wild dance. If you're wondering why on earth a pseudo-African tribal dance should take place in a club in Harlem performed by individuals hailing from St Louis and the Caribbean, well, as Baker would famously quip: 'the white imagination sure is something when it comes to blacks'.[20]

To the sound of tom-toms Baker appeared, upside down, doing the splits, balanced on the bare back of her partner, Joe Alex. Their costumes were cockamamie tribal gear, dreamed up by the show's white producers – both dancers almost naked apart from some strategically placed feathers and beads. Nudity might have been nothing new for the Parisian music hall at that time, but it was for Baker. The idea of bearing her small breasts to all of Paris didn't appeal at first, but it grew on her, and she'd soon cast her inhibitions aside enthusiastically.

Sliding off Alex's back, with her feet on solid ground, she launched into a sensual, ecstatic routine – throwing herself into his arms and wriggling away, tilting her hips, shaking her ass. 'We've hidden our asses away for too long,' she'd later remark. 'I don't see that there's anything wrong with them.'[21] According to contemporary accounts, Baker's behind was spectacular. The dancer Mura Dehn, who saw her in *La Revue nègre*, said it moved like a hummingbird. Georges Simenon, the Belgian writer with whom Baker would have an affair in 1927, rhapsodized about its bouncing gaiety, 'its lascivious quivers and wild convulsions'. It was, he said, 'a laughing butt'.[22]

Baker's trailblazing twerk brought the show to a close and the audience to their feet. Some stomped out, outraged at the obscene display; many more stood and applauded. Baker had signed on as the show's comic relief, but overnight she was its star. The lesbian photographer Berenice Abbott remembered how 'Josephine came out with these feathers on her tail and this beautiful little body, and people went wild. The French were kind of tired and a little bit decadent, it's hard to get them excited, but everybody just wanted to leap over the balcony; a great spontaneous combustion took place.' According to André Daven, the director of the theatre, 'it was like the revelation of a new world'.[23]

Baker's appearance in *La Revue nègre* was a sensation, and soon everyone in Paris was talking about it. According to the *New Yorker*'s Janet Flanner, within a half an hour of the final curtain 'the news and meaning of her arrival had spread by the grapevine up to the cafés on the Champs-Élysées, where the witnesses of her triumph sat over their drinks excitedly repeating their report of what they had just seen – themselves unsatiated in the retelling, the listeners hungry for further fantastic truths'.[24]

The excited, hungry discussions that started in the bars and cafés of Paris in 1925 hardly abated in the years that followed. For almost a century, people have told and retold the story of Baker's startling contribution to what was, in truth, a muddled variety show. *La Revue nègre* was thrown together at the last minute by a few white people who knew a lot about the mind of the white Parisian but very little about black culture: the *danse de sauvage* was invented a few days before the opening night by the show's director, Jacques Charles, who felt that his audiences wanted to see more 'authentic' black dances.

Over the years, many of these discussions have centred on ideas of primitivism and negrophilia – how Baker played up to white stereotypes of black as 'other'. For critics and scholars, her appearances in the Théâtre des Champs-Élysées show literally embodied white fantasies about exotic, primitive blackness. The primitivism of her costumes and performances fulfilled racist expectations that black people were naturally more sensual and physical, less rational and civilized, than their white counterparts – objectifying the black body in the process. According to Phyllis Rose, the best of Baker's biographers, 'Josephine Baker's body should be understood as one of many African "objects" which suddenly seemed beautiful to a Parisian avant-garde whose enthusiasm for African art had been developing for two decades.'[25]

In terms of their racial politics, Baker's early shows have been explored at length, but hardly anyone factors in her sexuality, which is rather surprising. Josephine Baker was a black bisexual woman: how can we understand any one of these facets of her life without considering the others? Her bisexuality and its implications are at least as interesting as her racialized performance, and are to a certain degree bound up with it.

There's no end of comment on her sex life, of course. In the weeks and months that followed the premiere of *La Revue nègre*, she became a true celebrity – which presented her with the opportunity to have as much casual sex with her admirers as she liked. Apparently she liked it a lot – in as many permutations as possible: 'she liked lovemaking on the spur of the moment, standing up, alfresco, under water, *n'importe comment* [any which way]', writes one biographer.[26] 'For Josephine Baker, sex was a pleasurable form of exercise, like dancing, and she wasn't notably fussy about her partners,' deduces another.[27]

In these descriptions, we get titillating glimpses of a promiscuous Baker, but we don't see much of a bisexual Baker. Jean-Claude Baker, determined to make his mother's bisexuality plain to her fans, is more forthcoming than most about her attraction to both men and women. But even in his sensational *Josephine: The Hungry Heart* (1993), there's little sense of what her bisexuality might have meant to her, or indeed if it coloured the way she viewed the world. And if she *did* view the world differently – from a bisexual angle – does that change the way we should understand Josephine Baker? Did her bisexuality influence how she lived or where she lived or how she danced? When Monsieur Daven gasped that seeing Baker dance was 'the revelation of a new world', I wonder if what was revealed to him was simply the world as a bisexual sees it.

I want to put a different spin on Baker's story. I'm drawn to thinking about her bisexuality as a new way of interpreting her life – a life that was so inextricably linked to the city of Paris. In a very simple but important sense, arriving in Paris offered her many occasions to explore her sexuality away from the segregated and piously prohibiting United States. Few places in Europe at the time could match Paris in terms of its sexual freedoms and relaxed moral standards, save perhaps Weimar Berlin, which Baker would visit shortly after *La Revue nègre* finished its French run. For this reason alone, Paris had a huge impact on Baker, how she expressed her bisexuality and who she expressed it with.

But there's a lot more to being bisexual than who you sleep with. For one thing, bisexuality puts you at odds with a prevailing mentality. Most people grow up in an environment where monosexuality, or the attraction to members of only one sex or gender, is the norm. For generations, institutions like the family reinforced the idea that one is born heterosexual; in the last few decades, culture and society have increasingly come around to the idea that a few of us might be born homosexual. In both cases, a monosexual bias holds sway. From this perspective, bisexuality has to be a phase or an experiment because desiring more than one sex or gender is not just unnatural, it's incomprehensible.

In other words, a monosexual mindset is defined by limits, an either/or state of thinking where desire and identity are carefully circumscribed. Bisexual desire, by contrast, is an excessive, both/and kind of thing. When I told my mother I was bisexual, she was flummoxed. 'Wait,' she said, trying to get her head around it. 'You're gay *and* you're straight?' For some, bisexuals are excessive in their desires.

As we will see, this idea of excess is key to understanding Baker and her life in Paris between the wars. A black bisexual woman who saw beyond a narrow, monosexual perspective, she lived extravagantly, forever going beyond constraint and limitation in the way she lived, in how she performed and in the public personae she created. People always said she was *un peu too much*.

La Folie du jour

Baker's triumphant premiere in 1925 set her on course to win the kind of fame and celebrity many have dreamed of but few have ever achieved. In a couple of years, she would become the highest-paid entertainer in all of Europe and the first international black star. Paris was the key to her success. Later asked to describe her relationship to the place, she said: 'I understood Paris immediately, and loved it passionately. From the very first evening, Paris adopted me, celebrated me, filled me up. Loved me also, I hope. Paris is a dance, and I am a dancer.'[28]

La Revue nègre was a hit, and audiences returned to see it multiple times. Its run at the Théâtre des Champs-Élysées was extended twice before it moved to a new home at the Théâtre de l'Étoile. Baker suddenly had more than enough money to get by, so she began to indulge her extravagant tastes – renting out a suite of rooms with a private bathroom at the Hôtel Fournet in Montmartre and decorating it in a lavish style. She was especially proud of her bed, 'draped with flowing red, white, and blue cretonne in an attempt to duplicate Napoleon's royal couch'.[29] In the mornings she luxuriated in it, awaking to the scent of freshly baked croissants and eating breakfast in bed.

She'd always loved animals, so she filled her new apartment with exotic pets: lime-green parakeets, parrots in a stunning range of colours, baby rabbits, a snake called Kiki, a pig named Albert. When one of her lovers, the artist Paul

Colin, came to visit her, her menagerie appalled him: 'The animals behaved as they would in a barnyard. The rabbits hopped around the room. The pig wiggled his bottom and shook his ears. He relieved himself on the floor and the carpets.'[30] The hotel staff didn't seem to mind too much – especially when Baker was so liberal with her favours. As she remembered later: 'the room waiter was the first Frenchman to truly savour my charms. I'll never forget his face the day he found me soaking in the tub. He almost dropped the tray.'[31]

With each performance her renown also grew. Potential lovers lined up to set expensive gifts at her feet: diamond rings, antique earrings, strings of enormous pearls, fur coats, exclusive perfumes . . . She wore haute couture by the finest Parisian fashion designers – Paul Poiret, Madeleine Vionnet, Elsa Schiaparelli – and drove a luxury sports car upholstered in snakeskin. Her fortunes seem to have shifted abruptly and accelerated fast; in less than two months, she had gone from hard-up vaudeville comedienne to the toast of Paris.

In November, *La Revue nègre* travelled to Berlin. It was well received and Baker liked the city, where the nightlife was as raucous as in Paris; for the couple of months she was there, she gave herself over to the sexual libertinism of the place. 'She was looking for the perfect penis, and she looked hard,' recalled one of her charming acquaintances.[32] At a party thrown by Count Harry Kessler, attendees remembered her dancing by herself, almost naked apart from a pink organza jacket and high heels. She ended the night in the arms of Ruth Landshoff, a cross-dressing actress and writer who wore tuxedos and sometimes went by the name of René.

As exciting as her German visit was, Baker yearned to return to Paris: 'Why must I take trains and boats that would carry me far from the friendly faces, the misty Seine, the colour-ful quays, hilly Montmartre, the Eiffel Tower, which seemed constantly ready to kick up a leg?'[33] The producers of *La Revue nègre* were getting ready to ship the company out to Moscow, but she had other ideas. Abandoning the show without warn-ing, she headed back to Paris, where she had signed up to star in an all-new extravaganza at the legendary Folies Bergère. Staged in 1926, it was called *La Folie du jour*, and Paris went bananas for it.

At the time, the Folies Bergère was one of the most cele-brated music halls in Paris. Immortalized in Édouard Manet's last masterpiece, *Un Bar aux Folies Bergère* (1881–2), with its realist depiction of a bored woman tending bar during a per-formance, and in the writings of Émile Zola, who called it 'a bizarre, exquisite, unorthodox place . . . as Parisian as possible', by the 1920s the theatre was known all over the world for its big-budget, risqué performances.[34] Being a French music hall, nudity was essential, but under the direction of Paul Derval a Folies Bergère show of the 1920s also had glamour, opulence and a little art, along with the requisite froth and silliness.

Baker's new show opened in May. Like the previous one, this was also a revue, made up of a series of entertain-ing vignettes, including gentle satires of Louis XIV's Versailles and present-day Paris, overrun by American tourists (the sheer number of them in the city by this point had started to grate on the nerves of native Parisians). But Baker was the highlight, or *la vedette*, and her appearance didn't disappoint.

The curtain opened on a jungle scene. In the back-ground, wrapped in vines and obscured here and there by huge palm leaves, a large fallen tree lay at an angle to the stage. In the foreground, a white colonial type dressed in khaki ordered about some bare-chested black men before retiring for a nap. Then, as if from an imperial dream, Baker emerged.

Inching down the tree, she alternated between making faces at the sleeping man below and concealing herself from him – before leaping onto the stage, where she started cavorting: doing the splits, stretching out like a cat, flinging her arms in the air, wiggling her ass. She was wearing very little, except a skirt covered with sixteen bananas 'pointing comically toward the ceiling'.[35] They jiggled about wildly and bounced lewdly up and down as she shook her hips and gyrated coquettishly.

The way she moved her body was superficially seductive but, with her wide, toothy smile, there was a lot of humour in it too – and maybe even a little menace. According to the American author bell hooks, Baker saw the black body 'as a site where nakedness and eroticism are not considered shameful realities to be hidden and masked'.[36] With her belt of severed phalluses, she seemed to be threatening the sleeping white explorer, taunting him with her body, her nudity and her shamelessness.

The banana skirt became Baker's trademark, and she would wear variations of it in different shows for the next forty years. Its origins are somewhat obscure (as indeed are many details of Baker's life – she was as likely to ornament her personal history with embellishments as her rooms at the Hôtel Fournet). Some say Poiret came up with the idea, but Baker always claimed it was the artist and filmmaker Jean Cocteau, which seems more likely – the costume was vulgar and irreverent in a way that was much too modern for Poiret.

In any case it was inspired, and her fans were delighted and titillated by it for decades. Indeed, the skirt continues to captivate years after Baker's death, and black celebrities as different as Diana Ross and Laverne Cox have worn it in tribute to her. Beyoncé wiggled a more demure version of it during her performance at a Fashion Rocks show in 2006 – flaccid gold bananas dangling from her waist as she thundered through the choreography for her single 'Déjà Vu'.

We might well wonder at the appeal of the banana skirt a hundred years after it made its appearance in Paris – and, indeed, why black performers have been so especially keen to pay homage to Baker while wearing it. Surely the primitivist context in which it first came on the scene – a jungle backdrop where a black woman danced naked for a white oppressor – is enough to convince us that the costume should be confined to the dust heap of history? But the truth is that, compared with *La Revue nègre*, Baker's 1926 performance was a massive leap forward in terms of how a black person was represented on the white stage.

While the earlier *danse de sauvage* seemed to exceed the limits of what a body could do, the *danse des bananes* exceeded the limits of what a black body was allowed to do. Watching old recordings of Baker dancing, the racialized dynamic of the Folies Bergère show is appalling, but as our attention shifts from the context to the dancer herself, something more interesting starts to emerge: a highly idiosyncratic and individualized performance.

During the jungle scene, Baker's body oscillates wildly between comedy and sensuality, inanity and athleticism. Existing styles of dance like the Charleston and the 'Mess Around', and jazz moves like the itch and the trench, are cut up and remixed into unusual combinations. There seems to be little pattern to her performance, which is impossible to classify: she's surprising and spontaneous and above all *uniquely* Josephine Baker.

With each gyration, Baker pushes back against the constraints of racial stereotyping, which, at its core, swaps individuals for types, and personalities for categories. Even in such a hyper-racialized setting as the *La Folie du jour* show, through her wiggles and jiggles Baker created a space where a black woman might assert her right to selfhood, to individuality – to being a person and not a type. Maybe it's this (in addition to her enormous success) that Beyoncé and others celebrate when choosing to wear the banana skirt.

After her Folies Bergère premiere, Baker was unstoppable, and she was quick to cash in on her success. In December 1926, she opened her own club in Montmartre called Chez Josephine, plush Josephine Baker dolls went on sale, and she started promoting a range of hair pomades and skin creams that helped the ordinary Parisian to get the Baker look. 'I was learning the importance of names,' she remembered. 'Having them, making them.'[37]

It wasn't just the hoi polloi of Paris who loved Baker and wanted to be like her; the bohemian avant-garde was besotted with her too. After watching her at the Folies Bergère, the poet E. E. Cummings madly gushed that she was 'a creature neither infrahuman nor superhuman but somehow both; a mysteriously unkillable Something, equally non primitive and uncivilized, or beyond time in the sense that emotion is beyond arithmetic'.[38] She modelled for Picasso, who referred to her as the 'Nefertiti of now'.[39] Alexander Calder made sculptures of her in wire – suspended, kinetic forms that moved gently in the air and tried to evoke something of her movement and vivacity.

Women artists and writers also adored her – especially Colette, the bisexual writer and one of France's most celebrated novelists. A model of the sexually liberated Parisienne, as an actress Colette delighted in scandalizing pre-war audiences on stage at the Moulin Rouge. When she performed a skit in January 1907 that ended with her stripping off and giving her partner, Missy de Mornay, 'a lingering and unfeigned kiss', the audience rioted, shouting, 'down with the dykes!'[40]

By 1927, Colette was fifty-four years old and had long given up her career on the stage. She went looking for Baker at Chez Josephine, and they struck up a close friendship. 'Of all the women I knew, she was the only one who seemed completely open, deeply attuned to animals and growing things, a potential soul mate,' Baker said. Colette wrote her affectionate letters on lacy paper embossed with flowers: 'This sentimental writing paper is designed for gentle hearts, children and poets. Which is why I address it to you with a kiss,' she wrote.[41] Baker would keep this correspondence with her all her life.

Baker's friendship with Colette connected her with the queer demi-monde of interwar Paris. On the other side of the Seine from the Folies Bergère, a thriving lesbian subculture composed largely of American exiles and heiresses had made the Left Bank their home.

At 27 rue de Fleurus, Gertrude Stein, writer of such pioneering works as *Tender Buttons* (1914), who, with her partner, Alice B. Toklas, could be said to have midwifed modernism, such was the support they lent to young writers and artists in Paris in the early decades of the twentieth century.

At 12 rue de l'Odéon, Sylvia Beach, the founder of the Shakespeare and Company bookshop, which sold and loaned out English-language literature, and her partner, Adrienne Monnier, the proprietor of La Maison des Amis des Livres;

together they built the infrastructure that made Paris such a powerhouse of literary experimentation in the 1920s.

At 9 rue Saint-Romain, Djuna Barnes, the witty chronicler of Paris's lesbian scene, who arrived in 1921 already a renowned journalist, with a self-destructive streak (people whispered that she had voluntarily undergone force-feeding in order to write about the trials of imprisoned suffragettes).

At 70 rue Notre-Dame-des-Champs, the gender-bending photographer Claude Cahun and her partner and collaborator, Suzanne Malherbe – about whom more in the next chapter.

And at 20 rue Jacob, the lynchpin of the scene, Natalie Barney and her famous weekly salon, which, by 1927, had become something of a sapphic idyll and the centre of lesbian Paris to which queer women regularly flocked.

One of these was Radclyffe Hall, who first met Barney in 1924. Born Marguerite Radclyffe Hall on 12 August 1880, like many of the other English lesbians she associated with (Jack Holme, Christopher St John, Tony Atwood), she was known by a male nickname, John. Rich, imperious and, by the time she arrived in Paris, a celebrated English novelist, Hall was a snooty upper-class type, conservative in everything except her sexual orientation. She was accompanied by her partner, Una, Lady Troubridge, a similarly rich, conceited woman with fascist tendencies who dedicated her life to supporting Hall's genius.

Both women cleaved to patriarchal norms, playing them out across their otherwise unconventional relationship. Hall fashioned herself as the masculine head of the household who exerted order and control, while Una embraced the role of a subservient wife. They were also resolutely traditional in their tastes, and considered modernist experimentation to be little more than a fad that had no bearing on good (i.e.

conservative) literature and art. They were, therefore, hardly the most radical of couples – and certainly not the most likely to have become queer icons. Next to some of the bohemians who turned up at Barney's salon, they must have seemed positively out of place.

The salon was held every Friday afternoon from four o'clock until eight at 20 rue Jacob, accessed through a pair of large double doors on the street that opened onto an interior cobbled courtyard. At the end of this was Barney's large, two-storey seventeenth-century home, the interior of which was decorated in earthy browns and reds – all scarlet interiors and crimson velvet cushions. Sombre portraits by her partner, the misanthropic Romaine Brooks, glowered from the walls. Nestled among the trees at the bottom of the ever-overgrown garden was a small temple in the Greek style with four Doric columns supporting its entrance. Above the door, À L'AMITIÉ was carved in large capital letters – *to friendship*. Barney was herself dedicated to cultivating intimate friendships with women and recreating Sappho's circle in twentieth-century Paris. Openly, shamelessly queer, she is reported to have said: 'I am a lesbian. One needn't hide it, nor boast of it.'[42]

For Sylvia Beach, Barney was an Amazon – albeit a gentle one. 'She was charming, and, all dressed in white with her blond colouring, most attractive. Many of her sex found her fatally so.' Colette was one of those who fell for Barney's charms and the two had a brief affair in 1906, which turned into a lifelong friendship. She, along with Beach and Monnier, and others like Stein, Toklas and Brooks, regularly attended Barney's salons. Beach recalled that 'at Miss Barney's one met the ladies with high collars and monocles, though Miss Barney herself was so feminine. Unfortunately, I missed the chance to make the acquaintance at her salon of the authoress of *The Well of Loneliness* . . . '[43]

Although they didn't meet, Hall's novel would have given Beach a good idea of what she thought of Barney and the 'rather splendid disorder' of her home.

> There was something blissfully unkempt about it, as though its mistress were too engrossed in other affairs to control its behaviour . . . The odour of somebody's Oriental scent was mingling with the odour of tuberoses in a sixteenth-century chalice. On a divan, whose truly regal proportions occupied the best part of a shadowy alcove, lay a box of Fuller's peppermint creams and a lute, but the strings of the lute were broken.[44]

For Beach and so many queer women like her, Hall and her book (and indeed the book's controversial reception in Britain) were enormously influential. 'I wished to offer my name and my literary reputation in support of the cause of the inverted,' Hall wrote, and perhaps more than any other work of fiction or non-fiction, *The Well of Loneliness* would set the tone for how same-sex love between women would be seen and discussed in the century after it was published.[45]

Hall's quasi-autobiographical story is about a woman named Stephen Gordon, born into an upper-class family in England in the late nineteenth century. Her parents are so certain they're going to have a boy that, even when Stephen turns out to be female, they give her a boy's name. As Stephen grows up, she gravitates towards male interests and habits: she likes to cut her hair short and wears men's clothes. She also harbours deep passions for other women, like her family's maid and a neighbour's American wife. She spends time with a woman she meets during the war; like Vera Holme and Evelina Haverfield, who were part of the Scottish Women's Hospital unit in Serbia, she works for the ambulance services, which seemed to attract many queer women.

All of Stephen's relationships are shot through with shame and self-hatred. As we saw in the previous chapter, before the 1920s there really weren't any prominent examples of homosexual women, and Stephen is at a loss as to why she is how she is. Over and over, she asks herself, 'What am I, in God's name?'[46] Searching for answers, she draws on the work of sexologists like Richard von Krafft-Ebing and Havelock Ellis, and concludes that she is a 'congenital invert'. She thinks that homosexuality is a disability, and inverts like herself deserve pity, not scorn. In the final lines of the book, she makes a plea: 'Acknowledge us, oh God, before the whole world. Give us the right to our existence.'[47]

The book was published in July 1928, to mostly positive reviews. But on 18 August, the *Sunday Express* newspaper denounced it as 'filth' for its depiction of depraved acts between women. The writer James Douglas asserted: 'I would rather give a healthy boy or a healthy girl a phial of prussic acid than this novel. Poison kills the body, but moral poison kills the soul.'[48] The newspaper then launched a campaign to have the book banned, which was taken up by other newspapers and a Tory government that was heading into a general election. The home secretary charged Hall's publisher with obscenity; after a long trial, all copies of the book were ordered to be destroyed. All the fuss only made the book more popular: it went on to sell millions of copies, and made an icon of its authoress and the lesbian identity that was the focus of the novel.

Things wouldn't be the same for queer women after 1928, which in retrospect was something of an *annus mirabilis* for lesbian literature and also saw the publication of Woolf's *Orlando* (a fictional biography of Vita Sackville-West), Djuna Barnes's *Ladies Almanack* (a fictional biography of Barney and her circle) and Compton Mackenzie's *Extraordinary Women* (a fictional biography of Romaine Brooks). The trial of *The Well of Loneliness* made the lesbian visible as never before.

This had the effect Hall had planned, where other 'inverts' could now see themselves represented in Stephen's tale. For many queer women this was a revelation, and Hall was inundated with letters of thanks and praise from other lesbians. One reader remembered: 'I identified with every line. I wept floods of tears over it and it confirmed my belief in my homosexuality.'[49]

But the novel and the response to it also had the effect of fixing that image of homosexual women for queer people and the public at large in much the same way as Wilde's trial had fixed the image of a homosexual man. The days of ambiguous romantic friendships were passing away as, for better or worse, same-sex love between women was now exposed to scrutiny. The public was newly armed with a scientific vocabulary that could be used to describe and delimit female homosexuality. All of a sudden, parameters were imposed on queer desire between women; and it set most quickly into the figure of the mannish lesbian.

Le Beau Chêne

Even as lesbian identity started to cohere around limits and lexicons, in her life and love and work the bisexual Baker continued to exceed every constraint. In 1929, she moved to Le Vésinet, a suburb of Paris, where she bought a gigantic thirty-room, turn-of-the-century mansion called Le Beau Chêne.

It was luxurious and over the top; every lily gilded, as was her wont. According to Bricktop, 'Josephine had to have been here before as a queen or something. She traipsed around her château just like she always lived that way.'[50] In the grounds of the villa flourished an ever-growing zoo, which now included chickens, ducks, rabbits, monkeys, thirteen dogs and a cheetah called Chiquita. A quarter of a mile from the house, in an area hidden by trees and bushes, Baker built a temple; marble columns in the Roman style were arranged in a semicircle around a large pool and decorated with statues of Diana, Venus and Circe. Like the temple at the bottom of Natalie Barney's garden, Baker's was also dedicated to love.

Inside, the house was filled with expensive antiques and dozens of life-sized portraits of its owner. The walls of her large bathroom were all mirrors, which filled the space with an infinity of Bakers. The bath itself was coated in a polished metal that reflected her body in absurd, elongated proportions. The sheer quantity of Baker that could be found at Le Beau Chêne could be seen as evidence of the star's narcissism; viewed in a different light, it also resonates with her stage performances and her desire to push beyond the limits of the solitary and self-contained body. She would live among this multitude of Bakers until 1947, when she moved into a castle in the Dordogne.

In her career, too, Baker began to multiply her personae such that within a few years she was not merely a dancer, bar-owner and model but an actor and a singer too. With the help of Pepito de Abatino, her partner and business manager, she trained her voice and was soon recording hits like 'J'ai deux amours', which was released in 1930 and sold 300,000 copies.

Composed by Vincent Scotto, the song is in the French chanson style, with Baker's pure soprano embellished with occasional coloratura – florid ornamentations of trills and runs going up two octaves from middle C and back again. The lyrics are written from the perspective of a foreigner, who views Paris from a distance. 'Over there' is an 'enchanting' place where she wishes to go, even though she adores her own home and its 'beautiful savannah'.

J'ai deux amours
Mon pays et Paris
Pour eux toujours
Mon coeur est ravi

[I have two loves
My country and Paris
For them always
My heart is full of joy]

The song is about having two, qualitatively different loves. Another pop song might find in this a cause for suffering – the singer might be in search of the one true love, for example, and torn between two. But an abundance of love is here a cause for celebration and joy. It's as if 'J'ai deux amours' gently exhorts us to move beyond the limitations of our thinking about love and relationships, and makes room for both bisexuality and polyamory within its story. The song would become Baker's anthem and she would sing it at every performance for the rest of her life.

Although Baker had performed in films as early as 1927 (she starred in a silent movie called *The Siren of the Tropics*), her first speaking part came in 1934 with the film *Zouzou*. In this quasi-autobiographical rags-to-riches story about a young laundress who is plucked from obscurity to become a singing sensation, Baker played the eponymous Zouzou opposite French stalwart Jean Gabin. African-American scholar Bennetta Jules-Rosette calls it 'Baker's best personal and professional achievement in film'.[51]

In *Zouzou*, Gabin, an established comic actor in the mould of Spencer Tracy, approaches his performance with a louche realism leavened by a smidgen of irony; Baker, by contrast, explodes onto the screen. Within two minutes of her first appearance, she tap-dances on a table, pulls funny faces and clowns around, performs a puppet show with her fingers and sings a song with a ukulele. A trapeze appears out of nowhere and suddenly she's swinging on it to the delight of a little girl in her charge. Such is Baker's energy and exuberance, it's as if the screen struggles to contain her. Her gestures throughout the film are also exaggerated and intensified: she squeals and pouts and thrashes about with joy; she juts out her chin, dances for no apparent reason, screams hysterically. Phyllis Rose takes a dim view of all of this, remarking that Baker 'overdid almost every move' in the film, and wondering why the director, Marc Allégret, didn't rein in his star.[52] Where it comes to Baker, however, overdoing things was precisely the point, and perhaps Allégret understood that her excessive performance was less a failure of realism than an attempt to conjure an individual style in itself.

Baker was committed to the idea of excess: given a choice of either/or, she chose both, a choice that found expression in all parts of her life. She loved abundantly, without shame and with both male and female partners. Her performances on stage and screen also surpassed all prescriptive notions about what the human body could do – and what a black person was allowed to do. Her lifestyle was conspicuously, extravagantly over the top, and her ambitions for her career were so huge she had to invent different personae in an effort to contain them. Such an individual could only have emerged in interwar Paris, a city of excessive appetites and ideas, where limitations in literature, art and music were consistently being violated and transcended. Only this place could have created the larger-than-life figure of La Baker.

Cultural historian Marjorie Garber writes that 'bi is not between, but beyond the heterosexual-homosexual divide'. For Garber, bisexuality isn't a sexual orientation; it exceeds the idea of orientation and undermines its usefulness. For many bisexuals, sexual orientation one way or another really makes no sense; to use it to talk about bisexual desire is to employ monosexual norms that are actually pretty irrelevant. Likewise, bisexuality isn't a category of sexuality; it exceeds categorization – specifically, the kind of categorization that started to solidify around Western ideas of sexuality in the nineteenth century (for men) and in the early twentieth century (for women), and have continued to dominate our discussions ever since. Considering things from a bisexual perspective, according to Garber, 'threatens and challenges the easy binarities of straight and gay, queer and "het," and even, through its biological and physiological meanings, the gender categories of male and female'.[53]

There may be even wider repercussions to Garber's reflections. To view things like a bisexual, to look beyond the heterosexual–homosexual divide and beyond the limitations of such monosexual thinking, is, perhaps, to be equipped to see beyond other divisions, other limitations. To see, for instance, that life is made up not of polarities but of spectra, or to see that black and white are divided from each other only by a way of thinking that sets them apart.

When the *Normandie* docked in New York, all did not go according to plan. Baker, Abatino and their friends piled into a Rolls-Royce that drove them across town to the luxurious Hotel St Moritz, a thirty-three-storey tower that loomed like a cliff over Central Park. The star and her entourage swept into the lobby of the hotel, but were turned away at the front desk. In deference to the hotel's white Southern visitors, black guests weren't allowed. Her fame in France counted for nothing. In America, she was a black woman and the implication was that she should know her place – which certainly wasn't at the Hotel St Moritz, or indeed any of the dozen other Manhattan hotels they drove around that afternoon. Finally, she settled for the Bedford on East 40th Street, a mid-range hotel for actors and artists, where she rented the most expensive apartment in the building.

More humiliations would follow as her fellow Americans – white and black – cruelly reminded her she was no longer in Paris. At a party for the composer George Gershwin, she arrived, elegance incarnate, dressed in sleek yellow satin. As her white mink coat fell to the floor, Beatrice Lillie, a white actress from whom all eyes had turned when Baker walked in, shouted, 'Who dat?' in her best imitation of a Harlem accent. The attendees tittered. Later, at a dinner party thrown by songwriter Lorenz Hart, a black maid took umbrage at Baker having the temerity to speak in French. 'Honey, you is full of shit,' the maid declared. 'Talk the way yo mouth was born.'[54] It was as if both Lillie and the maid had decided to make it clear to everyone that, underneath all her expensive style, Josephine Baker was just a Negro wench.

Which was, in fact, exactly what *Time* magazine called her, when it reviewed the *Ziegfeld Follies* in January 1936. The piece insisted on dispelling the reader's illusions that Baker was anything more than a 'St Louis washer-woman's daughter'.

> In sex appeal to jaded Europeans of the jazz-loving type, a Negro wench always has a head start. The particular tawny hue of tall and stringy Josephine Baker's bare skin stirred French pulses. But to Manhattan theatre-goers last week she was just a slightly buck-toothed young Negro woman whose figure might be matched in any nightclub show.[55]

Her white co-stars received plaudits while she was panned. 'Some people like Josephine Baker,' wrote one generous reviewer. 'I don't.'[56] There seemed to be universal outrage among white critics that she had dared to transcend the clowning pickaninny of her *Shuffle Along* days. The *New York Times* announced that 'Miss Baker has refined her art until there is nothing left'.[57] White audiences were also appalled by her final number in the show, where she danced provocatively with four white men; they objected to seeing such adoration lavished on a black woman and, according to one onlooker, 'at the end of the number, the boys lifted her into the air and ran off the stage with her, and there was total silence. Nobody clapped.'[58]

An either/or mentality found its apotheosis in American-style segregation, which could not countenance, and indeed violently refused, Baker's efforts to exceed its limitations. The result was heartbreaking for her, and for the rest of her life she refused ever to talk about the 1930s trip. The *Follies'* run had to be cut short when Fanny Brice fell ill; Baker was offered the chance to appear in a second run starting in September but she declined. The show closed on 9 May 1936, and not long after Baker boarded the *Normandie* once again to make the return trip across the Atlantic.

France was now her only home. In a few short years, she would renounce her American passport and become a French citizen; during the Second World War, she would put her wealth and property at the disposal of the French Resistance. For its part, France loved her as America never would, and when she died on 12 April 1975, she was given an enormous state funeral, complete with a twenty-one-gun salute.

In November 2021, France's President Emmanuel Macron would elect to transfer her remains to the Panthéon, where she would take her place beside the likes of Voltaire and Rousseau, the only black woman to have ever been granted France's highest honour. As the official notification from the Élysée Palace declared: 'France honours this exceptional individual, who was born American but who, in the name of her lifelong struggle for freedom and emancipation, chose the Eternal France of Universal Enlightenment.'[59]

At the train station in Paris in May 1936, crowds greeted her with bouquets of flowers in celebration of her return. Someone with an accordion struck up the tune of 'J'ai deux amours' and, to her fans' delight, Baker gave an emotional rendition of her theme song – with lyrics modified to suit the occasion. 'J'ai deux amours,' she sang. 'Mon pays, c'est Paris.' *My country is Paris.*

Self-portrait circa 1927 by Claude Cahun.
Courtesy of the Jersey Heritage Collections.

4.

Neither: Claude Cahun's Jersey

Night shrouds the island in darkness by the time we reach the Jersey coast. From the ferry's observation deck, I look out across the English Channel, where pinpricks of phosphorescent light in the harbour mirror the stars winking in the sky above. Over our heads, the moon is holding water, its thin crescent lit from below so that it resembles a large, delicate bowl. The tranquillity of the scene is disturbed only by the ominous thrum of the ship's turbines and the sound of the waves churning, churning away beneath us as we approach St Helier more swiftly than I can imagine.

Soon begins the docking: lurching, interminable, cacophonous. As the mammoth vessel reverses towards the pier, the air fills with diesel fumes and a deep engine rumble that makes me feel nauseous for the first time in this long voyage. Warning sirens beep and blare arrhythmically, and, down in the hold, steel clangs infernally against steel. Reds and greens are shattered and elongated in the black waters of the bay – harbour lights reflected in pop-impressionist renderings. Inland, the port looks eerie and empty. An unnatural amber glow envelops its warehouses and shipping containers, silhouetting the enormous cranes that stand about like unmoving sentries, barring access to the town.

From some land-side attendant hidden in the shadows, a

shout goes up announcing our arrival. It's echoed on board by a voice that comes across the loudspeaker, issuing a welcome in two different languages that remains garbled and unintelligible in both. Finally we're released, and I join the small band of foot passengers descending into the terminal. Once inside, each of us in turn recoils at the harsh fluorescent light, our pupils contracting to reveal the bounty of Elizabeth Pier: unmanned car-hire desks and shuttered souvenir shops. Abandoned reefs of chairs dressed in pleather blue.

Suddenly, stinking of beer and cheap aftershave, a quartet of middle-aged men in pastel-coloured shirts barges through the crowd, pushing me aside easily. They weave and stagger loudly through the doors, making for the taxi bays at the front of the building, gurning, bellowing. *I need a fackin' drink. Give us a fag, you cheap cunt. Keep your knickers on, love, we're only havin' a laugh.* An awaiting van reluctantly admits them and, as it disappears into the night, I exchange sympathetic looks with a couple of other recent arrivals. We are relieved to finally be rid of them.

They came aboard two hours earlier when the ship briefly docked in Guernsey, one of the other Channel Islands about two dozen miles north west of here. Obnoxious and already drunk, they set themselves up by the large porthole-shaped window by the door to the dining area. From there, they could monitor access and roar suggestive comments at any young woman who had the temerity to pass through. I watched them warily from the other side of the restaurant, as the humiliation of others and the insults they threw at each other shored up a type of aggressive, straight masculinity I have learned to loathe. My body knows all about the violence meted out to those who reject it or are incompatible with it.

In reaction to their arrival, I found I'd hidden my book in my lap in case it might somehow catch their eye.

I escaped their attention this time, but two young teenage boys a couple of tables away weren't so lucky. I'd seen them chatting together conspiratorially before; now, as one of the drunks stood up and tottered over, they turned silent and watchful. I braced myself for a confrontation, but there was something unexpectedly tender in the older man's approach that caught me off guard. He told them about his sons, who were of a similar age; he wanted to know how they were getting on at school; he asked them what football team they liked. His conversation was slurred yet cheerful; any response from the boys was soon drowned out, however, by the man's companions roaring from the corner. *Paedo! Nonce! Leave their little pricks alone! Yeah leave their peepees alone, you paedo!* Red faces turned beetroot as they howled with laughter and, chastened, the stray returned to the fold, screaming invectives. With the boundaries of acceptable behaviour successfully policed, they all submerged themselves once more in their pints and banter.

I've always been, as Boy George might say, a man without conviction. Growing up cisgendered but queer as much in terms of my interests and outlook as my sexuality, I never understood how young guys my age were able to *be men* with such apparent ease. They seemed to have no problem embodying a kind of masculinity that looked so normal and natural: they played sports and drove cars, shaped wood with their hands and lost their virginity and blabbed about it. I, on the other hand, was bookish, bad at sports and romantic. I loved musicals and played the lead in school productions, but I knew that offstage a convincing performance of straight masculinity was beyond me.

Which isn't to say that I didn't try, of course, or that I didn't fail repeatedly, but over time (if I can be forgiven for over-extending a metaphor) I realized the role wasn't for me. More importantly, I was left with a bone-deep understanding of how gender works. The kind of masculinity I was surrounded by passed itself off as the norm with the consent of the masses. If I could fail to achieve it and distance myself from it, however, then perhaps it wasn't as authentic as it first appeared. Slowly the realization dawned on me that it was all an act; that all gender is learned behaviour – something social and cultural, not natural and biological.

So even before my encounter with the drunks on the ferry, I was sensitive to how gender is acted out, especially among straight men; how it has to be affirmed constantly in a multitude of ways by the individual, by the people they surround themselves with, and by the cultures they're immersed in. On the way to Jersey, these ideas played on my mind more than ever. After all, I was on the trail of a gender-bending surrealist who had made the place her home. Using a deeply unsettling kind of drag, years ahead of its time, Claude Cahun's photographs show just how much gender is masquerade. Breaking the syntax of gender and rearranging its signs (those gestures and affectations assigned to femaleness and maleness – the belching bravado of the men who had just barged past, for instance), in Cahun's hands, on film, gender ceases to seem natural, and becomes instead a strange and uncanny spectacle.

Cahun was a queer anarchist and a gender renegade. She was also a visionary writer and a performance artist before anyone had heard of such a thing – the art historian Hal Foster called her 'a Cindy Sherman avant la lettre'.[1] At the age of fourteen, she fell in love with Marcel Moore (born Suzanne Malherbe), who later became her stepsister when Cahun's father married her mother, and the two of them fled to Paris where they moved among the radical, artistic sets of the interwar city. Surrealism, dadaism, communism: Cahun flirted with them all but signed up to none. For her, group-think was the enemy of the individual imagination, which had to be protected at all costs.

With war on the horizon, the two set sail for Jersey, a small island off the coast of France, in 1937. In a few years, the place was crawling with Nazis, and Cahun did what came naturally to her: dissented in any way that she could. She and Moore secretly distributed hundreds of anti-Nazi pamphlets and artworks, encouraging German soldiers to rise up and desert their leaders. The two women were finally arrested and sentenced to death, but the end of the war came just in time. They were released in time to join the jubilant crowds that thronged St Helier on 9 May 1945, the first day of Jersey's Liberation.

On my way to the hotel, I pass through an empty Liberation Square. Spectacularly illuminated in the centre of the plaza is a war memorial commemorating fifty years since the end of Nazi occupation. It consists of seven life-size bronze figures, which tonight look marvellously lifelike, clustered together, their arms upraised in celebration. A few members of the group hold onto the edges of a huge flag, also made out of bronze, which seems to hang, fluttering, in the air. It's hard to make out the markings on it at first, but I soon see it's the Union Flag of Britain; the sculptor has captured the movement of cloth so keenly, it looks like it might tug from the islanders' grasp at any moment. There's something in the symbolism of this that stays with me as I make my way through the streets on this autumn evening, and Jersey begins to reveal itself as a place that's clinging to its British heritage, all the while being pulled in different directions.

As a Crown Dependency, Jersey is a self-governing island, separate from the United Kingdom but still legally dependent on it. Its laws have to be approved by the British government, Britain is responsible for the island's defence, and Britain and Jersey share the same currency. This unique constitutional status is the result of shifting territorial claims between England and France over the centuries. At one time it was owned by William the Conqueror, the Norman duke who defeated the English in 1066 and crowned himself king of England; his successors lost Normandy to the French, but Jersey remained an English possession. The island is eighty-five miles from the coast of England and only nineteen from France, so it was regularly invaded by the French and reclaimed by the English in the Middle Ages, during the Hundred Years' War and the War of the Roses. As a testament to this historical toing and froing, both French and English are official languages of Jersey (along with Jèrriais, a native language spoken only by a few).

In St Helier you can feel the competing influences of England and France. Some of the town seems very French to me – the built environment, mostly, especially the concrete apartment blocks four or five storeys high that remind me of ones in the towns of northern France where I used to live. They stand, squarish and inoffensive, painted in washed-out yellow, pink or peach, looking like a municipal building where one might wrangle with a French bureaucrat over the terms of a *carte de séjour*.

The layout of the town is also similar to Caen or Brest or other places where French esteem for public amenities is in evidence – the footpaths wide, the roads well maintained, the signage excellent. It's an uncanny similarity, however. Here cars drive on the left, not on the right, and those excellent traffic signs are all written in English, not French. I'm also pleasantly surprised to find that, as I'm walking along, I don't have to pirouette around piles of dog shit. In contrast to, say, Lille, the pavements of St Helier are mercifully free of *crottes de chien*.

The sense of place here can turn on a sixpence. A street with the quintessentially English name of Kensington Place opens out onto a building with the French words 'Maison du Coin' emblazoned above the first-floor windows. Walking down Journeaux Street, I'm suddenly transported to the English seaside by the smell of fish and chips that comes wafting out of a chippy called Gerry's. It's strange and disconcerting, and difficult to get your bearings while moving between two different designations, definitions, languages . . . I suspect this is one of the reasons why Cahun liked the place so much.

Until the early 1990s, few people had ever heard of Claude Cahun. Her art wasn't recognized when she was alive, and after she died it was all but forgotten, fated to remain no more than a footnote in the major histories of surrealism. But then the French art historian François Leperlier started investigating marginal surrealists and her name came up; his research led him to Jersey, where he unexpectedly found a huge cache of her work. Acquired at auction for half-nothing after she and Moore had passed away, Cahun's photos emerged out of Jersey attics and lumber rooms, and quickly gained international acclaim as groundbreaking art objects, decades ahead of their time.

Nowadays, she's most famous for her bizarre, slyly humorous photographic self-portraits that play with norms of masculinity and femininity. Her photographs from the 1920s in particular seem to anticipate postmodern theories of gender by at least half a century, and have consequently been celebrated in the halls of academia. As lesbian critic Terry Castle comments acerbically: 'In the baleful little world of academic "gender studies" (strap-ons and piercings strongly advised) the cross-dressing Cahun has been a cult heroine.'[2]

In one of the most well-known of these photographs, Cahun stares seductively out of the frame with smoky eyes, her cheeks adorned with love hearts and lips pursed together as if getting ready for a kiss. She assumes, in other words, a hyper-feminine pose. But the costume she's wearing is jarringly hyper-masculine – dressed as a circus strongman, complete with prop dumbbells, and the words I AM IN TRAINING / DONT KISS ME scrawled across her vest. In this portrait, visual cues of gendered identity are all mixed up, collaged, juxtaposed. Cahun might simply say that they're shuffled. In her experimental memoir, *Disavowals* (1930), she wrote:

> Shuffle the cards. Masculine? Feminine? It depends on the situation. Neuter is the only gender that always suits me. If it existed in our language no one would be able to see my thought's vacillations.[3]

In recent years, people have looked to Cahun as something of a transgender icon. In my bag, I've brought along a lovingly handmade zine I found called *Another Mask*, created by a queer British couple who see Cahun as a trans or non-binary forebear. The authors criticize the way that the artist's gender presentation has previously been written about, and in deference to the apparent embrace of 'neuter' in *Disavowals*, they conclude that it's best to refer to Cahun using they/them pronouns. Given the viciously anti-trans sentiments that circulate online and in the British media, it seems right to me that trans and genderqueer people should reach out and connect with Cahun in this way, even if there's no indication in their writings or correspondence that she or Moore were personally uncomfortable with gendered pronouns.

Cahun's life is rich with contradictions, however, and I'm more wary than the creators of *Another Mask* of choosing her apparent alignment with 'neuter' over what she calls the 'vacillations' of her thought. In her cunning, paradoxical, symbolist-inflected writing, it's often difficult to pin down exactly what Cahun means, but in the lines quoted above, she seems to acknowledge that her thinking and her work are only made visible in the alternation – i.e. the movement – between masculine and feminine; in the transgression of both. *Neither* masculine *nor* feminine. I'm reminded of what the great 'gender outlaw' Kate Bornstein calls her 'borderline life':

Do you think you have it in you to be a man?
Do you think you have it in you to be a woman?
Have you ever thought what it might be like to be neither
for a day? An hour? One minute?[4]

To me, Cahun is a kind of Bornstein *avant la lettre* – a line that's traced as boundaries are obliterated and categories are negated. *Trans* means *across, beyond, through*; choosing they/them feels to me like it puts a halt to that movement and prematurely answers the provocative questions that Cahun's life and work raise about gender and sexuality. In short, whenever I use she/her pronouns to write or speak about Cahun,

I imagine the words in quotation marks – placeholders for an individual who was too nuanced for the brute approximations of language.

If Josephine Baker's queerness could be described in terms of both/and, then perhaps Cahun is best characterized as *neither/nor*. This thought comes to me while walking around St Helier at night, observing this place between England and France, that's neither in England nor in France, which Cahun loved so much and defended with her life. The island would reveal much more to me in the days that followed.

Masquerade

Under this mask another mask. I'll never be finished removing all of these faces.[5]

These words appear towards the end of *Disavowals*, in one of the book's fantastical photo-collages that were co-created by Cahun and Moore. Written in the kind of beautiful, meticulous cursive that French children are especially good at, the words snake around a distended head that fills the left-hand side of the work. Looking like a huge modernist totem pole, it comprises a stack of eleven faces – all Cahun in different guises: with bug eyes or lipsticked bow lips, wearing black welding goggles or smoking a cigarette or made up to look like a devil. One face follows another in an apparently endless series. The illustration and the script that frames it like a thought dominate the piece, which has no shortage of other startling images: embryos gestate in the bellies of a line of Russian dolls; a plant grows out of the navel of a statue; a naked family zoom through space in a geometric prism, Superman-style.

Masks and mask-wearing were recurring preoccupations for Cahun, especially in the early period of her life. The relationship between society and the self was at the heart of it: how, in the words of T. S. Eliot's famous 'Love Song of J. Alfred Prufrock' (1915), you 'prepare a face to meet the faces that you meet'.[6] Like Eliot's Prufrock, Cahun was keenly aware of society's injunction to conform. She used her writing and photography to explore the ways that outer conformity could harden into what she called an 'inflexible, implacable mask' that twisted up the inner self, but also how wearing a mask might allow something like a true self to slip away, unseen by the masses.[7]

Born Lucy Renée Mathilde Schwob on 25 October 1894 in Nantes, France (she would give herself the name Claude Cahun in 1917), Cahun had a rather nonconformist upbringing. Her family were well off but far from conservative. Cahun's father, Maurice, was the Jewish publisher of a leftist newspaper who permitted his daughter to read widely. Unusually for someone of his standing, he also discouraged her from getting married; to be exempt from this pressure was an enormous relief to her, and a privilege not many young women like her were permitted. Her mother, Victorine Mary-Antoinette, seems to have had a personality disorder, and spent long periods of Cahun's childhood in hospital. Although this was a source of profound pain, her absence meant further freedom from any requirement to wear the mask of conjugal femininity.

Marcel Schwob, Cahun's queer uncle, was a famous symbolist writer who counted among his friends the most celebrated authors of Belle Époque Paris, including Guillaume Apollinaire, André Gide, Colette and Oscar Wilde. Cahun deeply admired Schwob, and it's likely that it was through him she first started to read Wilde and Gide, before expanding her horizons to embrace the likes of Lord Alfred Douglas ('Bosie') and John Addington Symonds.

The latter were part of a group known as the Uranian poets – Victorian men who wrote poetry about that lofty Greek love between men we read about earlier (needless to say, all were educated at either Oxford or Cambridge). These homosexual male writers had a monumental impact on Cahun, and she would entitle her first book *Les Jeux uraniens* (Uranian Games), which was written around 1916. Reading the work of the Uranians, especially Bosie's poem 'Two Loves' (1892), which is famously about 'the love that dare not speak its name', Cahun had an early insight into society's investment in sexual conformity.[8] Wilde's fate, of course, was a tragic reminder to her of what lay in wait when such a love was openly expressed.

In the absence of any readily available literature that dealt with same-sex love between women, gay male poets also helped Cahun to make sense of her queer desires. In 1909 she met Moore, born 19 July 1892, an artistic teenager a couple of years older than she was, and much more calm and stable as a person. She became Cahun's collaborator, camera operator, friend and lover. Cahun remembered:

> From 1909 to 1917, we, Suzanne and I . . . managed to see each other secretly in the countryside (we had bicycles) and openly at one or other of our houses, usually my house where we were alone . . . We even travelled together on vacations with or without our parents: Brighton, London, Parsons-Mead, Holland, Italy, Brittany, Le Croisic, Roscoff . . . Switzerland . . . Saint-Malo and Jersey.

Their families were close and became even closer in 1917, when Moore's father died and her mother married Cahun's father. From that point on, the relationship between the two young women was able to flourish under their parents' noses, as they assumed the pretence of loving half-siblings and disguised their passion for each other as innocent, sisterly affection. 'The strange coincidence that brought us together as a family seemed to allow everything to turn out for the best,' Cahun wrote.[9]

Cahun's interest in masks, especially the straight masquerade queer people have to perform to survive in violently homophobic societies, emerges most forcefully in her self-portraits. To take a closer look at them, the morning after my arrival in St Helier I walk through grey streets to the Jersey Archive, which holds the largest collection of Cahun's artworks in the world. The vast majority of these were acquired from a rare-book seller on the island, who bought Cahun and Moore's library for £21 after they died. When he opened their old tea chests full of books, he also discovered hundreds of beautiful, remarkably strange photographs – an entire lifetime of radical experimentation with a camera.

The archive building is an angular, modern thing of steel and glass, tucked away on a quiet side street of St Helier, with a huge foyer that's three floors high and must be impossible to heat. The staff give me a warm welcome nonetheless, and direct me upstairs, where the photos I've asked for wait patiently to be viewed in their powder-grey cardboard boxes. I take a seat in the reading room, which is totally silent except for the light scratching of pencils on paper.

Sitting here, I remember how much I love the peculiarities of the archive. Call me a masochist, but there's something thrilling about its sense of order and control. I'm excited by the way the archive holds so much history that it often overflows with powerful emotions (in private letters, love notes, diaries, family records . . .) but one can only view parts of it, in pieces, for a short period of time, or lay hands on it in a very particular way – often wearing soft white gloves. I wonder to myself how many archivists moonlight regularly as dominatrixes.

Needless to say, I'm full of nervous anticipation as the archivist brings over the first item. I asked to see a photo I came across some years ago in an exhibit of Cahun's work in Paris. I remember it as a full-length snap of someone standing in front of a lace curtain, wearing a dark cape to which a dozen black-and-white eye masks have been affixed. The subject of the photo was presumably Cahun, but it was impossible to know for sure because of the eerie mask, like a porcelain doll, covering her face.

When I first saw it, I was struck by its paradoxical combination of openness and reticence. It felt like there was so much being communicated by the image – from the masks that appeared to float around Cahun, to the doll's dead gaze, to the arm beneath the cape that jutted out at an odd angle. At the same time, it felt secretive, withholding; I found it impossible to resolve all of its visual data into some kind of coherent message. If only I could see it again, I thought, then, surely, I'd make sense of it.

Which is why, when I open the archive box and its contents is revealed, I have to laugh. I'm aware of disturbing the reading room and earning the disapproval of its silence-abiding occupants, but I can't help it. In my hand I hold a piece of brown, semi-transparent plastic twelve centimetres by nine: instead of a photograph, I've been given a negative, in which

Self-portrait, circa 1928, by Claude Cahun.
Courtesy of the Jersey Heritage Collections.

the image of the masked enigma has been reversed. White is black, black is white; what was on the left is now on the right.

I'm laughing because there's something so very *Cahun* in this moment – so marvellous and mischievous. It's almost as if she somehow anticipated my desire to read her and turned the tables by insisting that I do it backwards. The doll's face with the inverted colours stares back at me implacably. I suppose if I'm given to understanding Cahun's queerness in terms of neither/nor, there's no better place to start my research than with a negative.

The archive's catalogue dates this photograph from 1928. By then, Cahun and Moore were in Paris. They moved there in 1922, and set up house together in a small apartment at 70 bis rue Notre-Dame-des-Champs at the northern edge of Montparnasse. I like to think that Cahun might have met Josephine Baker when they were both in Paris during the 1920s. I imagine these two iconoclastic performers coming together, perhaps after one of Baker's sensational shows, sharing secrets, goading each other, spurring each other on to even greater artistic heights. In *Never Anyone But You* (2018), a novel about Cahun and Moore's life, the English writer Rupert Thomson has the couple watching Baker dance at the Folies Bergère. 'We were sitting so close that her sweat landed on our clothes,' his Moore remembers.[10] But it's a novelist's fabrication; there's no record of anything like it ever having taken place.

Cahun and Moore's apartment was richly furnished in a personal, quasi-bohemian style evocative of their taste. On display around their home were cubist sculptures, Dada photomontages, a drawing by Joan Miró – flourishes that opened their private space to the art movements of the day. Framed photographs of friends and idols, including a famous double portrait of Oscar Wilde and Bosie, adorned the walls above the divan, where they received the host of influential avant-gardists who came to call: Georges Bataille, Jacques Lacan, André Breton, Tristan Tzara, Chana Orloff . . . Orloff, a Russian-born Jewish sculptor who was friendly with the couple, fashioned a bust of Cahun in bronze, which was proudly displayed in the living room. In her modernist interpretation, Cahun looks like a conceited Martian: her cheeks plumped and softened almost to abstraction; the curve of her nose still sharp and distinctive.

Although they lived near the homes of Gertrude Stein and Alice B. Toklas, Natalie Barney, and the other queer women we met in the last chapter, Cahun and Moore weren't really part of the scene. Apart from a glancing reference to 'the niece of Marcel Schwob' by Gertrude Stein, who also mentioned that she once saw Cahun at one of Natalie Barney's salons, there's no evidence that they were very involved with the Left Bank lesbians.[11]

Sylvia Beach and Adrienne Monnier were notable exceptions. Cahun, for one, spent lots of time hanging out on rue de l'Odéon at Shakespeare and Company and La Maison des Amis des Livres, reading and chatting about books with the proprietress of each bookshop. She seemed to look up to Monnier especially, whom she admired and whose literary tastes she considered impeccable. The woman's honesty and integrity were widely known – and so forthright was she in her opinions that she sometimes risked falling out with her celebrated friends because of it. She upset her pal Gide, for instance, when she called his 1925 novel, *The Counterfeiters*, cold and unkind. In 1931, when Beach's health and finances were severely overstretched by the demands of James Joyce, whose *Ulysses* she had published in 1922 when no one else would touch it, Monnier took it upon herself to confront him, writing to him candidly: 'In Paris rumour has it that you are spoiled, that we have ruined you with overwhelming praise, and that you no longer know what you're doing.'[12] Joyce's relationship with Beach and Monnier never recovered.

Following Monnier's advice, Cahun decided to gather together her short writing experiments into a kind of confessional memoir, which was eventually published as *Disavowals* in 1930. She warned her friend not to expect the same honesty from her in her book. After so long wearing society's masks, how can we know what a person looks like underneath?

Disavowals reads a bit like an adventure novel (Cahun calls it 'the invisible adventure'), but the treasure that the narrator hopes to unearth isn't gold or precious stones.[13] Instead, it's her true self. 'I want to hunt myself down, struggle with myself,' the narrator says.[14] We might compare her to Stephen Gordon in *The Well of Loneliness*, asking, 'What am I?' – but instead of looking to sexology for answers as Hall does, Cahun turns inward, forensically examining her past experiences and feelings. She then relays her findings, not with the cold precision of science, but with poetry, aphorism and eye-popping photo-collage.

Throughout the book, she probes deep into her personal history, trying to figure out who she is and how she got that way. Masks, naturally, play a large role.

I had spent my solitary hours disguising my soul. Its masks were so perfect . . . Beguiled by their comic ugliness I explored the worst possible instincts; I welcomed young monsters into myself and nurtured them. But the make-up I had used seemed indelible. I rubbed so hard to

remove it that I took off all the skin. And my soul, like a
flayed face, naked, no longer had human form.[15]

Cahun's memoir lays bare the self – flays it, even. Her
narrator courageously owns up to her less-than-attractive
qualities: she admits to being proud and cowardly; she's also
narcissistic and unfaithful. As a feminist book, the kind of self
that *Disavowals* describes – flawed, inquisitive, confident, uncertain what femininity is but intrigued by it all the same – is a
huge advance on, say, the great but one-dimensional women
we find in suffragette theatre a couple of decades earlier.

Cahun's narrator gains the reader's trust with these
revelations, but sometimes it's hard to know if she is being
entirely truthful. At one point, she writes, 'I'm lying anyway' –
which undermines everything that came before.[16] According
to her biographer Jennifer Shaw, 'Cahun denaturalises her
own identity and presents herself to the world as a visual and
literary enigma.'[17] For Cahun, writing – even confessional
writing – may be just another performance, another mask.

While Cahun's art and writing bear many of the hallmarks of surrealism (the long descriptions of dreams are a
giveaway), and she was friendly with surrealist writers during
the 1920s, she didn't actually become involved with the movement until after her book was published. In 1932, she met
André Breton, the leader of the surrealists, whose ideas for
radical art and literature echoed her own. In *Disavowals* she
had written: 'I have spent thirty-three years of my life wishing passionately, blindly, that things would be other than they
are'; Breton shared this wish and, like Cahun, had contrived
the artistic means by which such a transformation could be
achieved.[18] In one of his polemical manifestos of surrealism,

which inveighed against conservative French society and its institutions, Breton said: 'Everything remains to be done, every means must be worth trying, in order to lay waste to the ideas of *family, country, religion* . . . on this point there is no room for compromise.'[19] Surrealism proposed to do away with the old order by embracing spontaneity and unreason, the unconscious and accidental act.

If Breton sought revolutionary change in art, in person he could be a bit of a bore. For such a radical thinker, some of his views were also surprisingly unenlightened. He was disgusted by homosexuality, for instance, which he considered a mental and moral deficiency.[20] Cahun, on the other hand, was more of an anarchist, who spoke out in defence of sexual freedom and the rights of the individual. 'My opinion on homosexuality and homosexuals is exactly the same as my opinion on heterosexuality and heterosexuals,' she wrote in 1925. 'Everything depends on the individual and the circumstances. I call for a general freedom of morals, of all that is not detrimental to the tranquillity, freedom, and happiness of one's fellow man.'[21]

Given Breton's blatant homophobia and Cahun's queerness (not to mention her identification with a tradition of male homosexual writers), intimacy between them seemed unlikely. Breton didn't especially like Cahun's book when he first read it. Although he confessed to being 'captivated', he disliked the deviousness of her prose, which he contrasted with his own 'candour'.[22] Nonetheless, his admiration for it grew in time, as did his esteem for its author, and the two became friends regardless of their differences. They would remain close until Cahun's death in 1954.

The Vast Similitude

In the archive, my good humour has all but ebbed away. It's replaced by a mounting frustration that my attempts to get a sense of Cahun and her life – to hunt her down, she might say – are being blocked and frustrated at every turn.

The problem is the way her stuff is organized. Initially, I thought I'd be able to move through the collection chronologically, slowly building up an image of her from childhood to middle age, but the archive has other ideas. It seems strange to say it, sitting in a place that's synonymous with order and organization, but Cahun's collection feels very chaotic and haphazard. Photos from vastly different time periods sit side by side in the same folders: Cahun ages thirty years in an instant, then turns back into a child just as quickly. Carefully orchestrated self-portraits are mixed in with snaps of Cahun and Moore on holiday. Again and again, I expect to find a photo in one box, but instead discover a note written in blunt-nibbed pencil telling me to look elsewhere. It's impossible to bring the artist into focus. A line from *Disavowals* surfaces in my mind – 'at present I exist in another way' – and I wonder to myself if an archival collection might be a kind of self-portrait.[23] In this case, an elusive and misleading one.

At lunch, I meet Louise Downie, the Jersey art curator who oversaw the acquisition of Cahun and Moore's stuff, and she tries to set me straight. The collection is arranged just as it was found, she says. The photographs came out of those tea chests all jumbled up, and when they were transferred into the archive they were kept that way. We'll never know if the hands that shuffled the photos like cards belonged to Cahun or Moore or some anonymous other, but in any case, after our conversation I decide to change my approach.

Instead of resisting the chaos, I embrace it. In the spirit of surrealism, I give myself over to the involuntary and the accidental and open a random box at my elbow thinking that I'll take my lead from whatever it throws in my path. Unfortunately, it turns out to be the box of negatives I started out with and I'm confronted once again by dozens of semi-transparent brown plastic rectangles that hide their subjects in the gloom. But then something arrests my attention. It's the only negative in the box that's accompanied by a print, and the image is astonishing.

It's called *Je tends les bras*. Translated literally, it would be something like 'I hold out my arms', but the phrase has multiple meanings in French that English can't really capture. *Tendre les bras* is to extend one's arms, but it's also to offer assistance (such as 'to lend a hand') or to welcome (as in 'with open arms'). The image I'm looking at seems to have all of these connotations – and so much more besides.

Quite simply, it depicts a large stone pillar with human arms. The stone is rough, mottled, weather-beaten, ancient; it appears to tower above the viewer, immense and unyielding. The arms, by contrast, are lithe and expressive. The hands especially, with their splayed fingers, open themselves to a variety of interpretations, and seem simultaneously to resist, embrace and gather up an unseen partner. In this photograph, Cahun has literally inserted herself into the landscape of Jersey – through a small hole in a pillar hewn from the island's native granite.

The photograph dates from 1931 or 1932 – around the time that Cahun met Breton, and started working with him and other surrealists in organizations like the Association des

Je tends les bras, circa 1932, by Claude Cahun.
Courtesy of the Jersey Heritage Collections.

Écrivains et Artistes Révolutionnaires (Association of Revolutionary Writers and Artists). Indeed, the way Cahun's work takes a forgettable object you might find standing in a field, and gives it an aura of wonder and wit, shows that she was thinking along similar lines to the surrealists she encountered in Paris. The sculptor Méret Oppenheim comes to mind. Her *Objet (Déjeuner en fourrure)* (1936) is a china teacup, saucer and teaspoon covered in animal fur, which turns an everyday utensil startling and strange, and makes the domestic wild. It's also cheeky and loaded with innuendo.

Je tends les bras also shows that, like the surrealists, Cahun was interested in exploring the natural world and humanity's place in it. Dadaists, and surrealists in their turn, were critical of the opposition between humankind and nature, which had become even more pronounced as industrial modernity tightened its grip on the West. The sculptor and painter Hans Arp felt that the supremacy of reason was the problem, writing that it 'has cut off man from nature', and sought to reconnect the two by engaging with the irrational and nonsensical in his work.[24] Cahun seems to follow Arp's lead. By pushing her fleshy body through the cold hard granite and making a hybrid form on film, her work reconciles humanity and nature, while gently making fun of the distinction the modern world draws between them.

A plethora of other examples from the 1930s, all taken in Jersey, riff on a similar theme. In one from 1930, Cahun is stretched out on a sandy beach next to the outline of a feminine figure traced in seaweed. With her back to the camera, it feels as if we have stumbled upon a private moment between her and this sand-and-seaweed mother/sister/lover. In another, from 1939, Cahun stands in the doorway of a house next to a figure cloaked, like her, in black. Its head is a decorative white vase with an androgynous face moulded into it, and from its crown bursts a lush mass of light-coloured petals that resemble Cahun's platinum-blond locks. A work called *Self-portrait (with leopard skin)* (1939) is a riot of pattern and texture that finds Cahun lying naked among dense foliage. The smooth, tanned flesh of her face nestles among the razor-sharp shadows of palm leaves and the stippled effect of a furze bush.

These photographs, and many others, illustrate Cahun's fascination with nature and her desire to connect her body with it. Strangely enough, in spite of all the academic and art-world interest in Cahun's work, nobody has written much about them or thought too deeply about what they might mean – beyond their parallels to the better-known (straight, male) Breton, of course.

Maybe it takes a queer eye to see how significant they are. To me, these aren't just surrealist artworks, they're queer artworks; they don't simply depict the relationship between nature and the human body in general, they also explore connections between rocks, the sea, plants and Cahun's queer self in particular. At the time these photographs were taken, as we have seen, queer people had started to come together in big cities like London and Paris. These proto-communities anticipated the emergence of the metropolitan gay, by far the most recognizable queer identity, and produced what the queer theorist Jack Halberstam has called 'metronormativity', or the normative urban-based narrative of coming out. The metronormative story, according to Halberstam, is a deeply engrained tale of migration from country to town, where the queer subject 'moves to a place of tolerance after enduring life in a place of suspicion, persecution, and secrecy'.[25] Just as modern queer identity and the urban landscape were becoming forever intertwined, how-ever, Cahun and Moore went in the opposite direction: back to the countryside and nature. Back to St Brelade's Bay.

I follow a winding track that hugs the coast in twists and turns. It leads me through a thicket of windswept cypresses, all cling-ing desperately to a hillside that drops sharply into the sea. I hear its soft sibilance down on the rocks, and the tune is picked up by the wind as it moves through the tops of the trees. The sea air; the citrusy scent of cypress; the sound my boots make on the leaf-strewn earth; the horizon: I'm glad to be outside today. I've felt like an outsider many times, but rarely when I've been outside.

The path curves sharply to the right, and I come upon a blasted tree denuded of branches and bark. It looms like a massive wizened finger, pointing skywards. The old Buddhist saying comes back to me, that truth is like the moon and lan-guage is like the finger that points at it. Both truth and the moon have been slow to materialize, but by now it's early even-ing, so I figure it's just a matter of time.

Suddenly, laid out before me, is St Brelade's Bay, the sun's last rays streaming through cumulous cloud, casting the entire scene in the light of a revelation. High above, gulls circle and send out staccato screams, while down below, the tide is drawn back like a curtain, revealing a pristine expanse of beach. Signs of human life appear here and there: tiny couples gathered in conference, children playing, someone sweep-ing the sand with a metal detector. Craggy headlands that descend haltingly into the Channel on either side shelter the bay from the elements. It's quiet and I can hear myself think.

I take the steps down to the promenade, which runs

along the top of a concrete sea wall left over from the German occupation (before they arrived the beach wasn't so heavily circumscribed). It arcs round the bay, passing cafés and ice-cream shops besieged by septuagenarians. At the end of its parabolic curve, over in the distance next to the church, lies a beautiful fourteenth-century house with a long gabled roof: La Rocquaise, Cahun and Moore's home.

The couple had holidayed in Jersey since they were teenagers, but they moved here for good in 1937. We don't know for sure why they chose to relocate, but it's clear that, by the second half of the 1930s, Paris was no longer the wild, permissive city of *les Années folles*. In the wake of the Great Depression of 1932, French politics became increasingly polarized, and the far right made massive gains, especially among the Parisian middle classes. This was accompanied by a rampant anti-Semitism, which would have unnerved and dismayed Cahun, who was Jewish, though she rarely set foot inside a synagogue. She and Moore would also have been appalled by the creeping homophobia of the time, which took the form of a suspicion among French intellectuals and commentators that effete homosexuality had infected the social body of the Republic. Whatever their reasons, in March 1937 Cahun and Moore packed up their stuff, put their cat in a Hermès handbag and bid adieu to France.

In one of only a few surviving letters by her, Cahun describes their first, peaceful years at La Rocquaise. It had felt like 'the wonderful fantasy of an endless holiday; the garden already in bloom. It seemed like all we had to do was tame the trees, the birds, the doors, the windows; pulling out of our trunks the appropriate clothing (the shortest and lightest), plunging into the sunshine and the sea.'[26] She remembered long lazy afternoons spent reading and writing and sunbathing naked in the garden, observed only by their grey cat named Kid. Whenever storms hit the Jersey coast, the couple delighted in the spectacle, watching the waves battering the bay and sending up spumes of sea foam to crash down upon their lawn. They started a vegetable patch and fertilized it with seaweed harvested from the beach; they painted the house and furnished it; they had their literary friends to stay. 'Nothing seemed to be pressing, or overdue.'[27] In short, they had a lovely time. La Rocquaise was, she said, 'our little island within an island'.[28]

The house and its surroundings nourished Cahun's creativity, and in her photographs from this time the coastal environment of St Brelade's Bay is a fixture. She basks in the rockpools; she caresses the sands; she mingles her naked body with the rising sea; she sequesters herself among fields of poppies . . . Natural phenomena are not merely a backdrop for her strange, surrealist performances; they are implicated in it as partners and collaborators. The Jersey Archive calls such works 'self-portraits' but in fact they portray much more than the self; their subject is, rather, the act of communion, between species and beyond binaries. They depict an encounter between the natural world and a queer, gender-dissenting body, which social norms and the laws of the time considered aberrant and unnatural. In photographs like *Je tends les bras*, Cahun is discovering a place for her queerness in nature. She found that place in Jersey.

Approaching La Rocquaise from the beach, I see that Cahun and Moore's massive old farmhouse has been divided into two homes. As I'm lingering about, trying to assess the other changes that have taken place, I attract the attention of one of the more recent residents, a blond in a button-down shirt unloading a snot-nosed child from an Audi. At least I assume he's a resident: he declines to tell me whether or not he lives there at all, and in spite of my explanations seems affronted by my interest in the house. He keeps repeating the word 'weird'; my being here is 'weird', he says, as are my questions. If this guy thinks I'm weird, I say to myself, I hope he doesn't find out who used to live here; he might never sleep again. In any case, clearly there's nothing to be done with him, so I leave him to his paranoia, and take my weirdness down onto the beach where the light on the surface of the water has faded and the tide inches slowly in.

Cahun wasn't always in love with nature. She could actually be quite dismissive of it in the years when she lived in the city and was narrowly, narcissistically focused on herself as an artistic subject. In *Disavowals*, she wrote: 'I'm obsessed with the exception. I see it as bigger than nature.'[29] Nature represented the rule, and, as a rule-breaker, she represented the exception. But over the course of her career, Cahun's outlook evolved; as she spent more time on Jersey, she seemed to distinguish between the idea of nature defined by scientists and reinforced by social norms, and nature as it actually existed around her – and had proved such an eager participant in her art. In other words, she stopped mistaking the finger for the moon.

A sliver of that celestial body now hangs over St Brelade's Bay, dimly illuminating the beach, which is deserted apart from a lone figure turned towards the sea. As the waves wash up the beach before me, I find myself concentrating on their slow, meditative rhythm – in and out, in and out – matching my breathing to it. I think about Cahun's photographs, some of which were taken on the sands beneath my feet; how, in them, queerness is the most natural thing in the world. I think about how, fifty years later, Derek Jarman would undertake a similar kind of project, implanting his queer self into the shingle of Dungeness, along with the hardy perennials of his garden. I think about Walt Whitman, the good grey (gay) poet of America who had a profound influence on Cahun's beloved Uranians. Long before either Jarman or Cahun, Whitman spent his life writing celebratory poems infused with ideas akin to theirs.

One of these is titled 'On the Beach at Night Alone': 'As I watch the bright stars shining,' he writes, 'I think a thought of the clef of the universes and of the future. / A vast similitude interlocks all.' The poem was written in 1856, possibly after a bad break-up; with the connection to his lover severed, Whitman seems to console himself with the knowledge that, regardless of appearances, everything is connected. 'All gaseous, watery, vegetable, mineral processes, the fishes, the brutes' are part of the same one-all, he says. As I stand there, feeling my chest rise and fall with the lapping of the waves on the shore, Whitman's lines come to me, and I speak them aloud:

A vast similitude interlocks all,
All spheres, grown, ungrown, small, large, suns, moons,
    planets,
All distances of place however wide,
All distances of time, all inanimate forms,
All souls, all living bodies though they be ever so
    different, or in different worlds,
All gaseous, watery, vegetable, mineral processes, the
    fishes, the brutes,
All nations, colors, barbarisms, civilizations, languages,
All identities that have existed or may exist on this globe,
    or any globe,
All lives and deaths, all of the past, present, future,

This vast similitude spans them, and always has spann'd,
And shall forever span them and compactly hold and
enclose them.[30]

Not quite symbiotic like Baker and her Paris, the relationship of Cahun and Jersey is characterized less by mutual dependency than mutual cooperation. The artist and the island are independent of each other yet they are held together by a similitude – an underlying identity.

Occupation

'I believe from 37 to 40, I *felt* the arrival of war (without wishing to believe it).'[31] Cahun's sense of impending doom was prompted by the snippets of news she and Moore received from their friends in Paris: of Germany's tearing up the Treaty of Versailles; of Italian aggression. The occupation and ownership of space seemed to be at the heart of it. Most alarming was Germany's appetite for territory – expanding relentlessly, far beyond its own borders into Austria and Czechoslovakia in pursuit of what Hitler called *Lebensraum*, or 'living space'. His appeasement by France and Britain did little to persuade Cahun that such territorial disputes would not end in catastrophe.

On Jersey, life continued largely unchanged for months after war was declared. Some inhabitants left the island for Britain, where they signed up for the war effort, but most simply went about their business as usual. British tourists were still arriving on the island as late as May 1940, feeding the island's summertime economy as they always had. Cahun and Moore were fearful of what the war might portend, but developments in mainland Europe left them feeling numb: 'The series of military defeats on a national level – from Norway to France – did not surprise us, but left us in a strange, mechanical state, as if we'd been "doped".'[32] Observing the war from afar, they felt powerless and unable to resist; this would all change as soon as it arrived on their doorstep.

The first sign of the German invasion came at the end of June 1940. Cahun remembered the final moments of their idyllic 'holiday' at La Rocquaise: 'I was sitting out in the sun by the mimosas when the German reconnaissance planes were sighted. I could see them as they turned, leaving huge circles of smoke like cigarette smoke rings that become distorted, little by little.'[33] Thousands had been evacuated from the island in a panic in the preceding days, but Cahun and Moore declined to join them; this was their home, and besides, they relished the prospect of rebellion. In England they would have been even farther from the front lines, and the British army was hardly desperate to recruit middle-aged Frenchwomen with bad English. What was necessary, according to Cahun, was *situated* resistance. She would later declare that if fascism 'had been beaten by everyone in their place and according to their means with an uncompromising heart . . . all postwar imperialisms would have been impossible'.[34]

In truth, there was little organized resistance in Jersey. Hitler vastly overestimated the strategic importance of the island and sent 11,000 troops to take it. Given that the entire population was 40,000, this was a huge occupying force on an island of only forty-five square miles. Non-resistance was one thing, but blithe acceptance was quite another. Cahun was so appalled by the calm in St Helier in the days after the invasion and the joy she saw on the faces of many, she found herself inventing scenarios to make sense of it. The young woman who hung on the arm of that handsome German soldier must be a spy, she thought. For her part, when addressed by any German, she relished the opportunity to be as rude and unhelpful as possible.

Her contempt wasn't personal, it was ideological; for Cahun, the rise of Nazism was further proof of the evils of group-think. She never stopped believing that the individual was fundamentally good, and that bad decisions were made only when one gave oneself over to dogma. This would be the key to Cahun's sedition. Among the crowds in St Helier, she would sometimes catch a glimpse of a soldier who seemed out of step with his fellows: 'Some of these guys seemed morose, closed-off. They didn't mix with the others. Was it possible there were antifascists in their midst? Unlikely, but not impossible. I also noticed young men with romantic faces: were they dreamers?'[35] Moments like this fuelled the campaign of resistance and subversion that Cahun and Moore ran from 1940 to 1944. They targeted the quiet dissenters and the dreamers, encouraging them to think for themselves and abandon the fascist cause.

It started small. Cahun was out walking with Moore, and as they went along, she collected empty cigarette packets from the side of the road and stuffed them into the pockets of her coat. She'd become fascinated by an aphorism she read in a German newspaper early in the 1930s, when the country was lurching towards fascism: 'Schrecken ohne Ende oder Ende mit Schrecken' (terror without end or a terrible end). For her, the idea of 'terror without end' was less a slogan than an observation about the state of the world under Nazism; so she took the phrase 'ohne Ende' and scribbled it on all the empty cigarette boxes. The next day, she surreptitiously littered the roads of Jersey with her anti-war propaganda.[36]

Cahun and Moore's resistance quickly graduated to pamphlets, manifestos and collages, filled with poetry, satire and news surreptitiously gleaned from the BBC. Over the course of the war, they created hundreds, perhaps thousands, of seditious tracts. Cahun wrote the text, Moore translated it into German, and together they pushed them through letter boxes, deposited them on church pews and inserted them into magazines at the local newsagent's. They secreted tracts inside unlocked German cars and into the pockets of Nazi uniforms left unattended on the backs of chairs. Cahun wrote 'Nieder mit Krieg' (Down with War) in nail varnish on coins, and left them about the amusement park where German soldiers socialized. Soon they were signing their insurrectionary work DER SOLDAT OHNE NAMEN (The Soldier without a Name). By the winter of 1941, their action was 'serious, regular, systematic'; it became, Cahun said, 'an obsession'.[37]

Cahun's immersion in the worlds of Dada and surrealism – revolutionary art movements that sought to recalibrate the modern mind – had prepared her to make this kind of anti-fascist intervention. On an island so closely guarded, it was, in fact, the only kind that was possible. It also helped that, to all appearances, Cahun and Moore were just two strange, middle-aged French sisters who seemed to be forever tramping the roads around St Brelade's Bay in headscarves and Burberry coats. Once again, the queer art of masquerade they had perfected earlier in their lives gave them an advantage, and allowed them to disguise their dissent.

The Nazi occupation of Jersey is most noticeable in the huge fortifications and military installations that still suffuse the island. Jersey was part of what Hitler called his Atlantic Wall, and he threw endless amounts of money and manpower into securing it – building vast installations and defensive structures that continue to dominate the landscape many decades later. There are remains everywhere. On an uncharacteristically warm November morning, I head out along the coast from St Helier by bike, and soon come upon enormous lumps of a defensive sea wall, followed by cuboid anti-tank bunkers and blast walls that protrude incongruously into the beach. Down on the sand, people stroll by and a dog darts to and fro with a sodden tennis ball in its jaws.

The physical signs of German occupation only become more prevalent and menacing as I make my way south. Approaching a place called Noirmont Point to the south west of the island, I emerge out of a countryside of lush green fields and farms peaceful in the mid-morning sun into a brutalist nightmare. Alien objects and inorganic forms in cornered grey squat along the section of coastline comprising Batterie Lothringen: a poured-concrete monstrosity and one of the largest German artillery batteries on the island.

I wander slowly around the site, skirting the gun turrets jutting out from the cliffs and towers that look so ominous amid the knee-high heather and briars that tug gently at my clothing. I descend the two dozen or so steps down into a bunker until the sky is no more than a chink above me, covered over by a steel grill. It's cold down here, and an uneasy feeling starts to grow in my stomach, even before I read the commemorative plaque, which is dedicated to the thousands of slaves that were brought to Jersey from places like Russia and Spain, and forced to build these terrifying steel and cement structures.

This is the architecture of oppression. Whatever the defensive role played by places like Batterie Lothringen (which was, in the end, very limited), its featureless and abstract forms exert a tyrannical, inhuman dominance over the landscape. Over the furze-covered hills. Over the rust-coloured stones and cracked, flinty boulders. Over the sea, here flinging spray up the face of the cliff. I find so many more examples during my stay: the fortresses that surge up out of the rocks of La Corbière in the south; the ones that loom over the peaceful bay of St Ouen in the west; the network of tunnels that honeycomb the island known as the 'Hohlgangsanlage', which attests to the German control of space under the ground as much as above it.

Even now, long after the war, these symbols of a terrible power are rarely out of sight. In this context, in the light of this near-total domination of the landscape, I find myself wondering again about Cahun and Moore's small acts of resistance. What would it have been like to have found one of their dissident tracts in the shadow of those hulking great triumphs of the proverbial will? Seeing the words 'Down with War' written on a scrap of paper lying in a ditch or along the roadside – then suddenly finding similar exhortations in a church or a café: what effect would it have on the finder's idea of space and its occupation?

Cahun and Moore's resistance may have been minuscule in comparison with the German war machine, but still it served to shift perceptions of space on the island – made them vacillate. Like graffiti that adorns the anonymous thoroughfares of a city (its bridges and tunnels, its rooftops and alleyways), their subversive works made a claim for a different kind of ownership, littering the highways and byways of Jersey with assertions of independence. Phrases that let freedom in.

At the time, it was difficult to ascertain if their work was having the desired impact. Cahun admitted that 'it was equally convenient, reassuring, disappointing, and annoying to know so little about the effect our distribution of leaflets had'.[38] They did succeed in attracting the attention of the Nazi command, however, which ordered a large-scale investigation into this secret group of seditionists 'without a name'. Cahun varied the style and colour of her writing from one piece to the next, such that it seemed as if lots of people were contributing to the cause. Indeed, when she and Moore were finally arrested, the Germans were under the impression that there were many dissenters, even a Jersey intelligence service, and refused to believe these two inconspicuous women could possibly be working alone.

They came for them at La Rocquaise on 22 July 1944. By that point, the tide of the war had started to turn (Allied forces had descended on Normandy in June), but it would be almost a year before the Nazis' hold on the island was broken. Cahun and Moore spent the remaining ten months in the cold, damp cells of St Helier's Gloucester Street prison. They were kept in solitary confinement for the most part – the first time since they were teenagers that they had been separated for so long. Fearing prolonged imprisonment and the death sentence they were sure to receive, both attempted suicide on a number of occasions. Under the deplorable conditions of the prison, the meagre food and lack of human contact, their recovery was slow. Cahun's health had always been fragile, and in the prison she suffered terribly.

Finally, on 16 November 1944, they were escorted from their cells into the court; it was clear to Cahun that they were taking part in little more than a show trial. 'It was a spectacle,' she remembered. 'The décor and the actors didn't fool us at all.'[39] Of course, there wasn't much to decide, given that Cahun and Moore admitted that they were responsible for making and distributing the objects and tracts the prosecution presented them with. The Germans had found 350 such items, which, according to Cahun's calculations, amounted to less than one-seventh of the total they produced: 'Four years is a long time!'[40] When a representative sample was displayed in the court as evidence, it looked like the surrealist art exhibit in London she had contributed to eight years earlier.

The judges didn't take long to deliberate. Both were sentenced to death 'for propaganda undermining the morale of the German forces'; its grave portent notwithstanding, at least this indicated that their work had a considerable effect.[41] They were also sentenced to six years' penal servitude for the crime of listening to the BBC on a contraband radio, and nine months for owning a pistol and a camera. Cahun mischievously asked with mock naïveté: 'Are we to do the nine months and six years before or after we are shot?'[42] The court erupted into laughter, the judges vainly calling for order as the couple were hurried back to their cells to await their doom.

They waited and waited. At length, they found a way to write letters to each other, which kept the misery at bay if only for a while. New Year came and went, and still there was no word about their execution. At the end of February, they heard that the death sentence had been unexpectedly commuted, when a Jersey government official interceded on their behalf. As Germany's war losses mounted, restrictions in the prison became more relaxed; Cahun and Moore were finally able to see each other. On 30 April 1945, Hitler shot himself in his bunker in Berlin; in early May, the islands were finally liberated. Cahun and Moore walked free of the prison, into St Helier where Union flags flew once again over the capital.

The Jersey Archive holds a small number of objects from Cahun and Moore's time in prison, like cigarette packets with doodles of faces on them and an envelope covered in pencil sketches of mythical figures, every bit of available space filled. On the back of another cigarette packet, either Cahun or Moore has sketched the interior of the prison cell they shared towards the end of their stay. Two featureless stick figures lie in narrow beds with the meagre slit of a window high above their heads. It feels desperate and heartbreaking, the roughness of its composition and the lack of effort illustrating little more than simple exhaustion.

There are other items too, including a stack of letters to Cahun written by Moore in pencil. 'Goodnight, my love,' she writes in one. 'Sleep well. Be brave.' Elsewhere, she calls her 'mon pauvre poussin' (my poor little chicken), and doodles two interlocking hearts at the bottom of the page. A message written in English on the back of one of Moore's letters reads: 'Will you please put this away for us?'[43] These thin, yellowing pages and parts of an unfinished memoir Cahun wrote about their incarceration were entrusted to their English friend, who smuggled them out of the prison in the lining of a coat and kept them safe until the couple could return home to La Rocquaise.

According to Louise Downie, Cahun has now come home for good. She tells me that a recent condition report on the Cahun archive found some minor deterioration of the photos; fearing further damage, Jersey Heritage Trust has decided not to loan out any more materials from the collection. Original photographs and archival objects owned by the trust that have been displayed around the world for the past thirty years and have forged Cahun's international reputation, will no longer appear in exhibits outside Jersey. Anyone who wants to see her original artworks will have to make their way here, as I have. This curtailed circulation of Cahun beyond Jersey seems momentous to me, as if it confirms my sense of her deep associations with the island. It feels like a symbolic shoring-up of their shared connection, their similitude.

The archive is about to close, so I gather up Moore's letters, put them back into the plastic sleeve they came in and carefully transport it to the reception desk at the front of the reading room. I thank the archivist for his help, and slide the folder towards him, as if I'm passing him a note in class. Cahun and Moore's message is face up, legible to us both through the folder's transparent cover.

Will you please put this away for us?

James Baldwin in Saint-Paul-de-Vence, 1985. Photo by Ulf Andersen.
© Getty Images.

5.

Exile: James Baldwin between America and France

In the end there was just so little left. Of the three-hundred-year-old farmhouse in the south of France that was once the home of James Baldwin, the queer African-American writer and civil rights activist, only a couple of the original walls remain.

A chic new apartment complex that looks out across the rolling landscape towards the Mediterranean has absorbed them into its concrete planes and shining glass surfaces. Repointed and repainted, the old stone walls add an element of tasteful authenticity for those who can afford to buy a connection to the region's past for more than a million euros. Baldwin's place, where he spent the last sixteen years of his life, has almost entirely disappeared. If I hadn't been so sure of my research, I'd wonder if I'd come to the correct address at all.

Baldwin came here first on holiday, at the end of 1970. At the time, he was living in Paris – a city where he had spent much of his life since he left his native New York in 1948. In the intervening years, he returned to the United States many times, travelling to and fro across the Atlantic with such frequency that he came to consider himself a 'transatlantic commuter'.[1] His writing, like his life, seemed to be suspended between America and Europe: his first book, *Go Tell It on the Mountain*

(1953), was a fictionalized account of his childhood in Harlem, written from a distance in the cafés of Paris and a small village in Switzerland.

Baldwin once said that he was 'a stranger everywhere', and the perspicacity of his writing seemed to derive in part from his rootlessness.[2] It may have also been the key to his early success, and he followed his debut with a string of best-selling works of fiction and non-fiction, including the queer classic *Giovanni's Room*, which was published in 1956. During the 1960s, his fame and fiery eloquence turned him into a somewhat reluctant spokesman for the civil rights movement and he became friends with Medgar Evers, Malcolm X and Martin Luther King. All three were gunned down within the space of five years, and the effect on Baldwin was devastating: 'something has altered in me', he wrote. 'Something has gone away.'[3]

By 1970, the peak of his popularity seemed to have passed. His latest novel hadn't been well received, and a new generation of black writers had come out against him. It became fashionable to Baldwin-bash, which in print was often indistinguishable from gay-bashing – especially in the case of Eldridge Cleaver, the Black Panther leader, who aimed deranged homophobic remarks at him. Accusing him of being a race traitor, Cleaver ranted: 'Homosexuality is a sickness, just as are baby-rape or wanting to become the head of General Motors.'[4] In October, Baldwin had a nervous breakdown in Paris, and a friend arranged for him to recuperate in Saint-Paul-de-Vence, a medieval town in the shadow of the Maritime Alps about twelve miles west of Nice.

He first stayed in a hotel called Le Hameau, before renting the downstairs rooms of the large house he'd spied across the road. By all accounts, Jeanne Fauré, the French landlady who lived upstairs, was a bigoted woman, but over the course of their long relationship she came to love her black tenant and he counted her among his closest friends. When she eventually moved out, Baldwin took over the whole place, which also included the gatehouse and ten acres of surrounding farmland filled with olive and cypress trees.

'I want a place where I can find out again where I am and what I must do. A place where I can stop and do nothing in order to start again,' Baldwin once said, and his house in Saint-Paul seemed to be the answer to his prayers.[5] Over the years, many well-known French and American guests came to stay with him: Maya Angelou, Josephine Baker, Miles Davis, Yves Montand, Toni Morrison, Nina Simone and a host of others received a warm (and often boozy) welcome at the place they referred to as *Chez Baldwin*.

He had intended to buy the house but never completed the purchase, so when he died, on 1 December 1987, it reverted to Fauré's family. They couldn't afford to maintain it, and Baldwin's estate seemed to have no interest in acquiring it, so the house and land were sold off. With the approval of the town's mayor, who seems never to have read a book by Baldwin, developers built the sprawling, multilayered complex, glimpses of which are visible through its imposing steel gate. Landscaped to within an inch of its life and centred around some insipid abstract sculpture, Chez Baldwin is now known as Le Jardin des Arts. The name is well chosen. It does actually look like a lot of contemporary art galleries I've come across: concrete, cold, geometric. Made by the rich for the rich.

If I seem a little hostile in my assessment of the place, it's because this vista hardly feels like much of a reward after all I did to get here. The journey to Saint-Paul had been long and dangerous – worthy of a true pilgrimage in fact. Even if it turned out to have been entirely unnecessary.

Some hours earlier, I had boarded a bus in Cagnes-sur-Mer, an unremarkable coastal resort near Nice, which, because it was April and off season, was shuttered and unwelcoming. Giant pastel-coloured apartment blocks lined the boulevards of the town like cruise ships jostling for a berth. From there the bus ascended through the suburbs, puttering through the swirls and eddies of traffic around American-style shopping malls and superstores, before dropping a gear and climbing up the roads that encircle the foothills of the Alps. Out of the window of the bus, over to the west, the sun-bleached citadel of Saint-Paul appeared. Perched atop a rock, towering above the surrounding countryside that lay lush and green, glistening with spring rain, the town looked like a large boat. How appropriate that, after his travels, Baldwin should finally have run aground there; or maybe, I thought, the receding tide had left him high and dry.

A widely used and, as I later discovered, quite unreliable travel app informed me that, without a car, the only route to Baldwin's house was a short bus ride, followed by a longer hike along country roads. Foolishly, I thought a walk would be a good chance to take in the scenery and get to know Baldwin's adopted landscape; I alighted from the bus, and the ordeal began.

What followed was the longest hour of my life, as I picked my way along the margins of treacherous mountain roads, literally courting death at every turn. On my left, a sheer drop down the mountainside. On my right, cars, vans, trucks zooming by at horrifying speed. (The French, even they will admit, *roulent comme des tarés* – drive like lunatics.) I was terrified, and the journey began to feel like some kind of epic trial, even before I came upon a cave hollowed out of the cliff face, hidden behind some trees. Inside there was a rolled-up mattress and a sleeping bag, which could have belonged to some ancient mythical hermit or guru of the mountain who, had they been around, might have bestowed a word of two of wisdom to help me on my way.

When I finally arrived at Saint-Paul, I was overtaken by a bus – different from the one I had boarded but also originating in Cagnes-sur-Mer. I wanted to scream, or sit down in the road and cry. Practically speaking, my circuitous trek had been pointless; I could simply have climbed aboard this bus and avoided the whole thing. As I made my way to Baldwin's former address, I still held onto the idea that somehow, spiritually, the journey had been necessary – that it had meant *something*. What an anticlimax, then, to arrive hot, dirty and wild-eyed, only to be faced with such a bland and soulless non-place as Le Jardin des Arts. Ironically, there was a certain Baldwinian quality to my absurd Provençal adventure: of all the individuals who feature in this book, his story best illustrates the fact that the journey is often far more interesting than the destination.

Baldwin was always moving around. Endlessly in pursuit of places and their attendant emotional states, he was often disappointed as soon as he arrived, and it wasn't long before he was off again. Even his time at Chez Baldwin was no more than a temporary sojourn: he had years to buy the house and settle here permanently, but the deal was never struck; the contract was never signed. Something in him seems to have held onto his itinerancy to the very end. In light of this, maybe it's fitting that little remains here to remember him by. I wonder if brick and mortar are really the best way to memorialize such a peripatetic life.

Viewed alongside recent research into the histories of the African diaspora and a black sense of place, Baldwin's life-long rootlessness seems to be symptomatic of the long legacy of the slave trade. According to the radical black geographer Katherine McKittrick, 'transatlantic slavery, from the slave ship and beyond, was predicated on various practices of spatialized violence that targeted black bodies and profited from erasing a black sense of place'.[6] The first, formative efforts to sanction black placelessness – whose traumatic effects black people continue to live through – came from the forced removal of Africans from their homelands and a plantation system that continually worked to rupture any sense of belonging to a place (moving and trading slaves between farms in order to destroy any emergent community, for instance). Baldwin's placelessness in this context is inseparable from his black cultural inheritance and related trauma – but his queerness also has a pivotal, and largely unacknowledged, role to play.

I'm curious to find some trace of Baldwin, like Forster's incongruous old mantelpiece, that would prove he once lived here, so I head down a dirt track that skirts the estate, where the view through a wire fence affords a better perspective. The complex, I realize, is huge, and must be made up of at least a dozen or more separate residences, complete with swimming pools and a children's playground. It all appears unoccupied, however, and an eerie silence lingers around the swings whose shadows are still and unmoving in the afternoon sun. Everything in view is clean and tidy and utterly devoid of personality. I reach the end of the road, where a large locked gate blocks any access. The days of breaking into Baldwin's property are long gone.

I'm not the only one to have made their way to Saint-Paul looking for Baldwin's house, and I'm certainly not the first to write about it. As you'll read in this chapter, Baldwin was preoccupied with spaces. All kinds of spaces: small spaces like the eponymous room of *Giovanni's Room*; the city spaces of Harlem and Paris; political and imagined spaces like America and France. In his work, he obsessively investigates how we represent spaces in writing, how we relate to the memory of them, how they influence our sexuality and our sense of ourselves. Little wonder, then, that his readers are themselves so deeply attuned to the significance of space, and of Baldwin's own place in Provence.

In the years since his death, when the house had fallen into disrepair but hadn't yet been totally razed, many visitors came here and wrote movingly about the sense of loss they felt on finding the place abandoned. Some, like the Baldwin scholar Magdalena J. Zaborowska, found the crumbling house 'filled with furniture and objects, [which] seemed eerily full of life, as if vacated seconds ago'.[7] Later, the cultural critic Thomas Chatterton Williams hopped over the fence and found the place stripped bare; in the rubble of a demolished wing, he retrieved some saucers and coffee cups to take home as mementos.

In these essays, all written by pilgrims, Baldwin emerges as something of a saint. Simplified and sanctified, he is arrayed in the mantle of a prophet, whose words a stupid and immature world failed to heed but which have become ever more important over the years. Considering him with a less adoring eye, he looks a little different, however.

It may very well be the case that Baldwin's writing was ahead of its time, but some of his views were also rather backward. The misogyny of some of his work, for instance, or his less-than-progressive takes on homosexuality and the gay and lesbian movement: these troubling aspects of Baldwin's legacy are usually left unexplored by his fans. In the worst instances, their efforts to make the writer palatable to a contemporary reader portray a Baldwin that simply bears no relation to reality. Williams praises Baldwin's 'intersectionality before it was a thing', for example, but only a superficial reading of Baldwin's work would find it unequivocally intersectional.[8] According to the feminist theorist Kimberlé Crenshaw, who coined the term in 1989, intersectionality refers to the fact that gender, sexuality, class, race and other social categories intersect and reciprocally construct each other, such that any analysis of social identity must take a holistic approach. Baldwin was certainly attentive to the intersecting issues of race and class, but he prevaricated about gender and especially about sexuality, as we will soon see.

I'm wary of the partial appraisals of Baldwin and the retrievals of him, and I don't wish to repeat them here. Baldwin's work has been important to me for a long time, but I sometimes find myself disagreeing with or disappointed by him. I want to understand the nature of these disagreements, the difference between Baldwin's perspective and my own, between his time and ours.

I'm apprehensive about championing queer historical figures uncritically without acknowledging their faults. It's natural that queers like me should want to find a history to be proud of, but ignoring the facts obscures the very real impact of, say, sexist and homophobic ideas on the intellectual and emotional development of people – even queer people. This is one of the key ideas of the queer historian and theorist Heather Love. In her work on the politics of queer history, she argues that we should resist the temptation towards 'selectively affirmative' history-making.[9]

Queer past is 'a great unrecorded history', as Forster said; in our rush to set the record straight (as it were), it's important to pay attention as much to those difficult, sad, troubling aspects of past queer lives as to the more joyous and world-making moments. Baldwin's life was a courageous one, without a doubt, but it was also twisted by shame and trauma, and full of loneliness, grief and not a little vanity. Acknowledging these difficult parts of his personality treats him not as a saint but as a person; a human being as complex, fallible and multifaceted as the characters in his books.

His Father's House

> He had sinned. In spite of the saints, his mother and his father, the warnings he had heard from his earliest beginnings, he had sinned with his hands a sin that was hard to forgive. In the school lavatory, alone, thinking of the boys, older, bigger, braver, who made bets with each other as to whose urine could arch higher, he had watched in himself a transformation of which he would never dare to speak.[10]

Sin and shame, especially gay shame and the sin of homosexuality, are central to Baldwin's first novel, *Go Tell It on the Mountain*, which was published in 1953. The book is about a fourteen-year-old African-American boy growing up in Harlem, and his relationship to religion, his family and his sexuality – a coming-of-age tale of the kind that J. D. Salinger had popularized a couple of years earlier with his *Catcher in the*

Rye (1951). In its careful, sympathetic treatment of the young, 'frog-eyed' John Grimes, Baldwin's novel also takes seriously the psychological and emotional turmoil of the teenager, a distinct social category that had emerged in the years after the Second World War.

The first part of the book is all about John, who awakens on the morning of his fourteenth birthday one Sunday in March 1935. A sensitive, lonely and admittedly 'morbid' young man, he's a preacher's son, devoted to his local church. We follow him as he helps his beleaguered mother with the chores, and tries without much success to clean their dirty apartment. We read about his successes at school, and his failures in the street. Breaking off from sweeping the living-room carpet, he gazes down longingly at a group of boys playing stickball on the street corner. 'He wanted to be one of them, playing in the streets, unfrightened, moving with such grace and power, but he knew this could not be.'[11] Not for him the boisterous male group and the budding heterosexual bravado of the neighbourhood boys. John's interest in academic subjects, in reading and thinking, sets him apart from others his age. So, too, does his homosexuality.

He has a crush on his seventeen-year-old Sunday-school teacher, in whose presence the clouds seem to part and he becomes 'bold and lighthearted'.[12] When John looks at Elisha, his palms get sweaty and his heart starts pounding. His interactions with the older boy are charged with something he can only dimly perceive: a homoerotic desire to be overpowered and made submissive to the will of a stronger, more masculine boy. When they're roughhousing in the church before the service: 'He saw the veins rise on Elisha's forehead and in his neck; his breath became jagged and harsh, and the grimace on

his face became more cruel; and John, watching these mani-
festations of his power, was filled with wild delight.'[13] This
desire inflects the central event of the story, as John gives himself over to an ecstatic religious experience the faithful of the
church call the 'Power of God'.

Desperate to be absolved of the sin that so tarnishes
his soul but also, in a roundabout way, to win Elisha's love,
in the Sunday-night service John submits to a physical and
spiritual frenzy, a fit both painful and cleansing: 'Something moved in John's body which was not John. He was
invaded, set at naught, possessed.'[14] Viewed through his
homosexual longings, the eroticism of the event is obvious. Instead of Elisha being an instrument of God, here
the divine power becomes something of a proxy for the
trainee pastor 'possessing' John and leaving him thrashing
about quasi-orgasmically on the church floor. Hours later,
the two boys leave the church with the rest of the congre-
gation, walking out into the early-morning light, deliciously
exhausted body and soul.

> John, staring at Elisha, struggled to tell him something
> more – struggled to say – all that could never be said.[15]

Go Tell It on the Mountain is a semi-autobiographical
novel that draws on the author's own life and his experience
growing up as an illegitimate child in a God-fearing home in
Harlem. Baldwin was born in New York on 2 August 1924 to
a single mother, who married his stepfather when he was two
years old. His childhood was spent in a small apartment at
7 East 131st Street, which was home to a large family of which
he was the eldest.

Great demographic shifts were under way in the streets and neighbourhoods of Baldwin's youth, as the black population of Harlem ballooned from 84,000 in 1920 to 200,000 by 1930, making it the biggest black community in the US. Most had migrated from the South, according to the eminent black sociologist Kenneth Clark: 'millions of Negroes have come North seeking escape from the miasma of the South, where poverty and oppression kept the Negro in an inferior caste'.[16]

Baldwin's stepfather, who was born in New Orleans, was one of those black migrants who arrived in the cities of the North with so much hope. Searching for prosperity and freedom, they instead found poverty and the ghetto: neglected, densely overcrowded buildings, often with no central heating, frequently overrun with rats, and very little paid work to be done during the Great Depression. Reflecting on the Harlem of his childhood, a twenty-three-year-old Baldwin wrote in an essay in 1948:

> Now as then the buildings are old and in desperate need of repair, the streets are crowded and dirty, there are too many humans per square block. Rents are 10 to 58 percent higher than anywhere else in the city . . . All over Harlem now there is felt the same bitter expectancy with which, in my childhood, we awaited winter: it is coming and it will be hard; there is nothing anyone can do about it.[17]

The marginalization and neglect of Harlem and its black residents, coupled with his family's extreme poverty, seemed to stack the odds against Baldwin from the outset. As a child he was slightly built, malnourished and wasn't expected to live past the age of five. Somehow he managed to survive long enough to make it to school at P.S. 24 on East 128th Street between Fifth and Madison avenues. There he found sympathetic teachers such as Countee Cullen, the celebrated black poet, who would direct him towards the kind of intellectual stimulation he needed in order to thrive. Baldwin became an avid reader, visiting the local library every other day, where he would borrow books by the likes of Harriet Beecher Stowe and Charles Dickens.

The influence of Dickens on *Go Tell It on the Mountain* is most obvious in the name of its protagonist. *John Grimes* has a kind of nominative determinism to it that the creator of characters like Ebenezer Scrooge and Oliver Twist would recognize, given how the life of Baldwin's teenager is so bound up with grime and dirt of material and moral varieties. He lives in abject poverty (as indeed had his author) in a filthy apartment in Harlem.

> No labour could ever make it clean. Dirt was in the walls and the floorboards, and triumphed beneath the sink where cockroaches spawned . . . Dirt crawled in the grey mop hung out of the windows to dry. John thought with shame and horror, yet in angry hardness of heart: *He who is filthy, let him be filthy still.*[18]

Cleanliness is next to godliness, and as John's quotation from the Book of Revelation indicates, to his teenage mind the dirt around him is inextricable from his filthy conscience – and just as difficult to remove. To a certain extent he believes, as do many teenagers, that the world is created for him and reflects the way he feels about himself. In this case, the sin he

committed in the school toilets, pleasuring himself with day-
dreams of his classmates' cocks, has so besmirched his soul
that he has been condemned to live surrounded by filth. Here,
in Baldwin's first novel, is a glimpse of what would become a
recurring theme in his work, as gay shame takes on a physical
form, staining the places his characters inhabit.

Just as inner, moral states manifest in spatial terms in
Baldwin's writing, so exterior, physical spaces are also conceived domestically. Neighbourhoods and nation states are
frequently condensed by him, made personal and interchangeable with ideas of the house and the home. In the 1948 essay
I quoted above, he continues: 'All of Harlem is pervaded by
a sense of congestion, rather like the insistent, maddening,
claustrophobic pounding in the skull that comes from trying to
breathe in a very small room with all the windows shut.'[19] Baldwin often referred to the neighbourhood of his youth along
similar lines – as an airless, falling-down apartment its inhabitants yearn to escape. His analogy had some truth to it, without
a doubt, and many Harlem residences certainly were horrible
and dilapidated (a mid-1930s survey found 60 per cent of homes
in dire need of repair), yet his domestic imagery is particularly
bleak, contorted by memories of his own childhood home that
was presided over by a terrible, Bible-bashing patriarch.

Like John Grimes, Baldwin's stepfather was a preacher,
and an angry, abusive character with whom he had a very complicated relationship. In his famous essay 'Notes of a Native Son'
(1955), where he examines the racial background to his stepfather's descent into madness and death, Baldwin remembers
him as 'indescribably cruel' and 'certainly the most bitter man I
have ever met'.[20] At the apartment on East 131st Street and later
when they moved around the block to 2171 Fifth Avenue, his

stepfather seems to have ruled the place with an iron fist, full of paranoia and contempt for white people, none of whom he believed could ever be trusted. The family home was synonymous with him, and only after his death did it become in any way bearable. 'The younger children felt, quite simply, relief that he would not be coming home anymore,' Baldwin writes.[21]

The original title of *Go Tell It on the Mountain* was *My Father's House*, and the novel is, in part, Baldwin's attempt to understand his stepfather and reassess his relationship with him. In the section of the book about Gabriel Grimes, he comes across as a weak man, a misogynist in thrall to his sexual desires, a liar and a hypocrite. 'It was later to become his proud testimony that he hated his sins – even as he ran towards sin, even as he sinned.'[22] If Gabriel isn't a likeable character, Baldwin nonetheless encourages the reader to sympathize with this cowardly, conflicted man, who everywhere faces the threat of anti-black violence and confronts the duplicity of a country that only pretends to offer freedom and equality to all its citizens.

Gabriel doesn't seem to be aware of John's queerness, and Baldwin was similarly silent about how his own stepfather felt about his homosexuality. We are given no idea of how Gabriel would react if he found out, but the incompatibility between his oppressive Christian regime and the same-sex love John feels is played out in a scene towards the end of the novel. As John and Elisha reach the end of their early-morning stroll, we are told, 'they were approaching his house – his father's house'.

In a moment he must leave Elisha, step out from under his protecting arm, and walk alone into the house – alone with his mother and his father. And he was afraid.[23]

Here again, John's internal dilemma takes on a spatial form as he implicitly understands that there is no place in his father's house for the kind of love he bears for Elisha. To enter it, to enter into the family home, is to leave such a love on the doorstep, and commit himself to a heterosexist regime. Without words to describe his feelings and comprehend his predicament, John turns away from Elisha and enters the building. Baldwin himself would stay in his father's house until he was nineteen. In 1943, he headed south to Greenwich Village in search of another life, and his wandering began. He would never again live in Harlem.

Baldwin's debut novel isn't perhaps his best – *Another Country* (1962) is more narratively ambitious, for instance, and *Just Above My Head* (1979) is more formally exciting – but it's always been my favourite. I identify with the feelings of its young protagonist, and in spite of what seems on the surface like light years of distance between Harlem in the 1930s and rural Ireland in the 1980s and 1990s, of all Baldwin's characters, I feel closest to John Grimes.

Like him, I grew up in a religious household, and if the Christianity of my upbringing wasn't perhaps as strict as the one portrayed in *Go Tell It on the Mountain*, it was certainly as all-encompassing. I remember prayers every morning at school and decades of the rosary before bed. I remember the Angelus bell tolled out twice a day, at midday on the radio and at six o'clock on TV. I remember the highlight of my week was mass on a Saturday night. In that world of small-town Ireland, the Catholic Church was involved in everything. Priests and bishops, despite having no qualifications other than their collar, sat on sporting councils and boards of education and planning committees. I remember – and this is absolutely true – at the one and only sex talk we had at secondary school, the parish priest was in attendance and actually fielded questions from our group of confused teenage boys.

Homosexuality was a sin, of course, but something apparently so vile that it was hardly ever spoken about. On reflection, it may have been better if the priest had got up in the pulpit in that cavernous church in that tiny ex-coal-mining town, and denounced all the queers who were going to hell – at least then we would have had a word for it. Nothing stunted our sexual growth like the silence. As soon as I could, like Baldwin, I left, and I didn't come out until long after.

When I read *Go Tell It on the Mountain*, the claustrophobia of that place comes back to me: how much was determined by religion there and how it seeped into our minds. I feel in the pit of my stomach John's desperate struggle between love and guilt, and his fight to put a name to his feelings. I witness his shame and I know it intimately – just as I recognize the author's shame. I understand, furthermore, how it can colour the way you see the world, and how hard it is to move past it.

For Baldwin, home was not a place of love or protection but somewhere he had to escape from. His experience was not so different from many others'. From Edward Carpenter remarking that 'at home I never felt really at home', to Jimmy Somerville plaintively singing about never finding the love you need there, young queer people – then and now – have consistently fled homophobia and the threat of violence at home, in search of alternative, queer forms of kinship. For Baldwin, the problem was that he found himself forever searching for somewhere to call home, be it a physical space or a domestic relationship. But as soon as he arrived, he contrived some way to sabotage it and was off again. When the narrator of *Giovanni's Room* muses that 'perhaps home is not a place but simply an irrevocable condition', I wonder if by 'condition' the writer meant something chronic – home as an incurable disease.[24]

The way that Baldwin saw Harlem was tinged by this ambivalence towards home. His childhood experience of it as a claustrophobic, violent, heterosexist environment so influenced his portrait of Harlem that, based solely on his writing, it's difficult for us to imagine that any other kind of Harlem ever existed – one that might have been more hospitable to him. A queer Harlem, for instance.

In 1925, a year after Baldwin was born, the black academic Alain Locke published his landmark anthology *The New Negro*, which identified a new creative spirit among African Americans in the United States. This spirit derived, he said, from a new-found self-confidence and self-respect, which brought forth new forms of art and writing: 'Negro life is not only establishing new contacts and founding new centers, it is finding a new soul.' In his collection of fiction, poetry, drama and essays by young black writers, he included the likes of Langston Hughes, Zora Neale Hurston, Bruce Nugent, Countee Cullen and Claude McKay. These writers, and others like Wallace Thurman and Nella Larsen, were part of an exciting cultural scene based in Harlem in the 1920s and 1930s, which became known as the Harlem Renaissance. 'There is a spiritual and cultural focusing,' Locke wrote; that focus was located in Upper Manhattan.[25]

Locke was queer, and so were many of the writers included in his collection, like Cullen, Hughes, Nugent

and McKay. According to the historian of gay Harlem Eric
Garber, the Harlem Renaissance emerged in tandem with a
queer black subculture in the neighbourhood, and was interwoven with it: 'Throughout the Harlem Renaissance period,
roughly from 1920 to 1935, black lesbians and gay men were
meeting each other on street corners, socializing in cabarets
and rent parties, and worshiping in church on Sundays, creating a language, a social structure, and a complex network of
institutions.'[26]

These institutions included nightclubs and private
parties where queer men and women drank bootleg liquor
together, listened to jazz and danced till dawn. Speakeasies
were popular with the queer crowds. At Lulu Belle's on Lenox
Avenue, female impersonators could be found propping up the
bar, while well-heeled Harlemites frequented Club Hot Cha on
134th Street. One block over at the Clam House on 133rd Street,
people came to hear the bisexual Gladys Bentley, large and in
charge and dressed in a top hat and tails, growling out songs
like 'Worried Blues'.

Harlem's extravagant costume balls were a vital part
of the scene. Thousands of New Yorkers, white and black,
descended on ritzy venues like the Rockland Palace on West
155th Street and the Manhattan Casino at 596 Lenox Avenue,
where men dressed as women and women dressed as men.
In his autobiography *The Big Sea* (1940), Hughes remembers
looking down from above onto 'a queerly assorted throng on
the dancing floor, males in flowing gowns and feathered headdresses and females in tuxedos and box-back suits'.[27]

Balls like these were important, safe spaces where
gender nonconformity was not only tolerated, but celebrated –
prized, even. The annual Hamilton Lodge 'masquerade' in

particular featured a spirited drag competition where first prize was fifty dollars. One report from an attendee describes the splendid variety of drag costumes on display at the March 1927 event.

> Wigs, where necessary, were in evidence. From the garb of a biblical virgin, by way of the historic costumes of the early centuries, down to the very sparse attire only seen on the burlesque stage of today, accentuated with the feminine gesture and lingo, to say nothing of the contortions of the hip, formed the make-up of these male masqueraders. Color prejudice was thrown to the winds, as the Nordic contestants mixed freely with their dark-skinned brethren.[28]

Drag balls were glitzy, conspicuously queer events that were widely covered in local newspapers like the *Amsterdam News* and the *New York Age* right up to the late 1930s.

It may seem strange that, in all of his writings, Baldwin never acknowledged the existence of this openly queer community. Even though the biggest queer clubs and bars were all located a mere block or two from where he grew up, it didn't seem to register at all in his mental map of Harlem. In a late interview, he said: 'The word "gay" has always rubbed me the wrong way. I never understood exactly what is meant by it . . . I simply feel it's a world that has little to do with me, with where I did my growing up.'[29]

Granted, after the stock market crash of 1929 and the repeal of Prohibition, the scene shrank considerably. It would have been less readily visible during Baldwin's adolescence, when he was struggling with his homosexuality. He was

certainly aware of the Harlem Renaissance, however, and inter-
acted with many of its prominent figures: Cullen was one of
his schoolteachers; Hughes was a friend he liked to spar with in
person and in print; and the painter Beauford Delaney, whom
we will meet in a moment, would become something of a sur-
rogate father to him.

As a scene, however, Baldwin simply wasn't interested
in it, and disparaged the Renaissance as a worthless invention
of the white liberal. It was, he wrote, 'an elegant term which
means that white people had then discovered Negroes could
act and write as well as sing and dance and this Renaissance was
not destined to last very long'.[30] Implicit in this is a dismissal
of the social impact of the movement, the social context from
which it emerged (which we know was a very queer one), and
the very real effects it had on bringing together a queer community in Harlem. But, as we will see, sexual orientation was
always a private matter for Baldwin, which he felt had little
social importance. He never believed it should be the basis for
a community.

Baldwin's friendship with the artist Beauford Delaney gave him
the push he needed to finally leave home. More than twenty
years older than Baldwin, Delaney was black, gay and by that
point established as an abstract expressionist painter, who was
once part of the Harlem scene but now lived in Greenwich
Village. A fifteen-year-old Baldwin took the subway south to
visit him at his studio on Greene Street. Looking back in later
life, he remembers mounting the stairs with trepidation and
knocking on the door: 'A short, round brown man came to the
door and looked at me. He had the most extraordinary eyes I'd
ever seen . . . he smiled and said "Come in," and opened the

door.'[31] The older man soon became Baldwin's mentor and opened the door to the art and culture that would become so much a part of his life.

Delaney showed Baldwin how to be an artist. As a father figure, he also showed him how to be a man. In this regard, however, he was an unusual example to follow. Supportive and generous, Delaney was also private to an almost obsessive degree. Everything in his life was separated out: his black friends knew little about his white friends, and his queer friends knew little about his straight friends. His sex life was similarly compartmentalized. His homosexual desires repulsed him and he couldn't conceive of a romantic relationship with someone he respected, so he would prefer to have anonymous sex with hustlers he picked up on the street than run the risk of having it 'pollute' his relationships with friends.

As a model of how to relate to one's sexuality, therefore, Delaney perhaps wasn't the most progressive one for the young Baldwin, who was still vying with his Christian upbringing. But Delaney unconditionally loved the young black man who knocked on his door in 1940, and Baldwin found in him the kindness his stepfather withheld. The two were lifelong friends until Delaney's death in 1979.

When he first moved to Greenwich Village in 1943, Baldwin lived with Delaney for a while, before finding his own place in a succession of rooms nearby. The move downtown was necessary to his development as an artist and put some physical and psychological space between him and his home in Harlem, but his new neighbourhood was hardly the most hospitable of places. As Baldwin later remembered: 'racially, the Village was vicious, partly because of the natives, largely because of the tourists, and absolutely because of the cops'.[32]

In the Calypso, a popular Trinidadian restaurant, he found respite from the racialized threat of the streets. He worked there as a waiter, and, after hours, spent time drinking and getting to know the patrons – artists and writers like Henry Miller, Paul Robeson, C. L. R. James and Claude McKay. On his nights off, he and Delaney might find themselves at the White Horse Tavern, or the San Remo with the beat writers and other Village bohemians. Surrounded by this hive of creativity, Baldwin was inspired to work on a number of projects, notably *Ignorant Armies*, an unpublished novel with echoes of Patricia Highsmith in its depiction of murder and a queer romance gone wrong. Living in Greenwich Village, he also published his first work of fiction, a short story about the eviction of a black man from his Village apartment. Characteristically for Baldwin, the apartment assumes symbolic proportions and becomes something of a metaphor for white society.

Baldwin later referred to this period as his 'Season in Hell', after the French poet Arthur Rimbaud's visionary prose poem of 1873. In other words, it was creatively transformative, but personally traumatic. Baldwin's struggles with his homosexuality and the shame attached to it were exacerbated by the sexual freedoms of this most bohemian of New York neighbourhoods. Although he told his friends that he was gay and had a string of one-night stands with men, he also had relationships with women and seemed unwilling to give up on the idea of heterosexual happiness. In 1946, he had a year-long relationship with a woman named Grace; they lived together and he even bought her a wedding ring, but they never got as far as the wedding itself, as fate traumatically intervened.

Within a few months of his arrival in the Village, Baldwin had met Eugene Worth, a young black guy, apparently straight, with whom he became close friends over the next few years. 'We were never lovers,' Baldwin later remembered. 'I think I wish we had been.' In 1946, Worth ended his life by throwing himself off the George Washington Bridge. Before he died, he had declared his love for Baldwin, who couldn't reciprocate – he said he simply didn't believe anyone could love him. Baldwin looked back on their time together with guilt and regret: 'When he was dead, I realised that I would have done anything whatever to have been able to hold him in this world.'[33] When he and Grace broke up, he threw the wedding ring into the river not far from where Worth had jumped to his death.

Baldwin's relationships with men at this time were characterized by what his biographer David Leeming calls 'Eugene Worth syndrome' – the same complex of attachment and resistance, desire and shame represented by that unhappy friendship. Leeming writes: 'If [Baldwin] really loved a man, sex seemed impossible. Homosexuality involved "violation." It could take place only furtively with other "outlaws" of the night.'[34] This pattern, which so resembled the experience of his friend and mentor Delaney, would recur to varying degrees throughout Baldwin's life.

Traumatized by Worth's death, Baldwin feared he would suffer a similar fate. Five years after leaving home, he was no less conflicted about his sexuality, literary success had so far eluded him and he was increasingly driven to distraction by the racial injustices he witnessed all around him. He worried he might lose his mind, as his stepfather had. Moving to Greenwich Village evidently hadn't been far enough; he had to leave America altogether. So, in November 1948, he stuffed his unfinished book into a duffel bag, called in uptown to say goodbye to his mother and boarded a one-way flight to France, where he would live for most of the next decade.

Giovanni's Room

When Baldwin touched down in Paris in the winter of 1948, the rain was falling hard, as indeed it had been when Josephine Baker arrived in the city twenty-three years earlier. She thought rainfall was lucky on one's first visit to a new place, and indeed the Paris rain seems to have brought them both life-changing prosperity – although Baldwin would have to wait much longer for it than she did.

After the Second World War, Paris itself was hardly as prosperous as it had once been, and would prove a much trickier proposition for a black American expatriate who later claimed to have turned up in the city with only forty dollars in his pocket. 'Champagne has ceased to be drunk out of slippers, and the frivolously colored thousand-franc note is neither as elastic nor as freely spent as it was in the 1920s,' Baldwin wrote.[35] In fact, for most of the time he was poor and often hungry, writing in cafés to keep warm and, according to at least one account, occasionally resorting to sex work to pay the rent.

Of his early years in Paris, Baldwin recalled: 'I went through this period where I was very much alone, and wanted to be. I wasn't part of any community.'[36] Never before had he felt so much like an exile, uprooted from his birthplace, and set down in a strange, old city where he barely understood the language. And yet, as emotionally trying as the experience was, he had also never before been so productive. Some of his best, most keenly observed works were written far away from New York. Distanced from memories of abuse and feelings of guilt attached to his stepfather's house, he found a new sense of belonging in this state of homelessness. The more he inhabited his alienation, the more his writing came alive.

Before long, he became immersed in the bohemian literary scene of the Left Bank. He was a fixture at Les Deux Magots, a café in Saint-Germain-des-Prés made famous by the patronage of the surrealists and the Lost Generation of American writers. There, he rubbed shoulders with philosophers Simone de Beauvoir and Jean-Paul Sartre, whose existentialist ideas worked their way into his conversations with the likes of Richard Wright and Chester Himes – black American writers who had also fled the United States. Baldwin greatly admired Hemingway, and often found himself emulating 'Papa' by touring the same bars and cafés that had been frequented by him twenty years earlier, like the Brasserie Lipp and the Café de Flore in the Latin Quarter. As the night wore on, Baldwin and friends might go cruising at queer bars like the Reine Blanche or the more upscale Fiacre, finishing the night with breakfast at Les Halles as dawn broke over the city.

In spite of the busy, sometimes chaotic social life of the cafés, bars and clubs, exile was hard and Baldwin was often lonely and depressed. He missed his family. He missed being able to go up to Harlem on Sundays. He missed the food and the music he had grown up with. Living in a different area of Paris and on a different schedule to the black American musicians and entertainers, he also missed the ease and familiarity of being around black people. His lifelong struggles with alcoholism were most pronounced at this time too, and his depression deepened. In the winter of 1949, alone and in debt, he tried to hang himself from a water pipe in his hotel room. The pipe broke and he was saved. The water of Paris rained down on him from above, and all he could do was sit there and laugh at the absurdity of it.

His luck seemed to hold in the days following his suicide attempt, and shortly afterwards, while drinking at the Reine Blanche, he fell madly in love. Lucien Happersberger, a seventeen-year-old painter from Switzerland, was just as rootless as Baldwin was, but not half so morose – living on the streets, by his wits, giddy with the sheer abundance of stimulation and excitement to be found in the city. He was easy-going and masculine, and Baldwin fell for him.

From that night on they were inseparable, and spent all their time together: waking, eating lunch, drinking together in bars, and going home together at the end of the night to begin it all again the next day. 'All our time, all our life was ours. We had nothing else to do but live,' Happersberger remembered. 'We would see each other every day. We would talk, usually all night. We were in love with each other, being two young kids, both, in different ways, lost.'[37] Baldwin had never believed that love was on the cards for him, but now, he wrote, 'here it was, breathing and belching beside me, and it was the key to life.'[38]

The couple supported each other and shared everything. In 1951, when Baldwin needed a break from Paris to work on *Go Tell It on the Mountain*, Happersberger took him away to a tiny village in the Swiss Alps where his family owned a small château. According to Baldwin's essay 'Stranger in the Village' (1953), Loèche-les-Bains was like somewhere out of the Middle Ages, with no bank, no library and no cinema; there was only one typewriter in town – his. He was also the only black person who seemed ever to have set foot in the village. 'It's true that we must have been a very strange couple in that village,' said Happersberger. 'He'd be writing, and I would go do the shopping. I would take him out after the work, have drinks and have fun.'[39] Under Happersberger's care, Baldwin finally finished the novel – then they both trekked down the mountain to find a post office where he could mail the manuscript to his publisher.

If they were sometimes domestic, they weren't always blissfully so. For Baldwin, the young Swiss artist was *le grand amour*, and he would refer to him as the love of his life, but Happersberger seemed to hold their relationship more lightly. In fact, he was mostly straight and continued to date women while he and Baldwin were romantically involved; shortly after they came down from the mountain, he got married and had a child. For most of the next thirty-five years their relationship was not sexual and, from Happersberger's point of view, not romantic. They were, nonetheless, friends until the very end. In late 1987, when Baldwin was terminally ill with cancer, Happersberger arrived in Saint-Paul to care for him in his final days, and was at Baldwin's bedside when he died.

There's something tragic and inevitable (or, perhaps, tragically inevitable) about Baldwin's attraction to Happersberger and the other ostensibly straight young men he had short-lived relationships with during his life. For Leeming, 'permanence was all but impossible in Baldwin's love relationships because he was drawn not to other homosexuals but to men who were sometimes willing to act homosexually, temporarily, in response to a need for money and shelter, or to what can only be called his personal magnetism and persuasiveness'.[40] This pursuit of an unattainable love, which has elements of Baldwin's personal 'Eugene Worth syndrome' about it, is so similar to the experience of many men in the pre-liberation years.

Falling for someone who was incapable of committing to a stable, homosexual relationship; loving someone who could not reciprocate; finding oneself attracted only to men whose masculinity was unassailable – thus not queer: the stories of generations of queer men before gay liberation are marked by these kinds of impossible attachments. Their origin, according to the gay English writer and wit Quentin Crisp, was to be found in a devotion to gender stereotypes. In his memoir *The Naked Civil Servant* (1968), he writes that the 'problem that confronts homosexuals is that they set out to win the love of a "real" man. If they succeed, they fail. A man who "goes with" other men is not what they would call a real man. This conundrum is incapable of resolution, but that does not make homosexuals give it up.'[41] The conundrum faced by Crisp's community of homosexual men, which was the same conundrum Baldwin also faced, was rooted in a stubborn adherence to the idea of the 'real man', and exacerbated by shame and a misogynistic fear of feminization.

'If they succeed, they fail.' This paradox lies at the heart of Baldwin's second novel, *Giovanni's Room*, which opens on a town in the south of France where David, a blond American expatriate, reflects on his love affair with Giovanni, an Italian barman he met in Paris some months earlier. The model for the town is not Saint-Paul, which Baldwin wouldn't visit until much later, but nearby Grasse, the perfume capital of France, where he once took an ill-fated holiday with one of his lovers.

Miserable and alone, gazing out of a window of the house into the darkness beyond, David remembers a brief, formative night of love-making in New York with a teenage friend named Joey. He recalls the 'great thirsty heat, and trembling,

and tenderness so painful I thought my heart would burst'
(Baldwin writes great sex scenes), but how, in the morning,
overcome with regret, he gave his friend the cold shoulder.
'The sweat on my back grew cold. I was ashamed. The very
bed, in its sweet disorder, testified to vileness.'[42] As in *Go Tell It
on the Mountain*, gay shame is central to the story of *Giovanni's
Room*, and dirt and homosexuality are also interchangeable in
the mind of its narrator.

Flash-forward to Paris, and we find David broke, waiting for his rich father to wire him some money, borrowing cash
from his friends in the meantime. One of them brings him to
a swish gay bar, 'a noisy, crowded, ill-lit sort of tunnel' identifiable as Baldwin's take on the Fiacre. Looking around him,
David regards the bar's queer patrons with derision.

> There were the usual paunchy, bespectacled gentlemen
> with avid, sometimes despairing eyes, the usual knife-
> blade lean, tight-trousered boys. One could never be sure,
> as concerns these latter, whether they were after money
> or blood or love . . . There were, of course, *les folles*,
> always dressed in the most improbable combinations,
> screaming like parrots the details of their latest
> love-affairs.[43]

Screaming and flapping and addressing each other as
'she', *les folles* (from which we get *La Cage aux folles*, the 1973
French play and the musical based on it) are appalling to David
in their effeminacy – as are those who flout gender norms more
flagrantly, like the proto-trans post-office worker who puts on
make-up and earrings once the night arrives: 'People said that
he was very nice but I confess that his utter grotesqueness made

me uneasy; perhaps in the same way that the sight of monkeys eating their own excrement turns some people's stomachs.'[44]

As this horrible image makes clear, David is disgusted and terrified by any kind of gender ambiguity, and he's eager to distinguish himself from the queers around him, who might tarnish what a friend calls his 'immaculate manhood'.[45] He is, nevertheless, drawn to the new guy who's tending bar, 'insolent and dark and leonine' (and all-man and totally not-gay), standing over by the till.[46] Giovanni acts straight and is as contemptuous of his clientele as David is; later they both have a good laugh about how he beats his women. In other words, he seems to be one of those 'real men' described by Crisp, and David is weak-kneed for him. They retreat to have sex in Giovanni's apartment, a small, one-room flat on the ground floor of a building in the neighbourhood of Nation, in the east of Paris. 'He pulled me against him . . . with everything in me screaming *No!* yet the sum of me sighed *Yes.*'[47]

Giovanni and David's liaison is entwined from the beginning with David's shame, and here, as with John Grimes's house in Harlem, the dirt and disorder of Giovanni's flat is a physical reminder of it. The dirty walls, the dirty laundry, the mess and clutter of boxes, paintbrushes and musical instruments – this 'fantastic accumulation of trash' might as well be the contents of David's 'vile' conscience.[48] But it's only when he attempts to clean up the trash that things start to go seriously wrong.

Taking on the task of keeping their shared domestic space clean while Giovanni is away at work, he suddenly finds himself in the role of a housewife, and panics. 'I am not a housewife,' he gasps. 'Men can never be housewives.'[49] From then on, every time Giovanni takes him in his arms, David senses some of his hard-won masculinity slip away and feels less and less like the 'Butch' his father calls him in his letters. Unable to bear this assault on his manhood, he withdraws from Giovanni; as he does so, his lover also begins to act less like a 'real man' – turning melodramatic and cleaving desperately to David, afraid of losing him. By the time that David calls Giovanni 'outrageously and offensively effeminate', their relationship is over.[50] David returns to his fiancée and Giovanni embarks on a downward spiral that leads, finally, to murder.

Putting out a book like *Giovanni's Room* in 1956 required immense courage from its author – courage, indeed, that his publisher lacked. Terrified of something with so much queer content in it, Knopf turned it down, and Baldwin had to go and publish it in England. In the context of a virulently homophobic 1950s, the novel could easily have ruined his reputation and scuppered his career before it had really begun. It was almost without precedent at the time and, with the exception of Gore Vidal's *The City and the Pillar* (1948) and Mary Renault's *The Charioteer* (1953), hardly any high-profile books in English dealt so frankly with homosexual love between men. When *Giovanni's Room* became a success, outselling even his previous novel and solidifying his status as a brilliant young novelist, his courage was amply rewarded.

Baldwin claimed that he wrote the novel so that his homosexuality couldn't be used against him: 'It meant . . . I had no secrets, nobody could blackmail me. You didn't tell me, I told you.' If the motivation to write arose from a desire to protect himself, *what* he wrote also saw him exposed in a remarkably candid way. '*Giovanni's Room* comes out of something that tormented and frightened me – the question of my own sexuality,' Baldwin said, and the book is not simply reveal-ing of the author's homosexuality, but also of his particularly knotted form of queerness that was so laden with shame and so bound up with rigid ideas of gender.[51]

For David, Giovanni's apartment represents queer domesticity and ambiguous masculinity; staying there means giving up being a straight guy who just has sex with men and becoming one of those homosexuals he hates. In effect, the room isn't just a place, it's an identity, and David flees it because he can't confront his own misogyny and homophobia. This is the central tragedy of the novel; a tragedy which, consider-ing the author's biography, is a reflection of Baldwin's own. After all, these were the same terms under which he lived and loved: falling for straight men who couldn't love him in the way he wanted meant he couldn't achieve a stable domestic situation – he couldn't find a room to permanently share with someone else.

The novel was positively received when it came out, but reviewers were quick to reassure their readers that *Giovanni's Room* wasn't a homosexual book. It was, they said, a story about 'universal' themes of humanity and love, and this was some-thing that Baldwin was also keen to emphasize. '*Giovanni* is not really about homosexuality,' he said. 'It's about what happens to you if you're afraid to love anybody. Which is more inter-esting than the question of homosexuality.'[52] He held that his engagement with the subject of homosexuality was thus art-istic and literary, not political, and he always refused to have *Giovanni's Room* labelled a gay book.

At the time, Baldwin was critical of labels. Human beings, he wrote, 'cannot ever be labelled'; to label a person meant to lock them up 'in those airless labelled cells which isolate us from each other and separate us from ourselves'.[53] This applied as much to the label of black as it did to the label of homosexual. His logic, at least in the 1950s, was that assuming the label or category that one is given reinforces one's oppression and, in turn, the status of one's oppressor. This was a typical idea that was going around Parisian bars at the time Baldwin was there, when thinkers like Sartre and de Beauvoir were interested in the so-called 'master–slave' dialectic of G. W. F. Hegel's *Phenomenology of Spirit* (1807) – where binary identities, ostensibly oppositional, are shown to be mutually constitutive.

As he grew older, Baldwin's position on this would change – but only as far as blackness was concerned. After the collapse of the civil rights movement and the death of Martin Luther King Jr, he became more supportive of black separatism as a means of gaining political change. In his 1972 essay 'No Name in the Street', he wrote: 'To be liberated from the stigma of blackness by embracing it is to cease forever one's interior agreement and collaboration with the authors of one's degradation.'[54] Yet this about-turn never changed how he felt about the comparable stigma of homosexuality. 'Gay' rubbed him the wrong way, as we've seen, and until the end of his life he was cynical about the gay and lesbian movement. In an interview in 1980, he said: 'I have not really got to join a club in order to go to bed with a man or fall in love. My life is my life, and I have only one of them.'[55]

I can't help but feel disappointed when I read these kinds of short-sighted, individualistic statements by Baldwin. I want to understand why he was so unwilling to align himself with other gay people. Why he was so adamant that homosexuality was a private matter, when the laws of every country in the world had made it so much a public concern. Why, in his eagerness to excuse the homophobia of Eldridge Cleaver, he punched down, differentiating himself from 'all those faggots, punks, and sissies, the sight and sound of whom, in prison, must have made [Cleaver] vomit more than once'.[56]

Shame has a lot to do with it, of course. Take it from someone who was raised a Catholic: you don't grow up in a religious household without guilt and shame leaving a permanent mark on you. But so too does Baldwin's self-isolation: his idea of himself as independent and alone, which his relationship to the houses and rooms explored in this chapter reveals.

Baldwin's separation from his community in Harlem was necessary in order for him to write. It started during his adolescence and is encapsulated so beautifully in the image of the young John Grimes looking down at the boys in the street and realizing he's not like them; we witness his critical distance, his anguish, his resolve: 'If he could not play their games, he could do something they could not do; he was able, as one of his teachers said, to think.'[57]

Later, exile from America allowed Baldwin to flourish as an artist, permitting him to diagnose from afar the many ills of his country, and that of his adopted country too. At home and abroad, he embodied the role of the 'stranger' – a term first employed by the Austrian social scientist Alfred Schütz in 1944 to describe the status of someone who approaches a social grouping from a distance, who has a special ability to observe and anatomize its cultural patterns and unconscious investments. The essay Baldwin wrote about his time in Loèche-les-Bains in 1951 was called 'Stranger in the Village', but he was, as he later admitted, 'a stranger everywhere' – in every village.

Isolation and alienation – the artist's isolation and the exile's alienation – are what made Baldwin a great writer.

Consciously or unconsciously, he knew that in order to be able to write, he had to preserve his isolation, and he could never join a community or a 'club' without experiencing deep reservations. This gives us some idea why he was so reluctant to be identified as gay. In using the term, he would have consented to being part of a group, and this was something he found intolerable.

As an identity, gay is also a fixed position – however strategic or provisional. This was anathema to Baldwin, who was forever on the move, and whose sexual desires meant that he couldn't settle down and was ever in pursuit of an impossible love. He fled from fixity as he fled from his home, from Harlem, from all the claustrophobic little rooms he found with the windows shut, which prevented his escape; he fled as David fled Giovanni's room. 'I scarcely know how to describe that room. It became, in a way, every room I had ever been in and every room I find myself in hereafter will remind me of Giovanni's room.'[58]

It's safe to say that Baldwin's relationship to the places where we have found him contrasts markedly with that of the other individuals we have encountered. Forster, Baker, Cahun and the queer suffragettes of London all experienced the world around them differently, and responded to it in diverse, creative ways, but they are united in their shared status of being situated. All of the artists and writers we have considered thus far were *in place*. Baldwin, on the other hand, was always *out of place* – starting with his home in Harlem and ending with a town in the south of France where all trace of him has now disappeared.

Chances are if you hang around a place like Le Jardin des Arts too long, they'll set the dogs on you. So I leave it behind me, and make my way up the gentle incline that leads to the centre of Saint-Paul. Past the expensively dressed tourists loitering inside the doors of private art galleries. Past the busload of students pouring out of chic fragrance stores like L'Occitane and Fragonard. Past the group of deeply tanned men playing pétanque in the small town square, exaggeratedly shrugging at each other, shaking their heads. On into the walled town, its citadel gathered on a rocky outcrop that rises to six hundred feet above sea level.

Saint-Paul seems to draw me into it, and I'm conveyed by a kind of capillary action through the maze of tiny, cobbled streets that lead off in unexpected directions or narrow to the width of barely one person. Finally, I find myself on the rough stone battlements looking out across the countryside. The day is warm and the breeze up here is gentle and intermittent. Far below, where the ramparts meet the surrounding farmland, the slopes are strung with meandering lines of olive trees, interspersed with bitter orange – reminders of the town's perfume-making past. The land is lush and green, dotted with the tiled terracotta roofs of Provençal houses, gently undulating towards the turquoise haze of a distant sea.

I can make out some of Baldwin's old place from here, a little over to the west and partially obscured by giant cypresses that shoot up from the hillside like big green geysers. His moving to the town makes sense to me now. It's beautiful here, of course, and, with its quintessential Côte d'Azur scenery, who wouldn't want to live here? But I'm also struck by the splendid seclusion of Saint-Paul, which seems so indicative of Baldwin's character. Set way up on a hill, far from the beaten track, and in his time more inaccessible than it is now, the remoteness of the town reflects the kind of artistic removal

223

he cultivated throughout his life. Yet his living beyond the citadel seems significant too – as if he was protective of his isolation
yet unwilling to wall himself up in it. He was no hermit of the
mount, as the welcome he extended to many of his friends
while he was living here shows.

High on the parapet of Saint-Paul, I've been thinking
about the best way of approaching Baldwin's story. How do we
take account of his life and work, and at the same time respect
his self-imposed seclusion? How do we refrain from treating
him as a hero or a saint, and twisting his tale to our own ends?
Friendship may be the solution – coming to Baldwin in friendship, like one of those dear friends who came to visit him here.
To me, friendship is a special form of loving and supportive
connection, distinct from the intimacy of a romantic relationship, which retains an element of distance that is, to an extent,
always necessary. As friends, we can acknowledge each other's
flaws and understand them, without wishing that the other
person would change. Approaching Baldwin as a friend might
allow us to love him in such a way that he retains his difference from us.

In his *New Yorker* essay about breaking into Baldwin's
house, Thomas Chatterton Williams comforts himself by
writing that, even though the house is no more, Baldwin's
'monument is manifold, and we carry it inside us'.[59] What if
we refrained from swallowing Baldwin whole along with such
platitudes, and instead carried him *with* us, *alongside* us – as
an elder we've made the effort to listen to, compassionately,
and a friend who's dearly beloved not in spite of his faults, but
because of them.

Jack Smith
November 14, 1932–September 18, 1989
Legendary Filmmaker, Theatrical Genius
and Exotic Art Consultant

Jack Smith Memorial Service card, 1989. Courtesy of David C. Pace and the
Fales Library and Special Collections, New York University.

6

Utopia: Jack Smith and New York

New York has always been a place of dreams. For me, at least. Growing up, all I knew of the city was a televisual fantasy. American TV shows like *Cagney & Lacey* and *Moonlighting*, which my mother watched on a temperamental television in our kitchen, conveyed us on a saxophone theme across the Atlantic to an island of magical, oversized visions.

Enormous bridges, the likes of which I'd never seen in real life. Skyscrapers in polished steel and glass a hundred storeys high. Boulevards filled with noisy yellow cabs pushing along progress in lines of traffic like conveyor belts. Crowds of powerful all-American men and women with perfect teeth sailing through the streets in sharp suits. Later, still more shows propped up the fantasy: *Seinfeld*, *Friends*, *Sex and the City*. They all worked to confirm our collective illusions about the place: New York was quirky, intimate even in its vastness, romantic, fashionable. Culturally speaking, it was the most important place on Earth.

New Yorkers were all beautiful, of course, but unlike the stars beamed into our house from sunny California, they were also interesting, gritty – some sand in the oyster yielded these pearlescent beings, all quick-witted and fast-talking and go-getting. Based on the evidence of these TV shows, which rarely featured a person of colour, they were also uniformly white. Looking back, their attempts to represent New York as an all-white city and efface the true multi-ethnic character of the place would be laughable if it weren't so casually racist. But at that point, in the 1980s and 1990s in Ireland and everywhere else, the cultural ascendancy of basketball and hip-hop, and their attendant imagery of cool black New York crafted by the likes of film director Spike Lee, had given that pallid vision of the city some much-needed colour.

By the time I first arrived in the early 2000s, I'd lived with a fictional version of the city for two decades. So deeply embedded was the fantasy and so rooted was it in American film and television that, as I walked down Fifth Avenue or passed a recognizable landmark like the Empire State Building or the New York Public Library, all I could think to myself was, 'isn't it so much like the movies!' I expect everyone who lands here from other parts of the world can relate to this. Perhaps they, too, feel as I did: that simply by being in such an iconic space amid a procession of well-known images, one has somehow slipped the surly bonds of Earth and entered into a dream, a fantasy, a fairy tale. Magic, horror, romance, revenge . . . Here, at the epicentre of what the French Situationist Guy Debord would call 'the society of the spectacle', anything was possible because the images told us so.

Naturally, the more I returned to the city, the further away that initial impression felt. Realities intruded upon the ideal form: the sheer expense of the place; its appalling inequalities; the depressing sameness of so many parts of it. The rats! The dirt! Actually, the dirt I liked, or at least over time convinced myself to tolerate. When I did, it felt like I had gained access to *another* New York.

My gaze shifted south, from the bland, commercial

Midtown to the densely packed streets of Downtown Manhattan, and neighbourhoods with distinctive, characterful names. Greenwich Village. The Lower East Side. Alphabet City. From the slick, sanitized imagery spoon-fed to the masses in the 1980s and 1990s, to the authentic culture of the city. Naturally, this New York was another kind of dream – one of dirt and danger. A Downtown dream, which was inextricable in my mind from the queer history and culture of the place. Wasn't it Frank O'Hara, the gay poet of New York lunchtimes, who wrote: 'Is it dirty / does it look dirty / that's what you think of in the city.'[1]

New York, and Manhattan in particular, has long been home to a large (if at times underground) queer scene. According to the gay historian George Chauncey, 'fairies', 'queers' and other men who flouted the conventions of gender and sexuality were a highly visible part of Lower Manhattan's nightlife since at least the late nineteenth century. We might think that only isolation and loneliness characterized the queer experience before the conflagration of the Stonewall uprising. But Chauncey's masterful queer topography shows that, in fact, 'in the late nineteenth and early twentieth centuries, an extensive gay world took shape in the streets, cafeterias, saloons, and apartments of New York, and gay men played an integral role in the social life of certain neighborhoods'.[2]

In the 1920s and 1930s, this conspicuous queer presence came to be seen as a threat to American society, and anti-gay laws were implemented in the city and across the States that produced the very invisibility that the gay and lesbian movement would later struggle against. Loitering in a public place 'for the purpose of committing a crime against nature' (i.e. cruising for sex) was prohibited in New York City in 1923, and shortly afterwards any representation of homosexuality (or 'sex degeneracy') on the New York stage was also banned.³ Later, the Motion Picture Production Code (aka the Hays Code), introduced in 1934, made sure that any mention of homosexuality would be excised from the filmic landscape of the United States for almost thirty years.

With the Second World War came a brief reprieve, as mobilization brought huge numbers of men and women into urban areas like New York, and allowed more queer people than ever before to experience the gay world outside the small towns many of them came from. If the simultaneous departure of many young people overseas disrupted pre-existing gay social networks in the city, they were also enlarged by a massive transient population of servicemen and women who flooded the city's bars, clubs and parks from 1941.

These relative freedoms were quickly killed off in the 1950s by Cold War paranoia, however, and the susceptibility of queer people to blackmail and extortion. The Red Scare, led most infamously by Senator Joe McCarthy's witch-hunts, took on a lavender hue, and 'sexual perverts' were labelled a threat to national security. 'The homosexual menace continued as a theme of American political culture throughout the McCarthy era,' writes historian John D'Emilio in his landmark study of gay life, *Sexual Politics, Sexual Communities* (1983).⁴ During the 1950s and 1960s, homophile organizations like the Homosexual League of New York and the New York chapter of the Mattachine Society gently pressed for increased tolerance and recognition of queer people. Although their efforts met with limited success, they nonetheless paved the way for the emergence of liberationist groups by the end of the 1960s.

New York was, of course, one of the major hubs of gay liberation, and the riots that began on 28 June 1969 at the

Stonewall Inn are among the first major uprisings that led to the foundation of the gay and lesbian civil rights movement. In the following decade, queer people flocked to the city to organize, socialize, fuck and find love. In his witty travelogue of the 1970s, *States of Desire: Travels in Gay America* (1980), the writer Edmund White reflects on the unique opportunities afforded by the city, not least that 'New York permits homosexuals an unparalleled chance to assemble a mix-and-match life. If I lived in another city, I suspect I would belong to two quite different circles – one artistic, the other gay . . . In New York most of my friends are gay men and women who are almost all in the arts.'[5]

As White's assertion implies, the art and culture of New York have always been inextricable from its queer scene (even if the connection between them is sometimes conveniently overlooked or ignored), especially where it comes to influential movements like New York School poetry, pop art and punk rock. I often think about O'Hara, LeRoi Jones (Amiri Baraka), John Ashbery and James Schuyler drinking together at Greenwich Village watering holes like the Cedar Tavern. I imagine O'Hara's swishy literariness in particular must have come as a welcome relief from the aggressive machismo of painters like Jackson Pollock, who also used to drink at the Cedar – it's said that, in a drunken rage, he once tore the bar's toilet door off its hinges.

Such macho displays would have appalled the cool, queer crowd of the Factory, Andy Warhol's studio during the 1960s. Located first in Midtown, it moved south towards Greenwich Village in 1967, before finally shifting east to the Flatiron district in 1973. Here Warhol and his assistants, friends and hepped-up hangers-on made the ubiquitous imagery of American consumerism strange and vivid – not so strange or vivid that it couldn't be easily sold, however. We will have occasion to encounter Warhol and his consumerist vision again in a little while.

The nascent punk rock scene of the 1970s absorbed Warhol's glamorization of the underworld of gay hustlers and transgender performers. Proto-punk groups the New York Dolls and the Velvet Underground (who were managed by Warhol) revelled in the imagery of glamorous gender nonconformity, which later inspired the style of androgynous punk rockers Patti Smith and Richard Hell. If punk later became more macho and straight as it was assimilated into the mainstream, its early, arty, New York incarnation seeped into the queer culture being made in the neighbourhoods around CBGB's bar on the Bowery. Its sound radiated outwards to the apartments and studios of Downtown residents like the transgressive feminist writer Kathy Acker, queer poet Eileen Myles and the artist and AIDS activist David Wojnarowicz.

Among these better-known names, one figure arguably represents queer, creative Downtown more than anyone: Jack Smith. Radical, gay and quite weird, Smith was a performer and filmmaker who was as colourful and fizzingly flamboyant as his name was commonplace. An anti-capitalist whose work never made any money (at least while he was alive), he nonetheless had an important and enduring influence on performance art and independent film, especially on the likes of Warhol, John Waters, Federico Fellini, Guy Maddin and Ryan Trecartin. In 1966 someone asked Warhol what filmmaker he admired most. 'Jaaaacck Smiiiitttth!' he replied. 'I just think he makes the best movies.'[6]

Smith lived in various apartments and lofts in Lower Manhattan from the time of his arrival in the city in the early

1950s until his death in 1989. He was forever in debt and often couldn't pay the rent, but in these places where real and celluloid spaces overlapped and intermingled, he somehow managed to conjure up luminous, exotic, far-flung locations. Kitsch dreams of Basra. Misty approximations of the Lost Island of Atlantis. A heavenly somewhere called Montez-land, named in honour of the 1940s movie star Maria Montez.

Not only does Smith epitomize the Downtown dream, he was himself a master of dreams – an artist of hallucinatory visions and failed, fantastical realms that were all constructed out of the detritus of urban life. In his world, the common-sense assumption that reality and fantasy are distinct locales, *separate spheres* – that they somehow contradict each other – doesn't make sense. In his run-down lofts and apartments, as much as in his films, the dreamlike and the fantastical permeated reality to such an extent that those who visited him at home remembered it as a quasi-religious experience. Word became flesh.

Like the queer suffragettes of London, Smith's queerness gave him the opportunity to imagine space differently; through its occupation (and ornamentation) he attempted to make it mean something different, to bring another kind of place into being. Oscar Wilde once said: 'A map of the world that does not include utopia is not worth glancing at.'[7] In Downtown New York, in the bleakest of times and using the most unlikely of materials, Jack Smith put utopia back on the map.

Montez-land

Smith first came to New York in 1953 at the age of twenty-one. The details of his life before then are a little sketchy. The filmmaker Ken Jacobs, who worked with him in the early years, remembered that he 'seemed reticent about giving the real facts of his life. I never knew when he spoke about his childhood – was it a self-amusing fabrication or was it fact?'[8] This much seems true: he was born in Columbus, Ohio, on 14 November 1932, and grew up poor in a small family of immigrant stock. When he was seven, they moved to a coastal town in Texas called Corpus Christi, where his father died in a freak fishing accident.

This childhood tragedy is perhaps one reason for the abundance of sea imagery in Smith's work. In his personal symbology, the lobster, a resident of the watery depths that killed his father, represents the kind of repulsive, crawling avarice that one found, for instance, among the landlords of New York. The mermaid, half in and half out of the water, is a dangerous beauty, with drowned men for suitors. Uncle Fishook, meanwhile, is a recurring character: a light-fingered cretin otherwise known as Jonas Mekas, the underground filmmaker and archivist Smith accused of stealing his films. Smith's final, unfinished movie was called *Sinbad in the Rented World*, in which he played the title role. If anyone could avoid the fate that befell his father, surely it was the heroic, adventure-seeking sailor of *One Thousand and One Nights*.

Smith's mother remarried after his father's death, and moved the family up the coast to Galveston, a down-at-heel town south-east of Houston. They moved again after her third marriage in 1945, this time all the way north to a small city in Wisconsin called Kenosha. According to Smith, his mother was tyrannical and neglectful during his childhood, and he couldn't wait to leave home. After high school, he headed south along the shores of Lake Michigan as far as Chicago, where he soon found a job working as an usher at a movie theatre. It was here, in 1951, at a memorial screening to mark her recent death, that Smith had a life-changing encounter with Maria Montez. Consummate diva and queen of 1940s Hollywood, she would become his patron saint, his deity, his portal to a magical world he called Montez-land.

She was the luminous, glittering star of such Technicolor extravaganzas as *White Savage* (1943), *Ali Baba and the Forty Thieves* (1944) and *Cobra Woman* (1944) – wartime films with terrible plots and even worse dialogue, set in fantasy locations far from the bloodshed of Europe or the Pacific. Cast for her looks, rather than her acting prowess, she hams it up outrageously in all of her roles, chewing the scenery like it's a half-price buffet. According to Robert Siodmak, who directed *Cobra Woman*, 'Maria Montez couldn't act from here to there, but she was a great personality and she believed completely in her roles.'[9] A native of the Dominican Republic, she was called the 'Caribbean Cyclone' because of her exaggerated performances and behaviour behind the scenes (she sued any studio or producer who was foolish enough to undermine her). The studios were only too happy to exploit the exoticism of her ethnicity – if only for a short time. After just a few years as a leading lady, she fell out of favour at the box office, and was soon supplanted by a younger starlet, Yvonne De Carlo. Montez's untimely death came at the age of thirty-nine, and she was found in her Paris apartment, drowned in her bathtub, on 7 September 1951.

To say that Smith idolized Montez would be an understatement. His works for the stage and screen were dedicated to her, and, if you squinted, looked like delirious no-budget remakes of her glitzy movies. In his apartments in New York, he created elaborate Maria Montez shrines, to which he prayed and sometimes had his actors pray. 'Hail Mary full of grace, Delores with thee. Blessed are thou amongst women and blessed are one of thy fruits, Jesus.'[10]

He wasn't deluded, he knew she was a terrible actress – but the point was that she didn't. In his classic essay 'The Perfect Filmic Appositeness of Maria Montez' (1962–3), Smith wrote that 'M.M. dreamed she was effective, imagined that she acted, cared for nothing but her fantasy'.[11] She dreamed, she imagined, she fantasized; she was convinced that she was the greatest actress in the world and nobody could tell her otherwise. The critics who heaped scorn on her performances only showed themselves to be too wedded to reality, and were of no consequence as a result.

'I never fully understood his fixation with Maria Montez,' said the transgressive filmmaker Nick Zedd. 'It seemed to be an inside joke to gay people.'[12] As a gorgeous, spurned Hollywood diva who met a tragic end, Montez was almost ready-made for gay fandom. Like Judy Garland or Joan Crawford, she seemed to embody those elements that, according to the cultural historian David M. Halperin, gay male audiences before liberation deemed necessary for any gay icon: the 'singular combination of glamour and abjection (that is, extreme, degrading humiliation)'.[13] The response of gay viewers to flawed screen goddesses like these was full of contradictions. They cried with them and laughed at them; they celebrated their achievements and revelled in their misfortunes; they took equal pleasure in their successes and failures. This is what Halperin calls the 'double identification' of subcultural gay fandom, which arose as a response to the lack of representation of same-sex love between men.[14]

From the 1930s to the 1960s, mainstream images of queerness were all but non-existent as a result of the widespread adoption of the Hays Code. In the absence of any easily available cinematic representation, gay men looked elsewhere and came to identify with sirens of the silver screen like Garland or Crawford or Bette Davis. These women were talented and whip-smart, but they could also dramatically articulate the feelings their gay viewers had about men. ('Ah! Men!' Davis quips in *All About Eve*.) But with this identification came a resentment that it was necessary at all; that women could openly, easily express what, for gay men, dare not speak its name, and that gay men should *have* to identify with women and give up some of their patriarchal privilege as a result. Thus the strange mix of empathy and contempt gay fans had for their Hollywood divas.

There's something different about Smith's love for Montez, however. I can't detect any resentment or anger in his affection for her, and in his writing about her his deep sympathy appears genuine: 'One of her atrocious acting sighs suffused a thousand tons of dead plaster with imaginative life and truth.'[15] For Smith, being a fan of Montez seems less about the expression of desire by proxy, and more about the revelation of a world. This was, of course, the world of exotic fantasy, of places like Cobra Island and Temple Island, but it was also *this world* and all its phony ideas of good and bad, treasure and trash, that she revealed to him.

Sitting in darkened movie theatres from his teenage years, weeping real tears as his idol smooched with her paramour or plunged dramatically to her death, Smith's lifelong study of Montez *as a failure* showed him just how artificial artistic norms and values were. What did it say about him that he could feel so much about this actress everyone said was so bad? More importantly, what did it say about the society in which he lived? 'She is one of us,' he wrote. 'Is it invalid of her

to be the way she is? If so, none of us are valid . . . To admit of
Maria Montez's validities would be to turn on to moldiness,
Glamorous Rapture, schizophrenic delight, hopeless naïveté,
and glittering technicolor trash!'[16]

Ultimately, Smith saw that what was true of artistic
norms was also true of social norms. As a gay man who came
of age after the Second World War, when homosexuality was
condemned as an aberration, or an illness, or a moral failure, he
understood how arbitrary norms were – and how devastating
their effects. So why not give up trying to be normal altogether?
Turn on instead to failure, 'moldiness', trash: this is what it
meant to be an inhabitant of Montez-land.

The B train emits a long, irritating bleep and trundles off into
the darkness, leaving behind a sillage of grease and rubber,
and me standing on the platform of Grand Street station. If
not perhaps as filthy and neglected as it was in the 1980s, when
Keith Haring plastered its billboards with drawings of featureless caterpillars and UFOs, the New York subway is certainly
dirty, as the ancient grime that covers this station's once-white
wall tiles can attest.

Blackened stairs lead up and into daylight. I emerge in
the middle of an open space on the margins of Chinatown,
on an overcast afternoon in May. Four or five guys are playing handball in a court nearby, observed by a small group of
spectators in different-coloured face masks. I head east for a
couple of blocks, through the distinctive multicultural collage
of Downtown. Chinese restaurants and pharmacies, vibrant
awnings with names emblazoned in Mandarin, sit side by side
with Jewish fabric wholesalers and old-school men's outfitters.

An ambulance screams past, honking and grinding, and

on my right Ludlow Street appears. A quiet side street with a shuttered store on the corner, it's where Smith's first New York apartment was, and where he started to make films with the help of his friends. The ground floor of his old building at number 56 is now the premises of a company that organizes events for multinational corporations. They pride themselves on working closely with the financial services sector, which I suppose is another make-believe world, but the antithesis of those created on the upper floors when Smith lived here.

There's something weirdly familiar about the street, I realize; a sense of déjà-vu that's impossible to shake. I carry on past Smith's old place to the next cross-street, which, unbelievably, is called Hester Street. I ask myself if I'm dreaming. Is that why this place feels so familiar? Was my coming here somehow predestined? Before my imagination really runs riot, I spot a cinema a little way down the street and suddenly I remember: yes, I was here once before. A few years ago, I went to the Metrograph cinema with a friend to watch a movie. The strange thing is, it was a Jack Smith movie: *Flaming Creatures* screened in 35mm. I had no idea that he'd lived less than a block away, on this very street.

According to his estranged sister, Mary Sue Slater, Smith only became who he was 'after he got to New York City. Because before that he was OK.'[17] When he first arrived, he stayed at a hotel on 12th Street near Union Square, then moved around a few different places Downtown before settling into the flat on Ludlow Street. He shared it with Tony Conrad, the video artist and experimental musician, and the two frequently collaborated; Conrad and his friend John Cale (later of the Velvet Underground) were often roped into providing the soundtrack for Smith's films and spoken-word performances.

Smith's first job in the city was as a commercial photographer, taking portraits of fashionable New Yorkers at a West Side location called Hyperbole Photo Studios. His clientele expected him to produce conventional, flattering photographs, which could presumably be shown to their respectable families and friends. But he managed to entice many of them into the back room of the shop, where he kept his most extravagant costumes and backdrops. There, draped in silks, veiled in delicate muslin, occasionally flashing a naked breast or penis, they were unwittingly transported to Montez-land through his camera. Ken Jacobs remembered: 'Jack made these photographs, unlike any photographs I had ever seen! It was like they were stills from a movie. There was no movie, but there were these very evocative images that *suggested* a movie.'[18]

The long-imagined movie would finally arrive in 1963. *Flaming Creatures* was shot on a budget of $300, on expired reels of Perutz Tropical film ('trash is the material of creators', Smith once wrote).[19] The cast was made up of his friends and acquaintances, whom he filmed over eight weekends at the Ludlow Street flat and up on the roof of the old Windsor Theatre a few blocks east on Grand Street.

On its release, it was denounced by politicians and lauded by bohemian artists, banned by the government and acclaimed by the liberal intelligentsia. It was, as a result, probably the most-talked-about film of the 1960s. But talking about a film like *Flaming Creatures* really isn't all that simple. I admit that I find it almost impossible to translate its wordless, fleshy, voluptuous visions into words without demystifying them. Smith once called Maria Montez 'the bane of critics – that person whose effect cannot be known by words, described in words, flaunts words (her *image* spoke)'.[20] Like the screen goddess who was its inspiration, *Flaming Creatures* also resists easy description. Its *images* speak.

In the opening shot, the film seems to be covered in dust and debris and has the grungy look of a long-forgotten silent movie. Cymbals crash and trumpets blare, and an exotic theme cribbed from *Ali Baba and the Forty Thieves* announces a much-anticipated arrival. Faces surface in the haze: one raven-haired beauty, then another, emerging as if out of a sandstorm. Swaying to the music, they run their hands seductively through their hair, before exiting the frame to reveal a handwritten title card.

An actor with masculine features (Francis Francine) gazes into a pocket mirror, generously applying lipstick to a mouth that opens to reveal only a few rotten teeth. A fey voice on the scratchy soundtrack (Mario Montez) advertises 'a fabulous new heart-shaped lipstick'. A second actor puckers up and applies the lipstick, then a third, then a fourth: men, women and those one suspects to have transcended gender altogether rub colour on their lips enthusiastically, deliriously. As the camera pans along their intertwined, half-naked bodies, another voice (Jack Smith) asks: 'Is there a lipstick that doesn't come off when you suck cocks?' Someone jiggles a flaccid penis.

The lid of a coffin inches open to the mismatched accompaniment of 'It Wasn't God Who Made Honky Tonk Angels', a country song with an upbeat tune. Kitty Wells sings how 'most every heart that's ever broken / was because there always was a man to blame', while fingers with long painted nails curl around the wooden lid, shifting it aside to reveal a cross-dressing vampire (Joel Markman). Wearing an enormous platinum-blonde wig, she is submerged in a casket of white blossoms.

A gorgeous Spanish girl (Mario Montez), dressed in a black gown and a black lace mantilla, dances around smilingly with a rose between her teeth. As she laughs and twirls, she's joined by a big-breasted woman (Sheila Bick), who shakes her tits and giggles as she dances. The frame fills with a dozen people of indeterminate gender, all dressed in lace and flowing fabrics, turning, waltzing, laughing . . .

Like a lipsticked mouth full of rotten teeth, *Flaming Creatures* is gorgeous and gross, glamorous and freakish, rich and poor. Its images hold and contain these apparent contradictions – and many more besides. Visionary moments are undercut with amateurish errors, like when the vampire melodramatically leans in to drink her victim's blood and the stuffing of her bra falls out. For much of the film, even the soundtrack contradicts the tone and mood of the images it accompanies. The upshot of all of this is that, for the film's running time of forty minutes and forty-three seconds, the viewer is compelled to live in a world where contradictions make less and less sense. Queer or straight, shedding one's narrow, deep-seated prejudices about what's good and what's bad, what's normal and what's abnormal, is the price of admission to Montez-land.

It seems inevitable now that a film so invested in undoing contradictions would itself provoke such wildly different responses. It was first shown at midnight on 29 April 1963 at the Bleecker Street Cinema in Lower Manhattan. Some early viewers rhapsodized that it was 'a transcendental vision of some kind of heaven', while others weren't so complimentary, writing it off as 'replete with limp genitalia and limp art'.[21] Holly Woodlawn, the transgender actor famous for appearing in Warhol's films, laughed when she remembered watching it for

'Is there a lipstick that doesn't come off when you suck cocks?'
A creature applies lipstick in a scene from *Flaming Creatures*.

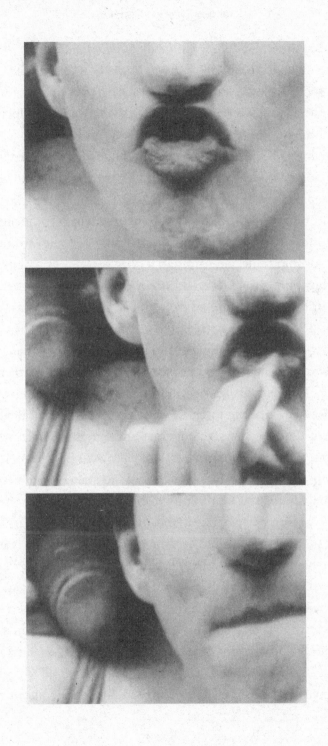

the first time: 'I didn't get it. *I didn't understand a thing!*'[22] The film's most famous supporter was Susan Sontag, who loved its embrace of visual contradictions, especially its chaotic, improvised scenes, in which 'bodies, some shapely and convincingly feminine and others scrawny and hairy, tumble, dance, and make love'.[23] This knotted confusion of gender was, she wrote, 'the poetry of transvestitism' – a poetry that yielded to the viewer 'a space of pleasure'.[24]

In her essay on the film, Sontag was also compelled to defend it against accusations of obscenity. '*Flaming Creatures* is not pornographic,' she argued; it was 'too full of pathos and too ingenuous to be prurient'.[25] By the time she was writing, in April 1964, the film had been pulled from cinemas in New York, prints of it had been seized by the police, and, when they tried to screen it illegally, a group led by Jonas Mekas had been arrested and charged with showing an obscene motion picture.

The censorship of the film had a special importance for Mekas. Since the 1950s, he had been the most vocal champion of the experimental, underground film movement, which encompassed the work of directors like Stan Brakhage, Maya Deren and Shirley Clarke. What was at stake in the case of *Flaming Creatures* was nothing less than the future of that movement in the United States, and his campaign was part of a much larger struggle at the time against social conservatism and what he called the 'enemies of free cinema'.[26] He appealed against the censorship of Smith's film all the way to the Supreme Court, only to have Chief Justice Earl Warren confirm in June 1967 that, yes, it was obscene. 'This film is not within the protections of the First Amendment,' Warren said; it was 'utterly without social value' and 'as a whole appeals to the prurient interest'.[27] The ruling has never been overturned, so screenings of *Flaming Creatures* in New York State are still technically illegal.

Somewhere in the middle of all the outrage, arrests and court cases, the original meaning of Smith's film got lost. A classic *succès de scandale*, it became defined only by its notoriety, and its creator was horrified: 'I started making a comedy about everything that I thought was funny. And it *was* funny. The first audiences were laughing from the beginning all the way through. But then *that writing* started – and it became a sex thing . . . there was no more laughter. There was a dead silence in the auditorium.'[28] He had been friendly with Mekas in the beginning, but now blamed him for the film's fate. For decades afterwards, he seemed to bear an enormous grudge against the man he renamed Uncle Fishook, Uncle Pawnshop, Uncle Roachcrust, Uncle Artcrust – who would figure in many of his subsequent performances as an arch-nemesis and the enemy of true art.

As a taste-maker and mouthpiece of a movement, Mekas represented cultural authority to Smith. His efforts to collect and preserve the history of underground cinema with his Anthology Film Archives (which Smith called 'Uncle Fishook's vault') symbolized elitism, the alienation of art from the world and, finally, its commodification. It was as a symbol, then, rather than as a person, that Smith hated Mekas. 'I've got to have something to hate,' Smith noted cheerfully. 'Uncle Fishook represents the idea of expectations from authority, which is also perfect for me, since I could spend the rest of my life demolishing [it] very happily. I can be happy this way.'[29]

Flaming Creatures was the last film that he would ever finish. Disgusted by what he called 'the sacred baby poo poo of art', Smith started exploring live performance and turned to forms of art that couldn't be captured and imprisoned by people like Uncle Artcrust.[30]

I've spent a lot of time in Manhattan over the years. I came here first on holiday, then to research a book, and ever since to stay with friends. Once I came back just to go to court. (Briefly: I was doing some urban exploration in the Freedom Tunnel under the West Side Highway; the traffic cops caught me and gave me a summons for trespass. Was it worth it? Yes. Would I do it again? No.)

Each time I return, I notice that something's changed: the bar or café I used to go to is now shut down or demolished; the bookshop I loved has been gutted and rebranded. Manhattan is, and always has been, a spatial palimpsest – but its non-stop reinvention has massively accelerated in recent decades under City-sponsored gentrification. Now it seems like the only thing that remains unchanged year after year is the dirt.

I often wonder what kind of culture can take root in these shifting sands. The Downtown culture that was so important to me – the music I loved, the literature that rewired my brain, the underground film that helped me to see – has mostly been shaken out of the place. I remember, for instance, one night a few years ago when the residents of Lower Manhattan asked me: 'Who's John Waters?'

I was working the door of one of the last real dive bars in SoHo. For a while, whenever I visited the city, my pal Brendan would get me to sit outside his bar and check IDs until 3 a.m. It was an easy gig and there was a lot of quiet time, so I'd bring a book and read under one of the street lamps. That night I was reading *Role Models* (2010) by John Waters, and almost every customer who came by asked me who the author was. The Pope of Trash? Nothing. *Pink Flamingos*? Nope. *Hairspray*? Hmmm, maybe. What hope can there be for Downtown, I asked myself, if the people here don't recognize John Waters any more?

Smith loved Waters' films. In his 1973 review of *Pink Flamingos*, he celebrated its 'gilded torrent of filth' that succeeded in confounding the critics, whom he branded 'pyorrheal piranhas'.[31] Such linguistic flourishes were characteristic of the way that Smith created his own, unique vocabulary to ornament his fantasies and skew the world to his peculiar angle. He plundered the imagery of marine life, as we've seen, making critics piranhas, turning avaricious landlords into lobsters, and giving 'crustaceousness' general connotations of superficiality and greed. 'Moldy', meanwhile, was something outmoded and unfashionable, cast aside by fickle consumerism. People were known as 'creatures', and his performers were 'superstars'. 'Exotic' was a superlative, the greatest compliment he could bestow.

The invention of worlds required the invention of words – or their reinvention. Yet some parts of Smith's lexicon weren't entirely his own, and in fact had their roots in the language of the pre-war gay world. 'Flaming' of *Flaming Creatures*, for instance, was another Smithian superlative. It meant the flouting of gender norms and resonated with previous, encoded uses of the word, where gay men referred to themselves as 'flaming faggots'. 'Normal', meanwhile, meant all those conventional, non-artistic people Smith had no interest in; his group of friends, by contrast, could have been drawn from the cast of Todd Browning's *Freaks* (1931), made up of drug addicts, scenesters, drag queens and sundry other sexual and social deviants. But the way he used the word was also consistent with gay New York, and his phrase 'pasty normal' in particular meant 'straight'. Chauncey writes that, in the 1920s and 1930s, 'queers referred to their counterparts as "normal men" (or "straight men") rather than as "heterosexuals" '.[32]

Normal Love (1963–4), Smith's follow-up to *Flaming Creatures*, was in some ways a parody of heterosexual romance, or at least the hackneyed, commodified version of it that circulates in mainstream culture. In his journal for 17 November 1963, he writes: 'I spent my summer out in the country shooting a lovely, pasty, pink and green color movie that is going to be the definitive pasty expression. All the characters wear pink evening gowns and smirk and stare into the camera.'[33] Yet Smith's approach to 'pasty normal' love could hardly be called a straightforward satire, and is, unsurprisingly, full of ambivalence and contradiction. Working in glorious reds, luscious greens and pastel pinks that tint and colour each scene, Smith pays homage to the Technicolor heterosexist Hollywood imagery of his youth, while also undermining it, remixing it and populating it with the freakish 'creatures' of Downtown New York.

Like the previous film, *Normal Love*'s visuals confound attempts to put them into words. Of Josef von Sternberg, the Austrian filmmaker famous for directing Marlene Dietrich in *The Blue Angel* (1930), Smith once wrote: 'His expression is of the erotic realm – the neurotic gothic deviated sex-colored world and it was a turning inside out of himself and magnificent. You had to use your eyes to know this tho.'[34] This seems like an excellent description of Smith, too, especially on the evidence of this film, which requires you to 'use your eyes'.

In one scene, a glamorous mermaid festooned with

pearls (Mario Montez) bathes in a lagoon of crimson flowers. She reverently lights the candles of a Maria Montez shrine, then plays suggestively with bright, cherry-red beads. Here, the colour red is everywhere – warm, passionate, amorous. In another scene, greens dominate, suggesting nature and luscious vitality, as we find the mermaid outside, languishing in a freshwater pond surrounded by glossy green water lilies. The next time we come upon her, she's washed up at the edge of a swamp, covered in dirt, with mud smeared across her face and chest. She swoons and is revived by drinking a Coke, which is sloshed all over her face. The scene is sticky and sickly – black filth filmed in a jaundice-yellow hue. Then, she is inside once again, dressed in an ivory swimming cap, bathing in a milky-white pool that perhaps signifies an innocence regained.

The mermaid is the main character in *Normal Love*, along with other recurring figures drawn from Hollywood genre flicks like the Mummy (Tony Conrad), the Werewolf (Eliot Cukor), the Pink Faery (John Vaccaro) and the Cobra Woman (Beverly Grant). But here, as in *Flaming Creatures*, the characters aren't that significant and the story is even less so. Far more important are the film's visuals, and how they transmit more on the level of sensory experience than plot or narrative. The effect of the film is a hallucination in vibrant, often overlapping tones; in Smith's words, 'something like the logic of dreams is deployed rather than the rigidly anecdotal chronology which is all that is known in film at present'.[35]

In his production of the film, Smith dispensed with the norms of chronological progress, and aimed for something more sensory and impressionistic – the movement from one scene to another is governed not by the logic of cause and effect, but instead by mood and tone. When he screened the movie, he would double down on this through what he called his practice of 'Live Film': 'some of the work goes on through the screening itself. . . I am experimenting with various records as the film is projected and making other small corrections'.[36] Because Smith's movie never had a set form, he was free to change scenes around according to his whim, splice them with others, cut out parts, paste in others, give the whole thing a new soundtrack . . . The permutations were almost endless.

In its openness, which seemed to channel the fluidity of sexuality through its very form, *Normal Love* is a riposte to the clichéd, cookie-cutter imagery of straight romance. It was also Smith's desperate attempt to make a work of art that would never be definitively finished and could, as a result, never become a saleable commodity.

He should have known, however, that, in New York, everything has a price.

In one of *Normal Love*'s most joyful and mesmerizing scenes, a dozen people dance, scantily clad, on an enormous pink cake. The scene was filmed in an orchard in Connecticut, on land that Smith's painter friend Wynn Chamberlain had rented for the summer. The cake was constructed by the sculptor Claes Oldenburg, another of Smith's friends.

In an amateurish riff on those tightly choreographed scenes from musicals of the 1930s, Smith's superstars run through some half-remembered dance sequence atop the battered cake. Busby Berkeley would be spinning in his grave if he saw it, but they all seem to be having a nice time. Francis Francine presides over the affair, laughing to reveal even fewer teeth than before. Beat poet Diane di Prima wobbles her enormous,

'The definitive pasty expression.' Andy Warhol and others dance
on a pink cake in a scene from *Normal Love*.

heavily pregnant belly. Beside her, in sunglasses and a bright pink wig, Andy Warhol clicks his fingers to his own rhythm. He appears out of step with the group, uncomfortable amid the chaos of Smith's shoot.

Smith and Warhol were friends during the early 1960s. They hung out together, collaborated, and appeared in each other's films. Whenever a new documentary about Warhol comes out, Smith invariably surfaces in old footage of the Factory, dancing around too excitedly to the Velvet Underground or at the margins of actor Dennis Hopper's photographs of the place. Although he's striking – tall, looking like a gaunt Errol Flynn and sounding like a queer Kermit the Frog – no talking head ever remarks on his presence; he might as well be a ghost for all the importance these Warhol bio-hagiographies attribute to him.

Yet Smith was hugely important to Warhol. He showed Warhol what a camera could do and was instrumental in his shift from painting to filmmaking in the 1960s. The second film Warhol ever made was a newsreel of Smith shooting *Normal Love* in Connecticut in the summer of 1963, which gives us an idea of the dynamic of their relationship at the time (the 16mm film was lost after it was impounded by the police during one of the *Flaming Creatures* raids). Warhol once claimed that Smith was 'the only person I would ever try to copy'.[37] As his filmmaking career progressed, he did copy Smith, incorporating various ideas and practices that were first used by him: not rehearsing, not using any storylines, roping anyone who was around into the film, continuing to film after everyone got bored . . . Boredom and duration, the signature traits of Warhol's films, were hallmarks of Smith's work first.

Warhol's Factory was itself modelled on the 'Cinemaroc

Studios' at Smith's Ludlow Street apartment, and featured many of the same faces that Smith had discovered. 'Creatures' like Mario Montez, Joel Markman, Beverly Grant and Francis Francine all went uptown and became part of Warhol's group; appropriating Smith's term, Warhol referred to them as his 'superstars'. Montez in particular was a hit there. A Puerto Rican native once known as René Rivera, he was renamed by Smith after his idol and the two were devoted to each other for years. He was 'a creation of Jack Smith', according to Smith's friend the writer/director Ronald Tavel: 'Smith fed Mario his vision, his psychology, his dream . . . Mario took on Smith's vocabulary, his costumes, and his fantasy.'[38] He went on to star in a number of Warhol's films, notably *The Chelsea Girls* (1966) and a series of films in which he slowly peels a banana and eats it, called, imaginatively, *Mario Banana* (1964).

In the beginning, Smith and Warhol seemed to have bonded over their shared freakishness. American society in the 1960s had nothing but contempt for sissy fags like them, and establishment mouthpieces like the *New York Times* lamented the growing visibility (which was, of course, a *renewed* visibility) of their kind of queerness on the city's streets. 'Growth of Overt Homosexuality in City Provokes Wide Concern', declared the front page of the *Times* on 17 December 1963. The article that followed valiantly proposed to investigate 'the city's most sensitive open secret – the presence of what is probably the greatest homosexual population in the world and its increasing openness'.[39] The focus in this instance wasn't homosexuality so much as identifiable queerness, and the fact that 'homosexuals have tended to be more overt, less concerned with concealing their deviant conduct'.[40] For the city's psychiatrists, religious leaders and the police, it seems, the only thing worse than a homosexual was one who flaunted it. Things weren't much better in the New York art world, where homosexuality was tolerated but queeny gays like Warhol and Smith were ostracized. Warhol was shunned by the likes of Jasper Johns and Robert Rauschenberg (who were themselves gay but straight-acting) because he was 'too swish'; to others he was known as a 'weird cooley little faggot with his impossible wig'.[41]

Even the emergent gay movement tried to draw a line between *us* and *them* – between the respectable gays who sought acceptance and assimilation into a society they believed in and the other parts of queer society who drew the wrong kind of attention. By the mid 1950s the homophile agitators of the Mattachine Society had shed their early leftist leanings in the face of the Lavender Scare, and abandoned ideas of collective action, in favour of personal responsibility and accommodation to social norms. As one Mattachine chapter declared at the end of 1953: 'homosexuals are not seeking to overthrow or destroy any of society's existing institutions, laws, or mores, but to be assimilated as constructive, valuable, and responsible citizens'.[42] Smith and Warhol and their (shared) superstars – 'the dregs of the invert world', as the writer of the *New York Times* cover story would have called them – were evidently the wrong kind of queers for everyone.[43] So, in their shared stigma, for a while they found a sense of camaraderie.

Beneath this connection were glaring differences, however. Stylistically, they couldn't have been further apart. The bastard son of Maria Montez, Smith was all tawdry, babbling flamboyance, while Warhol was poised and cool, in interviews monosyllabic and smirking behind dark sunglasses. If Smith's vision was feverishly colourful, as *Normal Love* showed, then

Warhol's was the machine-like monochrome of his disinterested *Screen Tests* (1964–6). Holly Woodlawn, who was friendly with both and moved between the Factory and Cinemaroc scenes, saw other differences:

> The difference between Jack Smith and Andy Warhol? One word: talent. Jack had talent. Andy didn't have a clue as to what he was doing. Jack, I always thought had a plan; he was focused. Andy never knew what the fuck he was doing. He didn't even know how to run a movie camera.
>
> A soup can? Gimme a break. Thirty-two soup cans . . . Ugh. I wish I had one, I'd sell it and buy a house. But if I had an original Jack Smith, believe me, I'd keep it.[44]

Her uncharitable assessment of Warhol and Smith's artistic merits aside, Woodlawn's insight is useful because it upends the presumptions one might have about the pair. Looking at their work, which in Smith's case was always unfinished, it might seem like he was the one who didn't know 'what the fuck he was doing'; as Woodlawn points out, this wasn't the case.

Their greatest difference lay in their attitudes towards art and commerce, which would eventually cause the breakdown of their relationship. Warhol, who by the early 1960s had made a fortune working in advertising and commercial illustration, was the quintessential commercial artist, infatuated by the iconography of American consumer culture ('Thirty-two soup cans . . . Ugh') and an artist-for-hire who churned out tons of portraits for wealthy clients. Smith was his polar opposite, an anarchist who once said, 'I think Nazism is the end product of capitalism', and who believed in creating work

that couldn't be pressed into the service of the market.[45] As
the 1960s wore on, and Warhol became the biggest star of the
New York art world (and the art world shifted to accommodate
his kind of queerness), Smith grew to despise him. He was a
'crust' – greedy and superficial. Tavel remembered how Smith
'had an abiding hatred for Andy as the almost summation of
the capitalistic artist'.[46] For his part, Warhol started to leave
the Factory's freaks and queerdos behind, and by 1967 drew
his material almost exclusively from celebrity culture and the
glamorous worlds of New York's rich and famous.

Atlantis

In December 1969, Smith moved into a loft on the corner of
Greene and Grand streets. He named it the Plaster Foundation
of Atlantis, and would live there for the next couple of years,
until he was finally evicted for not paying the rent. Built over
two floors, the apartment was his home, his film set and his
theatre – life interwoven with art.

During his occupation, Smith made substantial mod-
ifications to the interior, including removing half of the
ceiling so that he could hang stage lights from the rafters.
He also put in a lagoon (made out of an inflatable paddling
pool), and heaped up an enormous pile of assorted rubbish
in the centre of the space. Saturday performances starting at
midnight (or sometime after) had names like *Lobster Sunset
Christmas Pageant*, *Wait for Me at the Bottom of the Pool*, *Economic
and Religious Spectacle of Jingola* and *Gas Stations of the Cross*.
According to one audience member: 'The Plaster Foundation's
play, which varied wildly from performance to performance,
involved, in a general sense, listening to music, waiting for the

performers to finish dressing up, and watching the slow burial and exhumation of artefacts from the set.'[47]

Like the mythological island that gave it its name, which the Greek gods destroyed with fire and earthquake, and sank to the bottom of the sea, the Plaster Foundation's plays were all about failure and destruction. Smith's performances were catastrophic: he'd come on stage maybe an hour late, seem to forget his lines, go offstage, re-emerge and start again. In a rare video from 1970 shot inside the loft, he stands on stage, reading lines from his script excruciatingly slowly. Each word is pronounced with superhuman hamminess, as he presses his fingers melodramatically to his brow: 'See. What. The. Future. Holds. In. The. Future. Of. Your. Dreams . . . '[48] He would apologize endlessly to the audience for being so inept, while berating the other performers for their apparent failures. None of them had rehearsed, most were reading their lines and some were audience members coerced into being part of the event on the night.

The plays themselves were disasters, at least according to any existing standard, lurching from drama, to violence, to deadpan clowning, carrying on endlessly until the early hours of the morning. For long periods, Smith would do nothing except contemplate his trash heap. Mekas, who seemed to bear Smith's attacks on him with good humour, attended a piece called *Withdrawal from Orchid Lagoon*, and reviewed it for the *Village Voice* newspaper in July 1970: 'I suddenly was very conscious that it was 2am in New York, and very late, and most of the city was sleeping,' he wrote. 'At 2am only Jack Smith was still alive, a madman, the high priest of the ironical burying grounds, administering the last services.'[49] The film historian Jim Hoberman was at the same performance, and later remembered: 'What seemed most memorable at the time was the piece's stunning conclusion. As the audience left the Plaster Foundation for the deserted streets outside, Smith turned up the volume of his record player so that one walked away with the sounds of "Orchid Lagoon" slowly fading into the night.'[50]

There's something magical and extraordinary about these accounts. Attending a performance at the Plaster Foundation seems to have been an ordeal, to be sure, but one that had a ritualistic, even spiritual quality to it. Reading the recollections of Mekas and Hoberman, I can't help but think of all the Catholic ceremonies I was dragged to when I was a child, which were at least as long and boring as Smith's performances – but not half as sexy. Smith's audience members, who were often also co-celebrants and co-creators, exited his loft bleary-eyed but reborn. From failure and disaster comes transformation – which is quite a religious idea, when you think about it.

By the summer of 1970, the streets into which Smith's audience emerged had witnessed other monumental changes, as the Stonewall riots of the previous year had grown into a nationwide (soon to be international) movement centred on New York. On 28 June, between 5,000 and 20,000 people marched through Manhattan on the one-year anniversary of Stonewall. According to a front-page report in the *New York Times*: 'Thousands of young men and women homosexuals from all over the Northeast marched from Greenwich Village to the Sheep Meadow in Central Park . . . proclaiming "the new gay strength and pride of the gay people." '[51] It was the largest public demonstration for homosexual rights that had ever taken place, with queers descending on Lower Manhattan from all over New York, and from places farther afield, like Washington, DC, Boston and Cleveland.

The Gay Liberation Front (GLF), an organization founded in the aftermath of Stonewall out of which the gay and lesbian movement grew, proclaimed it 'Liberation Day', and announced:

Liberation Day – 1970 is more than just the First Anniversary of the Stonewall Riots. It celebrates a year in which a new spirit has entered the struggle for homosexual freedom – a new spirit both militant in tone and revolutionary in orientation ... Gay Liberation is for the homosexual who stands up, and fights back. And, as in the words of Nietzsche, 'What doesn't destroy me makes me stronger.'[52]

While the existing homophile movement wanted little more than social acceptance, the GLF, inspired by contemporary movements like Black Power, demanded the radical overhaul of society. It was anti-colonialist, anti-capitalist and anti-war; it critiqued traditional gender roles and denounced the nuclear family. As the first issue of its newspaper *Come Out!* made clear, liberation was an opportunity to interrogate all of society's givens. 'Does society make a place for us ... as a man? A woman? A homosexual or lesbian? How does the family structure affect us? What is sex, and what does it mean? What is love?' asked its editors. 'As homosexuals, we are in a unique position to examine these questions from a fresh point of view. You'd better believe we are going to do so – that we are going to transform the society at large through the open realization of our own consciousness.'[53]

This kind of idealism was everywhere in the early gay and lesbian movement. Out of the GLF came other radical groups, such as the Third World Gay Revolution, which addressed itself to the 'triple oppressions' of capitalism, racism and sexism; the Street Transvestite Action Revolutionaries, founded by Sylvia Rivera and Marsha P. Johnson, whose focus was homeless trans people of colour; and Radicalesbians, a lesbian feminist group that grew out of the Women's Caucus of GLF-NY.

These and other liberationist factions that emerged after 1969 applied themselves to the utopian idea of a radically transformed society. Smith desired this transformation as much as they did; although he wasn't a card-carrying activist, his art agitated for him, critiquing the social conditions his audiences were living under and attempting to shift their perceptions of normality – to turn them on, he might say, to 'moldiness' and trash. 'What doesn't exist is important,' Smith once wrote: like the GLF and its associated groups, and like his idol Maria Montez, he dreamed, he imagined, he fantasized – beyond the limits of a homophobic present and the constraints of so-called reality.[54] Of Smith's fantastical art, queer theorist José Esteban Muñoz writes: 'Queer fantasy is linked to utopian longing, and together the two can become contributing conditions of possibility for political transformation.'[55]

Unfortunately, by the mid 1970s, gay liberation's radical ambitions had turned into much more modest liberal and reformist ones. Conservative backlash and the increasing political power of the Christian right stymied radical change in America, and the movement became less committed to a revolutionary utopianism that would alter society as a whole, and more interested in achieving minority rights. A booming lesbian and gay economy, including queer commercial establishments, literature, media and film, which ostensibly challenged dominant heterosexist models, also reinforced this shift towards the notion of a homosexual minority that by then had become a distinct consumer group.

In many (but certainly not all) instances, the initial anti-capitalist fervour of gay liberation gave way to a bourgeois consumerism. Smith didn't waver in his radical commitments, but under these new conditions there were even fewer places for him and his work. When he was asked what he thought about the gay movement in 1978, he was irritated by the adoption of a minority politics and the removal of sexuality from a broader discussion of social change. 'They just want to talk about gay things. They're trying to cut it off from being in any context,' he said.

This turn also had ramifications for the kind of work that was being produced – and supported. According to Smith: 'I took my program to a gay theatre, and [the manager] couldn't understand how it was gay, because he was unable to see it in a context. If it wasn't discussing exactly how many inches was my first lollipop, well then it wouldn't be anything they were interested in.'[56] Gay culture wanted confessional, coming-out-style stories that shored up an emergent gay self, not fantastical queer contradictions hewn from trash. As the 1970s turned into the 1980s, Smith became more and more marginal, even in the Downtown scene around him. Lollipops were in, lobsters were out.

Basra

Sometimes I wonder if anyone actually lives in Manhattan. I look around at these iconic buildings – the Lower East Side tenements as much as the multistorey skyscrapers – and I feel like I might as well be in Disneyland looking at Cinderella

Castle. How much square footage do you think there is inside an image? Of course, it's now so expensive and rent controls have become so relaxed that in fact fewer and fewer people do live here – year round, I mean. There's no end of Airbnbs and pieds-à-terre for the globalized, jet-set crowd.

My friend Lynne Tillman does live here. Or rather, she did, before the pandemic hit and she moved from her tiny apartment on the edge of Greenwich Village to a small wooden house upstate. She's a writer, a native New Yorker and a sometime teenage acquaintance of the Factory set who lived in Downtown since 1978. The last time we hung out was a few years ago, at a café on the intersection of First Avenue and 10th Street. She inscribed a copy of her new book for me while I ordered us some fizzy water. The bottle was too warm when the waiter delivered it, so we sent it back; it was replaced, to our amusement, with one that was all ice. The third bottle was, of course, just right. I think I am condemned to imagine this city forever in terms of fairy tales and fantasies.

From the mid 1970s until his death from AIDS-related complications on 18 September 1989, Smith lived in a Lower East Side apartment at 21 First Avenue, a few minutes' walk south of the café where Lynne and I met. There isn't much to see there now; it's a nondescript building, except for the empty shell of an old tattoo place at street level that had to close sometime after the pandemic hit. Tragically, it seems to have been the oldest tattoo parlour in Manhattan, which survived for years underground when tattooing was illegal in the city, only to be killed off by the fallout from Covid-19. I would have asked them to give me a tattoo to mark the occasion of my visit. Smith garlanded with ostrich feathers perhaps, or even better, a portrait of Maria Montez: something permanent I could take away from this inconstant island.

As a result of his obscurity, friends say that in his later years Smith became more bitter and paranoid – but he was certainly no less creative. In this small, sixth-floor tenement flat, as in his loft on Greene Street, real and fantastical spaces were indistinguishable. The entirety of his living space was turned into Basra, a Middle Eastern-themed movie set for his last great, unfinished masterpiece, *Sinbad in the Rented World*.

In a short documentary film, *Jack Smith's Apartment* (1990), made less than a year after Smith's death, the artist and director M. M. Serra moves inquisitively through the densely packed space. Doorways have been turned into grand arches with a Moorish twist. Fake grapevines grow out of kitchen cupboards. Geometric designs in blue and gold adorn the walls. In the bathroom, a jungle of plastic palm trees, bushes and vines resembles a Tahitian garden; in the bedroom, there's a mural of Scheherazade with three breasts, one of which protrudes from the wall in a pointed cone. Smith's final residence became legendary. Chris Kraus, art critic and author of *I Love Dick* (1997), called it 'the Sistine chapel of the underground', while performance artist Penny Arcade described it as 'a room that by its very construction would expand your consciousness and make you weep'.[57]

Arcade was Smith's friend and confidante during his final years, and when he died she became the self-appointed custodian of his legacy. He didn't leave a will, so there was the very real danger that all of his art and personal artefacts would simply be tossed – much of it returning to the dumpsters of Lower Manhattan whence it came. After all, this was the era of queer trash, where the lives of gay and bisexual men were synonymous with waste. It had always been the case in the eyes of a homophobic Republican administration, but in this period became literally, *materially* so on the streets of New York. The writer and AIDS activist Sarah Schulman remembered seeing a huge hoard of *Playbill* in the rubbish outside an apartment building, and knowing instinctively that a gay man had died of AIDS there. Without Arcade's efforts, Smith's stuff would have ended up in landfill like the belongings of thousands of New York's AIDS victims in the 1980s and 1990s.

For eighteen months after his death, she tried to keep the apartment as a Jack Smith museum. No cultural institution cared enough about him to help preserve the space, so in the end she boxed everything up and took it to her building, where it stayed for years. With Jim Hoberman, she incorporated the Plaster Foundation (named in honour of Smith's Greene Street loft), and both worked tirelessly and voluntarily to secure Smith's reputation and place his archive at a museum that the public could access. In 1997, P.S.1 Contemporary Art Center launched a major retrospective called *Jack Smith: Flaming Creature*, exhibiting material taken in large part from the stuff that Arcade had salvaged. For the art critic Cynthia Carr, the show 'changed Smith's image from cult figure to visionary, and no doubt enhanced the value of his work'.[58]

By that point, Arcade and Hoberman hadn't heard from Smith's family in years. His sister had come by his apartment after his memorial service, and left with some bearer bonds, a small box of jewellery and a table; the table was, she said, 'the only thing of beauty that he had'. The rest was garbage. It would be more than a decade before she would contact Arcade again. In 2002, after she was alerted to the possible value of her brother's work, she wrote demanding her cut. According to a deposition she later filed in court, she had spoken to Smith only a handful of times since 1956. She said her husband 'did not approve of Jack's homosexual lifestyle and did not want [their] sons to be tainted by it'.[59]

A long court case ensued, with Arcade and Hoberman claiming Smith's possessions had been abandoned, and refusing to relinquish control unless they were guaranteed the archive would end up at a museum. In January 2004, after a six-minute hearing, ownership was handed over to Smith's sister and the whole lot was eventually sold to the Gladstone Gallery in New York for an undisclosed amount. Barbara Gladstone, the owner of the gallery, remembered: 'When we had the closing, and I was sitting at a table with something like seven lawyers, I thought: Jack should see this.'[60] One of the pieces she acquired was a colour photograph of Smith, lying down, blue glitter smeared around his eyes, with a thought bubble drawn on the wall above his head. It reads: 'How can a queer escape the mocking laughter of wealthy normals if they visit his very rejection-sewer home to get art?'

The most recent exhibition of Smith's work was a couple of blocks from his Greene Street loft in a New York gallery called Artists Space. I visited it on one of the show's final days – this was around the same time as my cinema trip to Metrograph. Escaping the assault of the mid-morning sun, I entered the cool, industrial chic of the gallery, where I was greeted by Smith's voice. By the doorway, a recording of one of his monologues played:

I have to live in squalor [chewing noises] all day long playing hide and seek with odors. I want to be uncommercial film personified. That's the . . . oh wait . . . *have to live in squalor all day long playing hide and seek with odors . . .* No kidding folks. They love dead queers here.[61]

Smith artefacts and ephemera relating to his performance work filled the interior of the gallery. Along with production shots and scripts in vitrines were some rare treasures, like the crab prop used in many of his works, an entire lobster costume and Yolanda La Penguina – the stuffed-toy co-star of his final performances.

Sweat cooling on my skin, a series of conflicting thoughts and feelings followed me around as I wandered through the exhibition. I was excited and grateful, of course, for the opportunity to see the imprint of Smith's loose hand; to examine up close his garish costumes and props; to bear witness to a phenomenal creativity that refused to be constrained by his poverty, his destitution. Yet how dead and lifeless it all was! All the static documentation of his ever-changing performances and Live Film events that had taken place, many before I was born. An untouchable record sitting now in perpetuity behind frames and vitrines. Smith might have said they were 'vaults'.

Catching a snippet of Smith again as I left the gallery, I remembered hearing his voice on a tape that Tony Conrad made in 1964. Smith and Mario Montez are sitting around in the Ludlow Street flat, chatting, performing, laughing. 'This is life!' Montez giggles. 'It isn't life!' Smith shouts in his distinctive high-pitched drawl. 'It's being recorded!'[62]

I wonder about my recording of Smith's life in these pages. How, in my attempt to preserve it, I've poured it like concrete into a narrative, complete with a beginning, middle and end. Trying to preserve Smith's legacy, and turn people on to ideas of 'moldiness' and trash, I've also packaged him within this book and turned him into a commodity. In order to preserve a thing in amber, we first have to subtract it from its context – the community and constituent relations that gave it life – such that what we're left with may be a greatly distorted version of what once was. In this regard, I can sympathize with Jonas Mekas, whose crusade to protect underground films like *Flaming Creatures* in some cases ended up alienating them from a place and time, warping their original intention.

Were he alive, I've no doubt Smith would call me an art crust. But perhaps he might also recognize something in my efforts to recycle – to retrieve and reclaim his life and work, which were treated like garbage for so long by his family, the American government and the New York art world. To contemplate this heap of trash. See how gaudy and impressive it is!

Kevin Killian with his collection of autographed head-shots, San Francisco, January 1988. Photo by Robert Giard. Copyright Estate of Robert Giard.

7

Niche: Kevin Killian's San Francisco

Through the window of the BART train, heading west into San Francisco, I watch the wide, empty spaces of Oakland inch by, slow as oil tankers. Outside, an enormous concrete monotony fills the view as far as the eye can see; all eerily unpopulated, save a couple of articulated lorries churning laboriously across it, turning in wide parabolas. Otherwise: emptiness, and the occasional cross-hatching of roads. Like something painted by Agnes Martin if she'd been very, very bored.

Then, all in a rush come the shanty towns of the homeless, by the side of the road, in the shelter of the freeways, underneath the overpasses. Pitched in temporary structures: sagging green tents, huts assembled from pallets, blue tarpaulin yoked to fences, rusty Toyotas, lean-tos encircled with trash . . . On this train of the future past, an automated marvel of the 1970s but by now a beleaguered relic, we zoom forward but can't shake them off. Out of the window, still more of America's homeless. The entire scene is bathed in an unreal golden light that turns everything hazy and pink – a ready-made Instagram filter for a photograph nobody will like.

The homeless of the Bay Area are remarkable for their sheer number. Shuffling by in half-shoes with dirty brown sleeping bags thrown over their shoulders. Pissing in the gap between train carriages. Panhandling, punctuating street corners. More than any other place I've visited, homelessness in San Francisco is ever-present and insistent: it mutters in your ear or to some ghost you can't see; it blasts a tinny pop tune on a bashed-up radio; it trails the deep rectal stink of the ever-unwashed. Yet the city's residents appear oblivious to it. Somehow they can breeze through the hordes huddled around subway stations, and ignore them completely as they pass on into Whole Foods, or Starbucks, or the Apple store. Some kind of adaptive tic allows them to leap over the chasm of inequality, to observe the multitudes of destitute and immiserated without registering them. *How else do you move through the spaces of San Francisco?* they might say.

The problem of homelessness preoccupied me in previous trips, but it's hitting me especially hard this time. I can't be sure of the exact cause, but the writing of this book seems to be at the heart of it. The homeless in San Francisco illustrate the precariousness of our connections to spaces; they are the living, breathing proof of how essential a home is to a *life*. All of the figures in this book had homes where they could live and work; even those who were peripatetic, like James Baldwin, or threatened with eviction at one time or another, like Jack Smith, had somewhere they could go where they could feel safe. Any time I see a homeless person, I can't help but think of them as some unknown queer genius who could revolutionize art or literature or film – if only they had a roof over their head. A recent statistic found that 20 to 40 per cent of homeless youth in America identify as LGBTQ+. How very different queer culture would be if those young people had a home and somewhere they could work and create.

My brooding on homelessness also has something to do with the reason I'm here: to visit my friend Kevin Killian's final resting place in a cemetery outside San Francisco. I've asked myself the same question for the past few days. What kind of world gives the dead more property rights than the living? As if in response to the sepulchral turn of my thought, the train plunges suddenly downward, howling and shrieking, racing beneath the waters of the bay.

The dead of San Francisco have in fact taken over a whole town. Colma, a couple of miles south of the city, has the distinction of being the only place that's ever been incorporated as a necropolis – literally a city of the dead. Almost 75 per cent of the town's 2.2 square miles consists of graveyards, where more than 1.5 million dead are interred. Kevin is now among them, and that's where I'm headed.

The origins of Colma lie in early twentieth-century disputes over the proper use of land in San Francisco. (*Plus ça change . . .*) By the late 1800s, the population of the city had risen rapidly and the cemeteries that filled its western quadrant were deemed a waste of increasingly valuable space. New burials were outlawed in 1901, and in 1914 all existing cemeteries were closed, with orders for the dead to be removed. The remains of more than a hundred thousand people were dug up and relocated, along with their grave markers; for decades, railcars hurtled down the same railway line that I'm now on, laden with precious cargoes of dirt and decomposition destined for Colma's new cemeteries.

Who was it that told me Kevin had died? Maybe it was my friend Sophie, or Eric, or Daniel who delivered the news; I forget now. That time's a bit of a blur. Looking through my emails, I find one from Dennis Cooper dated 17 June 2019 that says: 'It's bewildering and violently awful and very hard to get my head around.' But Kevin died on 15 June. What was I doing in the time in between? Spending a lot of time online, I suppose, grieving his loss with the rest of his fans and friends.

Kevin was a quiet giant of contemporary queer culture. The prodigious author of two dozen books, including novels, memoirs, plays and collections of poetry, he was also a biographer and editor who spent the greater part of his sixty-six years promoting underrated queer writers and artists, especially ones who were in danger of being forgotten. The biography of Jack Spicer he co-wrote put that most underground of gay poets back on the map – as did his co-edited collection of Spicer's poetry, which won the American Book Award in 2009.

He is perhaps best known as one of the original members of New Narrative, a queer writing movement that started in San Francisco in the 1970s. Its influence quickly spread south and east across North America, gathering fans and affiliates in the cutting-edge literary cultures of Los Angeles and Downtown New York. Kathy Acker was an early adherent, as was the novelist and AIDS activist Sarah Schulman. Chris Kraus's sensationally candid, self-reflexive *I Love Dick* was shaped by her association with the New Narrativists, whose work she described to me as 'erudite but colloquial, a very intimate but at the same time showman-like kind of writing that charms you but reaches deep inside your head'. Kraus also told me that Kevin and his Bay Area friends 'never exactly intended to become a genre or school, but you see their influence everywhere',[1] and writers like Sheila Heti, Maggie Nelson and Michelle Tea all claim a connection to New Narrative. It may be the most important queer literary movement of the twentieth century, so why haven't you heard of it? As we'll see, it was an avant-garde born into a time of crisis; on the cusp of widespread recognition, it was condemned to obscurity by death and disease. AIDS claimed its writers and devastated its readership, but Kevin lived to tell the tale – for a time, at least.

I remember logging into Twitter as soon as I heard about his death, bleary-eyed, still shocked and disbelieving. Kevin and I had emailed only the previous week. Or was it two weeks before? Anyway, he didn't mention anything about his treatment then and seemed his usual breezy, flirtatious self. 'I have more news about my upcoming photo books!' he wrote. 'I am going to make your body as famous as your mind, baby, if you let me.' The year before, I'd stripped off for his project called *Tagged*, where he took amateurish photographs of various artists and writers posing nude except for a Raymond Pettibon drawing of a cock and balls strapped over their loins. Somehow he'd convinced a gallery to put on an exhibition of his photos and a book of the show was in the works. Not now, of course. I thought, rather inappropriately: perhaps my body just wasn't meant to be as famous as my mind.

Kevin was sick, I knew that, but I deluded myself into thinking he'd pull through. The guy had survived the AIDS crisis. And a heart attack. And a previous bout of cancer. He was always so dynamic and vivacious, and had so much energy to give to his work and the work of others, even while holding down a day job as a secretary for a janitorial firm in San Francisco.

Reading the many tweets about him that flooded my timeline that morning, the truth finally started to sink in, and it was devastating. I'm normally cynical about public mourning on social media, but in that moment I needed to be part of it. To say: *Yes, he helped me too. Yes, I also felt his kindness. Yes, I lament his loss, which is unfathomable.* But I couldn't find the words.

Instead, I posted a comment I'd found online by Jarett Kobek, the author of *I Hate the Internet* (2016), who'd given Kevin a cameo in his bestselling novel. He described Kevin as 'a man who looks like a late period Caesar wandering through San Francisco, taking pictures of people while being the nicest and most helpful person you can imagine and occasionally saying something very, very disquieting'.[2]

I think Kevin would have liked being so much on our Twitter timelines and Facebook feeds that day and for days after. Social media seemed designed for his particular skills: a born networker, he'd post photographs of himself on Instagram with every writer or artist he liked who came to town. In these pictures, he would stand beside them, smiling and goofy, as if he was the fan and they were the icon, and not the other way around, and when he posted a snap of you, you felt enfolded into something much larger than yourself. His Instagram's disappeared now.

As tributes poured in from his famous friends and protégés in the following weeks, Kevin's true impact and the extent of his renown came into focus. Michelle Tea called him 'a giant sweetheart and incredible writer who was so open and loving to all us little writers and queerdos'.[3] Eileen Myles remembered his voice, which was 'explosively bright and gay and what you'd call an Irish tenor'.[4] Robert Glück, the founder of New Narrative and Kevin's former mentor, said: 'I used to say Kevin was the only person I ever knew who possibly could have come from a different planet – an enigma who possessed superhuman knowledge, baffling productivity, and later, superhuman kindness.'[5]

Before he wrote to me, Kevin wrote about me, on Amazon, in his review of a book that included one of my essays. It was a good book and a middling essay, but Kevin was kind. In any case, I thought it was an honour to receive an Amazon review by Kevin Killian and to know I was caught up in one of his writing projects. While recovering from a heart attack, he'd started composing meandering, poetic, invariably offbeat reviews of products on Amazon. All sorts of objects, not just books:

- men's briefs – 'Top scientists collaborated on the design for this product in two teams, meeting daily for three weeks'
- Disney's *Frozen* – 'I felt pretty heroic after watching *Frozen* and look forward to at least 14 other sequels – fingers crossed!'
- pink-coloured push pins – 'You'll see a soothing, almost angelic pink on their tips, as friendly as a dog's tongue licking your face'
- Brillo pads – 'We argued for several hours why Andy Warhol was so inspired by the Brillo Pad'[6]

In the end, he'd written 2,639 reviews and made it into Amazon's Reviewer Hall of Fame. Later, he'd publish three volumes of his selected reviews; in her introduction to the third volume, Dia Felix wrote that they are 'wise and have the perfume of the afterlife'.[7]

More than any figure in this book, Kevin is associated with the spaces of the internet. He was more attentive than most to the ways that the web, with its forums and chatrooms, apps and social media, would come to dominate our lives, on- and offline, and how queer people and communities especially would feel its ambivalent effects. How the internet gave those in homophobic backwaters somewhere to express their queer desires, while also circumscribing an arena of ceaseless self-objectification and self-commodification. How it created spaces where queer people could find solidarity and sympathy, while simultaneously ramping up the alienation of the individual under late capitalism. How it encouraged people to 'live their truth', while so much of what it was peddling was a pack of lies.

Although Kevin remembered being slack-jawed with amazement when his pal Acker informed him sometime in the 1990s that she often spent four hours a day online ('we couldn't believe her. What a devotion to the machine! Nobody could spend that much time online!'), he caught on pretty quickly that the internet was here to stay, and we would spend ever more time in its uncanny digital spaces.[8] Like it or not, the future of queer culture would be bound to its fate – so he decided to bind himself to it too. If he was a 'late period Caesar', as Kobek had said, then the online realms of the likes of Amazon and Instagram were his empire, and we were all his far-flung subjects.

Nonetheless, the physical spaces in which he lived and worked were once just as important to him. For most of his forty-year career, material worlds were the material of his writing; his fiction and poetry drew deep from the territories through which he moved; the ground beneath his feet grounded his queer politics. In short, Kevin was attuned to the vast range of possibilities afforded by certain spaces.

Chief among these was San Francisco, that great Emerald City by the Bay, where he relocated in 1980. Almost as soon as he arrived, however, the city was devastated by a combination of AIDS, earthquakes and rapid gentrification – all of which made it increasingly difficult over the years to hold onto those physical places that had held such significance for him.

When they started to disappear, his efforts turned more and more towards the internet. There, even hyper-commercialized, consumer spaces could be repurposed – hacked, in a gently subversive way – for art-making and community-building.

Loveland

I think about Kevin coming to San Francisco in 1980, wide-eyed and elated, his hair tousled by a light breeze blowing in from the sea. Stepping off a plane that had just touched down from somewhere in the east, like Mary Ann Singleton, the heroine of Armistead Maupin's *Tales of the City*. Long before I'd ever glimpsed the rainbow-coloured crosswalks of the Castro, Maupin introduced me – and so many others – to San Francisco's queer and transgender cultures through his bestselling series of novels published from the late 1970s. Kevin was also a fan and, as we'll see later, his last novel, *Spreadeagle*, is a kind of homage to what Maupin called his 'story without an ending'.[9]

In the first *Tales of the City* book, Mary Ann is a sweet, naïve twenty-five-year-old from Ohio who's never done any drugs and is sexually pretty repressed. She comes to San Francisco on vacation and of course decides to stay. Calling her alarmed mother back home in Cleveland, she excitedly tells her, 'You wouldn't believe it! The people here are so friendly.'[10] The city is gradually revealed to us through Mary Ann's eyes, as she begins her new life in this warm, relaxed and unambiguously queer place. As Michael Tolliver, Maupin's famous gay protagonist, announces: 'In *this* town . . . The Love That Dares Not Speak Its Name almost never shuts up.'[11]

Tales of the City offered a vibrant snapshot of the city's spaces and scenes to readers far beyond the Bay Area. I first read about San Francisco's gay ways in my parents' house on the other side of the world. Sitting in an overstuffed leather armchair in a bungalow on the outskirts of a grey Irish village, it felt as if I'd been teleported into the city's sun-drenched streets. All the sights and sounds and smells of the place in the 1970s were there for the taking: waving hello to the cute guys and girls on the corner; stopping by Café Flore for an espresso; sauntering up and down Market Street like Judy Garland singing, 'San Francisco, here is your wanderin' one, / Saying I'll wander no more'.

Maupin's city was a sexually liberated paradise that lent itself easily to my decadent dreams. There you could find the 'megasexual' Stud bar on Folsom Street, described in the books as a great place to pick up men – and women.[12] A few blocks north on the corner of 8th and Howard streets were the Club Baths, a 'discreet, dispassionate, noncommittal' venue with an orgy room where one might 'diddle away a frenzied hour or two'.[13] (In Maupin's version, there was also a chill-out room complete with a microwave – can you imagine anything more off-putting, sex-wise, than the smell of food being warmed in a microwave?) Farther north on 6th Street was the EndUp, where many nights ended up, hot young men in skimpy underwear dancing till sunrise (or so I imagined) to the disco beats of 'Cherchez La Femme'.

Such real-life spaces were an important part of Maupin's attempt to capture the feel of the 1970s and 1980s, and you could say the physical space of San Francisco is as much a character as any of the people portrayed in *Tales of the City*. But a fictional house on a fictional street also captured the imagination of Maupin's readers.

Number 28 Barbary Lane seemed to exemplify Maupin's

vision of the city. Located in Russian Hill, a part of the city so steep they had to cut the road into the side of the slope in wild zigzags, the house is 'a well-weathered, three-story structure made of brown shingles'. When Mary Ann sees it for the first time, it makes her think of 'an old bear with bits of foliage caught in its fur' and it becomes her home shortly after she arrives.[14] Presided over by the kind, motherly landlady, Anna Madrigal, who has a penchant for smoking cannabis and quoting Tennyson, the house develops over time into a sanctuary for its small group of inhabitants.

Gay, straight, bisexual, transgender – these occasionally flawed but generally good-natured characters are all given shelter on Barbary Lane. For many queer people – indeed, as we've seen, for many of the figures in this book – home and family are extremely fraught ideas. No wonder Maupin's story resonated so deeply. With its promise of unconditional acceptance and the way it evoked feelings of a perfect home (not to mention its excellent views), for many of Maupin's queer readers 28 Barbary Lane *is* San Francisco.

It's hard to believe that Kevin was ever as naïve as Maupin's Mary Ann, however; by the time he arrived on the west coast, he'd already had plenty of adventures, sexual and otherwise. He was always such an inquisitive boy.

Born on Christmas Eve in 1952, he was raised in Long Island, New York – a peninsula that extends from the northeast coast of the United States like a sentence, underlined by Fire Island and with Montauk a full stop at its tip. With characteristic flamboyance, Kevin described the place as 'a jewelled bracelet flung out into the sea from Manhattan'.[15] His home was Smithtown, his family middle class. From his surname you could guess he was of Irish immigrant stock, but that only really dawned on me when I met him in person. I'd seen his kind of broad Irish face looking back at me so many times before, shaded by the tweed caps of taciturn farmers standing by the side of country roads; between us, lines of slow-moving, shit-smeared cattle sashaying past for ever.

Kevin recalls his time growing up in Smithtown in his poetic memoir *Bedrooms Have Windows*. In the book, which was first published in 1989, the space of memory and the physical space of Long Island are conflated, brought together in the fictionalized form of a place he calls 'Loveland'. As the title of the opening chapter, it stands like a road sign in front of the rest of the book.

Loveland
Population: one gay teenager, infatuated with a much older man.

Out hitchhiking at the age of fourteen, Kevin gets picked up by a thirty-five-year-old guy named Carey, who whips out a map and asks him where he wants to go. It's an important moment, considering how central place and its representation would turn out to be in Kevin's work. He writes: 'The names of the roads on the map blurred before my eyes like sudden tears. "Show me where it is," he said once or twice, all the while playing with my prick. That's how I fell in love.'[16] He and Carey would stay together for six years until just before his twenty-first birthday.

The stories of many queer men include these kinds of early sexual liaisons with much older guys. If, in the late nineteenth century, John Addington Symonds might have regarded such encounters as incipient forms of Greek love, today we're more inclined to read them for signs of exploitation and abuse. Yet Kevin isn't interested in casting himself as the victim of a predatory adult. There's certainly blame here – as the striking image of 'sudden tears' hints at – but his memoir is first and foremost an attempt to survey the landscape of his adolescence and figure out his warped love for a married man, who also had a son his age.

'I really liked being desired,' Kevin says, and he offers us a vivid, impressionistic portrait of his feelings at the time, filtered through the territory of Loveland.[17]

> In Loveland, only a few colors stain the crystal radiance of the skies, gray, pink, white, black; someone holds you for a few minutes, then lets you fall to the rocks, and nothing hurts, and you're never betrayed. All your allegiances are holy. All the phones are tapped . . . Once you've made your way there, you never, never grow old. First he frightened me, then he made me come, then he amused me, then he left me, then he made me recall him.[18]

Here, radiant ecstasy mixes with plunging terror, trust rubs up against duplicity, and youth mingles with maturity. In these mesmerizing lines, Kevin-as-narrator takes the measure of his formative relationship with Carey, and admits to all its contradictions and his conflicted feelings about it. If *Bedrooms Have Windows* is a map, this passage is its key.

Small Press Traffic

Soon after he arrived in San Francisco, Kevin was out wandering around the Noe Valley area of the city, half a dozen blocks or so south of the Castro district, where most of the queer action was taking place. Turning a corner onto 24th Street, he saw a shop that looked out of step with the middle-class vibe of the neighbourhood and decided to take a closer look. His encounter with this tiny independent bookstore – and the encounters he had in it – would change everything. 'For years it was the centre of my life,' he remembered. 'I came nearly every day.'[19]

The shop had an unusual name: Small Press Traffic. Intrigued, he made his way up the short flight of steps, pushed past the piles of free newspapers and stuck his head in the door. It was a relaxed, unassuming kind of place, occupying the front of an unremarkable Victorian-style home. Sun poured in through the big bay windows and fell in slanted light across the rows of books that packed the space. All over the two high-ceilinged rooms, divided by sliding doors that never closed, were trays, racks, shelves, full to overflowing with limited-edition volumes and chapbooks made by people who put poetry before profit.

Kevin didn't recognize many of the titles, even though he was a big reader. 'So this was the "small press" . . . I'd never heard that phrase before and at first it struck me as precious. Not in a good way. I had the typical American view that large was the ideal and small was just a poor man's substitute for that.'[20] Very quickly, however, he discovered that where it comes to presses and communities, small can be precious *in a good way*.

Small Press Traffic was more than a bookstore – or maybe I should say that it was a bookstore at a time when that meant more than it does now. Not simply a purveyor of literature, it was also a social hub, a place to hang out with friends and meet like-minded people; somewhere to cruise cute, smart readers or bang out poems on the old-fashioned manual type-writer by the door. You didn't even have to buy a cup of coffee for the privilege. When Kevin arrived, it was also the base of operations for a free creative-writing workshop run by the gay author Robert Glück.

Kevin dropped into the workshop sometime in 1981 and, instantly, he was hooked. Every week from then on, he said, Glück's workshop had him 'racing up the hill from my pad on Guerrero past the ICA just to come to Noe Valley, to come to this quiet little bookstore'. In the small sunny room in the back, Glück and his collaborator Bruce Boone delivered glad tidings of what Kevin remembered as 'a new type of storytelling, in which poetry, theory, gossip, and porn would be intermixed in order to accommodate, *to treat* the big issues of the day'.[21] Here, along with a small group of mostly queer writers, Kevin was trained in the subtle arts of New Narrative writing.

To understand what New Narrative is, we have to go back to the beginning – to gay liberation and the friendship between Boone and Glück. Both were writers and gay activists, who met each other at the San Francisco Art Institute in the early 1970s when they were looking for a house. Boone was thirty and Glück was twenty-three or twenty-four, so these were two relatively young gay men who had lived through and been part of gay liberation. They'd been on the marches down Market Street and screamed themselves hoarse at rallies with the rest of San Francisco's radical queers.

In 1969, the influential gay liberationist Carl Wittman had written that San Francisco was a gay ghetto. 'More beautiful and larger and more diverse than most ghettos' maybe, but still a ghetto.[22] Gays living there were subject to police control and violence, and routine exploitation by greedy capitalists who had no interest in gay civil rights. Every day, queer people paid taxes to a government that pursued their oppression. It was time to fight back, and the battleground was the ghetto itself.

Wittman's idea was to turn San Francisco into a 'free territory' by focusing the efforts of gay people on the community itself. 'We must govern ourselves, set up our own institutions, defend ourselves, and use our energies to improve our lives,' he wrote. Practically, this meant creating spaces and an infrastructure that would support the community: 'political action offices, food cooperatives, a free school, unalienating bars and after hours places – they must be developed if we are to have even the shadow of a free territory'.[23] In time, the need for such a strictly defined gay space might not be so pressing, but until then, a community rooted in a gay-owned and -operated free territory was the best chance they had to fight oppression.

Boone and Glück wanted to be part of it. They wanted their writing to build the community up, draw it together and give voice to its most pressing issues. But some effort was called for to bring literature into line with their ideas, and old ways of writing embedded in oppressive, heterosexist thinking just wouldn't do. Radical ideas required radical new forms of writing, and new kinds of readers.

Like the queer social and political life it drew upon, this new literature needed first of all to be explicitly rooted in place. The streets and landmarks of San Francisco and its gay hangouts were a big part of this, but just as important were the authors' relationships with their friends, family, even enemies. In other words, the whole network of relationships that gave a place significance. As Boone showed with his short story 'My Walk with Bob', it all had to be part of the fabric of the writing.

Published in 1979, Boone's piece is an autobiographical story about an afternoon spent walking around with Glück in the area near Mission Dolores, an eighteenth-century basilica and the oldest structure in San Francisco. From the opening sentences, his tale is anchored in a concrete sense of place.

> I had picked up Bob from Denise's and we were heading on down to Market Street where we intended to do some shopping and have some pastry. As we passed Mission Dolores I explained to Bob that all through the time at the Perramont Hotel I was disinclined to visit the Mission because of the 25c entry fee. I thought it was an extravagance to spend money on beauty when you were poor. And as I was soon to discover the church was really beautiful.[24]

Noting details about the areas he and Bob move through, the narrator goes out of his way to guide the reader along and, when the two companions drop into the church to have a look around, he almost beckons us to follow. Objects he sees, like statues or monstrances, prompt reflections on youth and life as a gay man that wouldn't be out of place in a novel by Proust. (Imagine the narrator of *Swann's Way* owning up to his latent homosexuality and then subjecting it to gentle scrutiny and you get some idea of the tone of Boone's story.) However long or complicated these digressions, readers are never left in any doubt about where they are or who they're with. Character, narrator, reader – all are given a very firm footing.

But Boone and Glück's new queer literature needed

to do more than trace pre-existing connections to places or between friends; it also had to forge new connections. They figured that if their writing could encourage readers to relate to other queer people they'd never met (such as the narrator), they might feel like they were part of a queer community. The more readers came to think of themselves as part of an *imagined* queer community, the more they'd feel invested in the *actually existing* queer community: they might be more inclined to help their neighbours, or take part in community politics. Imagined connections could strengthen and help to create real ones.

To generate these connections, the reader had to feel involved in the narrator's story. Not in a Choose-Your-Own-Adventure kind of way (although years later, in 2019, Carmen Maria Machado would use that to great effect in her queer memoir *In the Dream House*). Rather, by recounting details a gay reader might be familiar with and drawing them in with salacious asides, the narrator could make the reader feel implicated – *included* – in the tale.

So when you're reading Boone's story, for instance, you can't help but think of yourself as his confidant. He tells you about his childhood, his dreams, his failures – his sex life. During a particularly promiscuous period, he remembers: 'There was sex at the bathhouses and sex at the public parks. There was sex on deserted beaches. There was sex in the azalea bushes along the dividers of expressways. Sex in groups, sex with a chosen other, sex by oneself. Sex in thought, word, and deed – to use the formula I remember nuns using.'[25]

Later, when he dishes about his recent break-up with a lanky harpsichord player named Jonathan, he begins: 'Ah dear reader! I'm afraid I must come to the question of Jonathan at last. How am I going to get along now, who's going to take care of me?'[26] Questions like this make him seem so vulnerable. Soon, not only do you care about the narrator, you feel a vague desire *to take care* of him – maybe in the way that he writes about.

Ultimately, this new queer writing was all about using language to weave connections: to a place (San Francisco's Bay Area) and between people (real or imagined). All in the service of queer community politics. In the late 1970s, Boone and Glück thought about calling it something. 'How about New Narrative?' Boone suggested as a joke.[27] It seemed a bit much to treat their experiments as a movement along the lines of, say, cubism, or surrealism, or the French New Novel, for that matter, which had been all the rage in previous years. There were only two of them, and they hadn't published much by that point. But if these two gay Americans understood one thing, it was the power of branding, so they stuck with the name. After a while, New Narrative did start to look like a movement, albeit a small one, local to San Francisco.

This was the writing that so excited Kevin when he turned up at the Small Press Traffic workshops. He immediately felt, he said, 'at the cutting edge of something entirely new' and his work flourished under Glück's supervision – and with Boone's help outside class.[28] Kevin's book *Shy*, which came out in 1989, the same year as *Bedrooms Have Windows*, wears their influence on its sleeve – as well as reflecting his love for all things kitsch and camp.

Shy plays with the form of the memoir, although it's certainly more of a novel than the other book. The narrator is one Kevin Killian, a writer with 'an amiable freckled face' who drinks too much and reflects that his name is 'so Irish that often, contemplating it and myself, I think of Yeats: *all is changed, changed utterly, a terrible beauty is born*: Kevin Killian'.[29] If you hadn't guessed, he's also a bit melodramatic.

Kevin narrates his queer reworking of the paperback thriller from the comfort of his home in San Francisco. In a tone that could pass for a drag king doing Humphrey Bogart, he says: 'I was twenty-five, and this was not San Francisco, now my home, but Long Island. The year was 1974, summer.'[30] No matter how wild the story gets (and it does get wild), Kevin regularly steps aside from the action to remind us that he's still there, narrating it all in the present from his apartment in the Spanish Mission District. It's like reading a version of Boone's story written by his excitable, flamboyant younger brother.

In *Shy*, characters with hardboiled names like Harry Van and Gunther Fielder roam the beaches of Long Island's North Shore, falling into murder mysteries and double-identity plots. Gunther is a straight, well-heeled New Yorker, hiding out under an assumed identity for reasons that are shrouded in secrecy. Harry is a gay, sexually adventurous teen with a penchant for BDSM and, in one of the story's many nods to Charles Dickens, also an orphan. Paula Theale, Harry's friend and love rival, is a fourteen-year-old, hard-drinking, chain-smoking vamp. At the centre of it all is Kevin, failing to write about it. 'Am I being entirely too Raymond Chandler about the whole she-bang?' one character asks, and it might as well be Kevin himself inquiring of his reader.[31] Not that he waits around for an answer; this sexually transgressive take on *The Big Sleep* just won't wait. All of which is to say it's a gas.

Boone and Glück's impact on Kevin's writing was huge and the emphasis on place in the novel – how the story's situated, and how it spins out and keeps returning to the narrator's apartment in San Francisco – reveals his debt to them. Under their guidance he would perfect the style that you might call Killianian. (Killianesque? Killianese?) Imagine a stream of campy chattiness going on and on, and then its surface is suddenly disturbed by something terrible – a traumatic memory or a terrifying episode bobbing up from the black depths like a bloated dead body.

As I realized when I went looking for it in 2017, Small Press Traffic bookstore has long since disappeared. It was October – still T-shirt weather in California – and I'd come to San Francisco for a conference on New Narrative. There was an anxious, excited energy about the whole thing; all the participants and attendees seemed to guess it might be the last hurrah. Many of the writers involved were getting on, but I suppose nobody could've predicted that Kevin would be the first to go.

Accommodation in the city was way too expensive, so I ended up renting a room in Oakland from a guy named Dragon. We never met, but Dragon's tastes preceded him. Red velvet drapes lined the walls of the room, which also contained a four-poster bed. A large dressing table that doubled as an altar held a marble bust and was covered in melted candles. Paintings of demonic women receiving oral sex from shaven-headed submissives were prominently displayed. While I was there I had the craziest dreams, and in my review I gave the place five stars.

Wildfires had engulfed northern California at the time, sending clouds of acrid smoke south to cover Berkeley and the campus of the university in a thick, suffocating haze. I fled out across the bay in front of it, taking the BART train to the heart of the city and getting off at the 24th Street and Mission station. Checking the directions on my phone, I traipsed the few blocks west on the shady side of the street to 3841-B 24th Street, the old address of Small Press Traffic.

Once the headquarters of New Narrative and the hub of a vibrant poetry scene, the building had reverted back to a private residence – a very middle-class one, by the look of it. I'd like to say that as I was standing in front of the house, bathed in the sepia glow of longing for a queer past, I felt over-whelmed by joy or sorrow. But the place was a blank to me. I wasn't disappointed, as I was in Forster's room, or frustrated, as I was when I found that nothing remained of Baldwin's house. I felt . . . nothing.

As I stood there reflecting on the flatness of my feelings, I listened to a short piece Kevin had recorded about his mem-ories of the bookstore. His voice was fey and comforting, and he seemed to acknowledge the powerful draw of the place to someone like me – a recently arrived queer in a strange city, interested in the history of the place and eager for a connec-tion to it. But he also seemed to insist that it wasn't worthwhile to linger too long, here in the remains of the past. 'I wish that all of you who are listening to this will find your own world just like the one I was once privileged to share,' he said. 'Some place you'll run to even if it's way up hill, because it will be your everything.'[32]

Minna Street

If the back room of Small Press Traffic was essential to New Narrative's beginnings, the relationships Kevin formed when he was there would endure long after the place closed its doors. His connections with writers like Steve Abbott, Sam D'Allesandro, Camille Roy and Dodie Bellamy were invaluable to this young queer writer who had recently arrived in San Francisco.

The group would quickly become a close-knit community that supported and challenged each other as writers, socialized together, wrote about each other and, yes, occasionally fucked each other too. This was San Francisco in the early 1980s, after all. 'We all formed a gang,' Dodie says, 'frequenting the same parties and readings, hung out at the Café Flore. Not for us the simple coming out and falling in love sagas of identity politics.'[33] The funny thing is, she did fall in love – and with Kevin, of all people.

Dodie came to San Francisco in October 1978. Born into a working-class family from Hammond, Indiana, she fell into a lesbian relationship at the age of eleven with the girl next door and they stayed together for the next fifteen years. When they finally broke up, she followed some of her gay friends to San Francisco. In 1981, she found out about the workshops that Glück was giving at Small Press Traffic and dropped into the session on Monday night. Like Kevin, she was hooked right away. Something about the combination of exciting, politically radical writing and the sense of close community kept her coming back week after week.

You couldn't say it was love at first sight between her and Kevin. He was a nice guy and she enjoyed his company as much as anyone else in the group, but she thought he was a drunk and a bit of a clown. He was also gay – *very* gay. She says: 'If you imagine a continuum from straight to gay, Kevin's sexuality was practically off the queer end of the chart.'[34] For his part, Kevin was impressed by her but he never seriously thought anything would happen between them. In his words, he 'was not the type of gay boy to have sex with a lot of women'.[35]

But something special started to grow between these two unlikely lovers and after a while they decided just to go with it. Reflecting years later on their initial attempts at love-making, Dodie writes:

> To test the waters we started making out and sleeping in the same bed. Sometimes our lovemaking felt like lesbian sex, sometimes like gay sex, but it never felt like straight sex. For one thing, with Kevin, fucking was an option, not an expectation. For another, the power dynamics were always shifting and circling back on themselves. With straight guys I felt like I was alone in the dark, being acted upon. With Kevin, it felt like we were two people in mutual need and at equal risk.[36]

They got married at San Francisco City Hall in 1986. It was an open relationship but hardly a marriage of convenience like the ones between gay men and women in previous eras. Dodie was ambiguously queer. Kevin was steadfastly homosexual – but his love for Dodie seemed to transcend everything. 'It's scary to want somebody so much,' he confessed.[37] In 2000, Dodie wrote: 'I haven't slept with anyone else for years, because I haven't felt the need to. Kevin satisfies me sexually and emotionally. Whenever he makes love to me, it's an act of adoration.'[38]

As a student of Boone and Glück, Dodie naturally chatted about Kevin in her writing, divulging intimate details about him and their relationship to her reader. He appears most explicitly as 'KK' in her experimental memoir-cum-novel *The Letters of Mina Harker*, which begins on the day of their wedding: 'He said I was standing in his kitchen one day and his

Kevin Killian and Dodie Bellamy, San Francisco, 1989.
Photo by Robert Giard. Copyright Estate of Robert Giard.

heart slid open like elevator doors. He let me in and after that nothing else mattered.'[39]

Published in stages throughout the 1980s and 1990s before finally appearing in its entirety in 1998, Dodie's book has since become a cult classic. In it, she riffs on the vampire genre in much the same way as Kevin had riffed on the detective genre in *Shy* – namely by queering it. Taking *Dracula* as the basis for her story, Dodie narrates the book as Mina Harker, from Bram Stoker's original. In this version, though, Mina is no longer the victim who needs saving from the evil count; instead, she's streetwise, seductive and sexually voracious. Dodie's deliciously bawdy and self-reflexive work moves between all the categories of literature and sexuality that you could ascribe to it: it's lowbrow and highbrow; fiction and autobiography; homo and hetero. Essentially, it's very hard to pin down but very easy to love.

A few years after they got married, Kevin and Dodie moved into an apartment on Minna Street in the South of Market district of San Francisco. Named after Minna Rae Simpson, a nineteenth-century child prostitute, the street – which, in reality, is little more than a filthy alleyway – has long been associated with squalor and sexual misadventure. What better place for these two queer radicals to settle down. The apartment would become their home for almost three decades.

It was also their office, their art gallery, their classroom. Over the years, it would achieve mythic status among Kevin and Dodie's fans and friends. Novelist and critic Andrew Durbin recalls how 'their apartment entertained screenings, readings, workshops, and tea with visitor after visitor, who crowded in among the art and books of friends and admirers'.[40] The writer

Megan Milks was astounded by the clutter in the apartment when they came by to profile Dodie for an article, finding the place 'stuffed to the gills . . . All surfaces in creative use.'[41]

The hallway, living room and toilet were all full of books: row upon row of them, some stacked two deep, many piles reaching above head height almost to the ceiling. Between the bookshelves and the ceiling were endless artworks: acrylics, watercolours, pencil sketches, photographs – many of them depicting Kevin and Dodie in their apartment, sitting on a couch that was covered in files and printouts. On the walls: art by Etel Adnan, Elijah Burgher, Joe Brainard, G. B. Jones, Raymond Pettibon, Seth Price, Brett Reichman . . . In their shared office, Kaucyila Brooke's photos of Kathy Acker's dresses (Acker was close friends with Dodie especially), and a framed photo of Kevin with Dennis Cooper. After almost thirty years of occupation, Kevin and Dodie's Minna Street apartment was full to overflowing; the sheer excess of art and ideas was breathtaking.

Over that time, from this third-floor, rent-controlled, walk-up apartment, Kevin and Dodie watched the city around them change beyond all recognition. It had been shaken by earthquakes and reshaped by relentless gentrification, but it was the AIDS crisis more than any other event that had the most tragic impact upon the San Francisco they knew and loved. Reflecting on the plague years and the catastrophic loss of life they caused, Kevin said: 'At first there was no way to predict how terrible AIDS was going to be.'[42] As a large gay ghetto, San Francisco was one of the epicentres of the disease, and the gay community that called the city home was hit especially hard.

As early as June 1981, small stories had started to appear in the media describing a sharp rise in the number of gay and bisexual men getting ill from a series of mysterious illnesses. Otherwise healthy, they were being struck down in their prime by rare forms of pneumonia and cancers that usually affected only the elderly and the very young. Yet the city's newspapers had little to say about the growing health crisis.

Outraged by their silence, Bobbi Campbell, a registered nurse and one of the Sisters of Perpetual Indulgence (a radical drag troupe that lampooned religious bigotry while dressed up in nuns' habits), took it upon himself to warn the public about this new disease. He made a now-iconic poster detailing the symptoms of what was being called 'gay cancer' and displayed it prominently in the window of the Star Pharmacy on the corner of Castro and 18th streets; the poster included polaroid photos of his Kaposi's sarcoma lesions – livid purple-brown splotches that covered his chest, his feet and the inside of his mouth. From December 1981, you'd see groups of gay men on the corner, all gathered around the window of the store, straining to read Campbell's handwritten warning – and straining to understand where this disease had come from or when a cure for it might be found.

It's likely that AIDS arrived in the Bay Area around 1976. By 1979, around 10 per cent of gay and bisexual men in San Francisco were infected. At the end of 1981, when people started to become aware of the problem, approximately 20 per cent were infected. In late 1986, when HIV testing finally became available, almost 50 per cent were identified as HIV-positive. 'At that moment, and for years afterward, it was roughly the same as a death sentence,' Kevin remembered. 'That's, like, *every other guy you saw* as you walked down the street.'[43]

There were far fewer guys walking around the Castro at that stage anyhow, and when Mayor Dianne Feinstein shut down the bathhouses in October 1984, it spelled disaster for social life in the gaybourhood. But the closure of the bathhouses did little to stem the rates of HIV infection, and the action came too late to save the lives of the thousands of San Franciscans who would die as a result. By May 1987, when President Reagan finally broke his silence on the subject, and delivered his first speech about AIDS (where he managed, remarkably, not to mention homosexuality even once), 36,058 Americans had been diagnosed with the disease and 20,849 had died. These were the darkest days of the epidemic.

Years later, standing on a podium at the University of Maine in 2012 as he delivered a speech at the National Poetry Foundation's annual conference, Kevin recalled this period and the countless memorial services for friends who died of AIDS. It was the small details that seemed to stand out in the fullness of time: the music, for instance. 'For some reason,' he mused, 'even Jewish people who didn't have Christmas, they chose "River" by Joni Mitchell. That was the song that was played at the most AIDS funerals I attended in San Francisco in the 1980s.'[44] In a quiet falsetto, as if to himself, he sang the first few lines of the song – Christmas coming and wishing he had a river so he could skate away. I don't know how many times I've watched the video of this speech, but every time Kevin gets to the line about making his baby cry, I well up. My vision swims with sudden tears as I think of all the funerals where this line was sung or played, its melody moving out among the crowd, the bereaved, sitting in the pews with their grief.

If the terminal illnesses, infections and AIDS deaths hit San Francisco hard, it devastated the young New Narrative movement. Losing the handsome prodigy Sam D'Allesandro in 1988 and New Narrative's greatest champion and publicist

Steve Abbott in 1994 were both harsh blows to bear – as were the deaths of numerous other artists and writers New Narrative had supported and been inspired by: David Wojnarowicz, Joe Brainard, Hervé Guibert, Derek Jarman, Cookie Mueller, Essex Hemphill, Tim Dlugos . . . Looking back, Kevin and Dodie reflected how 'AIDS made community all the more important, while decimating ours in particular'.[45] This is why the name New Narrative is known to relatively few. Just as it was about to break through into the mainstream, AIDS drained away its emergent energies and deprived it of a number of its key players.

At the time, it was impossible to know how to respond to the crisis as a writer (Kevin confessed to me that he made lots of false starts, all of which seemed too weak and sentimental). But with his poetry collection *Argento Series*, which came out in 2001, it seemed that he'd finally found a way of talking about his friends' deaths and his own grief; from that point on, he kept coming back to the subject of AIDS and its long-term effects. *Spreadeagle*, published in 2012 and the last novel Kevin wrote before he died, is in many ways the culmination of all of these efforts.

The book follows two affluent members of San Francisco's gay cultural elite. Danny Isham is a successful gay novelist who is repeatedly mistaken for the city's other famous gay novelist, Armistead Maupin. Although he started out as a queer punk writer, whose sexy, transgressive stories were published only in handmade zines, Danny now writes popular, heartwarming novels about a middle-class interracial gay couple called Rick and Dick. He lives in a huge apartment in the wealthy Pacific Heights neighbourhood with his husband, Kit, an alumnus of ACT UP (AIDS Coalition To Unleash Power – an activist organization formed in 1987) who was involved in the group's more outrageous stunts back in the 1980s. Somehow Kit's managed to parlay this radical past into a career as a fundraiser for an AIDS charity that counts the likes of Bill and Hillary Clinton among its donors; he organizes benefit gigs and galas, glad-hands rich white people and jets off on misguided humanitarian missions to places like Cuba.

At the heart of the novel is, of course, San Francisco – 'a city landscape of improbable hills and misty, blue sunsets, and the strange sweet and sour smell that rises up from the ancient wharves'.[46] Its landmarks (gay and otherwise) permeate the minds of Kevin's characters as they move like Woolf's Clarissa Dalloway through the city – dropping into gay sex clubs like Eros on Market Street and bars like the Stud (relocated from Folsom to the corner of 9th and Harrison streets), or passing by the cable car terminal at Van Ness and noticing iconic local characters the Brown twins at the corner of Leavenworth.

Right in the middle of this is Minna Street and a third-floor apartment where a gay writer who once showed so much promise now lives in relative obscurity. It's not Kevin Killian's place this time; instead it's the apartment of Sam D'Allesandro, the gifted New Narrativist who passed away in 1988. Kevin's novel revives his old friend but only barely, and Sam is cursed to live through late-stage AIDS once again; in fiction as in life, he dies in pursuit of a cure. Half alive, haunting the streets of San Francisco, Sam is Banquo's ghost sent to plague the conscience of a city that has forgotten about him and the thousands of others who died as a result of AIDS.

Written over a period of twenty years, *Spreadeagle* is Kevin's masterpiece. Eileen Myles called it the best book of the twenty-first century so far, describing it as 'a quintessentially California novel' – and one of the book's greatest achievements is the way it considers place and queer culture together, and casts a satirical eye over the gentrification of both in San Francisco.[47]

When we think about gentrification, we usually think about physical space and geography. The revitalization of run-down urban spaces prompts an influx of the middle classes, who then displace diverse low-income communities that used to live there. The condos and galleries spring up; the family-run shops and community centres shut down. Since the dot-com boom of the 1990s, San Francisco has experienced the worst excesses of gentrification, which has intensified in recent years. Locals now refer to an 'epidemic of eviction' in the city, which followed the arrival of multi-billion-dollar tech behemoths and soaring inequality in neighbourhoods like the Mission. Kevin watched it all unfold from a front-row seat. 'With the newest tech boom of Facebook, Twitter, and so on,' he said, 'the city began a program of gentrification as severe as London's, where nobody but a millionaire could possibly afford to buy a house here.'[48]

What kind of queer culture can persist in such a city? Kevin's novel confronts this question head on and it's remarkable for the way it connects the creeping conservatism of San Francisco's queer culture and politics with the gentrification of the city's spaces. Following the lives of Danny and Kit from the AIDS crisis to the post-AIDS era, Kevin dramatizes what his friend Sarah Schulman would call the 'gentrification of the mind': Danny renounces Queercore and the margins of queer culture in favour of the mainstream and wealth; Kit gives up the direct action of ACT UP to work for a charity funded by the likes of Bill Clinton (whose heel-dragging on AIDS while he was in office is conveniently forgotten). In both cases, radical politics are traded in for cosy liberalism, activism is swapped for philanthropy, and the scuzzy Tenderloin is forsaken for afflu-ent Pacific Heights.

Spreadeagle is Kevin's final testament. In its vivid, satirical style, the book bears witness to his lifelong belief that where it comes to space, culture and politics, what affects one affects them all, and a hyper-gentrified place like San Francisco, which increasingly excludes difference and danger in favour of uni-formity, safety and *money*, produces queer culture and politics driven by the same ideals.

Colma

Daylight rattles down the train track towards us, and we come up for air somewhere in the region of Balboa Park. The sun shines weakly through the windows and thick layers of dust mute the joyful pastel tones of the buildings that crowd the tracks. In faded yellow, light terracotta and duck-egg blue, square-shaped modern houses are arrayed in long, neat rows that stretch off into the distance and line the verdant foothills of the San Bruno Mountain. But the houses seem to recoil from Colma, and as we near the station they're replaced by anonym-ous grey buildings and six-lane freeways. A huge multiplex looms up ahead and I wonder to myself who on earth could be its clientele, given the town has only 1,509 (live) residents. We arrive and I step through the train's sliding doors, and out of the station, tramping for twenty minutes or so in the autumn sun to the Cypress Lawn Memorial Park.

Cypress Lawn was an important place for Kevin, ever

since he learned that Jack Spicer had been buried there. Spicer was a visionary queer poet who, along with other radical queer poets like Robert Duncan and Robin Blaser, launched a full-scale poetry renaissance in the Bay Area in the 1940s and 1950s, before falling into alcoholism and passing away in obscurity in 1965. To Kevin, Spicer was like a god, and indeed he'd co-written a biography of him called *Poet Be Like God* in 1998. Over the years, Kevin made many attempts to find Spicer's final resting place, before a tip-off led him to the columbarium at Cypress Lawn and a niche in the wall bearing the poet's birth name: John Spicer. The discovery, Kevin said, satisfied 'a huge longing' in his heart: 'for a man like me there's no closure unless I go to the grave and fall down on it . . . and embrace spectral memory as a living thing in my arms'.[49]

For Spicer, poetry was magic. He was fascinated by age-old ideas of the poet as a mystic, a vessel the universe could speak through. Allen Ginsberg and the Beats had similar notions around the same time (and were much better known for them), but Spicer wasn't into the cult of personality that surrounded their work. For him, true poetry wasn't something an individual could claim credit for; ego wasn't important, and true art was a kind of séance that channelled the spirits of the past. Connection, continuity, inheritance: these were the keys to his life and work. 'Poems should echo and re-echo against each other. They should create resonances. They cannot live alone any more than we can,' he wrote. 'Things fit together. We knew that – it is the principle of magic. Two inconsequential things can combine together to become a consequence.'[50]

Spicer died alone in poverty, and was forgotten for many years. When Kevin found out that he'd been interred at Cypress

Lawn, he seemed to take it upon himself to use the place to rescue Spicer's legacy from oblivion. Channelling the poet's own ideas, he wanted to give Spicer's inconsequential life a consequence by having it resonate intimately with the lives of others. Over the years, he drove dozens of young queer poets out to his tomb on pilgrimages intended to shore up continuities between the new and the old, the living and the dead; to 'echo and re-echo against each other'. The columbarium became a shrine and a space of magic and ritual, where Kevin and his pilgrims wrote or recited poems, or performed ceremonies, or stripped naked in tribute to the 'shy, gifted, covertly-romantic, brilliant' Jack Spicer.[51]

Considering all of this, Cypress Lawn was the only possible place Kevin could be laid to rest, and a crowdfunding campaign after he died raised the funds for Dodie to purchase a niche in the columbarium, two rows beneath Spicer's one. I thought of my journey to Colma as a small, personal tribute to both Kevin and Spicer; while I didn't think I'd fall down on their graves as Kevin had, I'd at least pay homage to the radical queer tradition they represented in the last spaces they would ever occupy. I had no idea what I'd do when I got there. A ritual of some sort seemed appropriate, but what kind?

Behind a large artificial lake and a grassy slope bearing the name of 'Cypress Lawn' in topiary, the great white columbarium sits way back from the main road. I make my way up the drive, through the cemetery's ornate archway, and, as I approach it, the building's facade suggests something Roman to me, with all its towers and columns. A quick internet search reveals that it was in fact designed with the palace of the Roman emperor

Diocletian in mind: what better place for Kevin – a late-period Caesar of San Francisco – to be laid to rest.

Passing underneath the shadow of the entranceway, I mount the granite steps with a flutter in my stomach and give the huge iron door a push. It creaks satisfyingly, like the door of a tomb should. But the interior belies the horror-movie introduction. Inside, I don't find cobwebs or dusty coffins, and I'm not greeted by a giant funereal butler; instead, a warm green glow suffuses the space, softening the edges of everything around me – rays of the afternoon sun tinged by a beautiful stained-glass dome in the ceiling of the atrium. Above my head, botanical patterns in greens and reds, and lavish Tiffany flourishes line the passage to Kevin's niche – the columbarium is decorated with the kind of kitsch extravagance that he loved.

Moving past lush, overgrown ferns and turning into a small room off the main corridor, I soon reach section F where rows of niches line the walls. Brass plaques about a foot square reveal the names of their occupants; some have small bouquets of artificial flowers attached, others simply bear the phrase 'In Everlasting Remembrance'. The compact, geometric organization of human remains is oddly reassuring: at least here each name has a place. Spicer shares his niche with thirty others; Kevin's will be his alone – until he's joined by Dodie some day.

Standing in front of both niches – Spicer's at eye level, Kevin's directly below it at my knees – I remember the stories I heard about Kevin's trips to this place: the spells he cast with the help of others; the poems he recited; how he used the space as an incongruous backdrop for his *Tagged* project. I imagine him, snapping photographs of naked youths lying prostrate or posing suggestively in the Pettibon loincloth in front of Spicer's tomb; then I imagine their being discovered by a group of septuagenarians in search of a long-lost ancestor. Kevin was so charming, he'd laugh, and turn their disgust to delight.

I start to wonder about the true effects of all of Kevin's Cypress Lawn ceremonies, and it strikes me that while the pilgrimages and rituals he initiated were ostensibly about paying homage to the life of a great gay poet, they were just as much about the bonds forged between those who were on the journey with him. Kevin's ceremonies manifested *both* a spiritual connection to Spicer *and* a connection between the participants. I recall the reverence and sincerity with which the young, mostly queer poets and writers Kevin brought here talked about their experience – the intimacy they had with him, the memoirs they wrote about the event, how it was something they shared. These are the tangible, terrestrial effects of the whole mystical shebang. This place is so much more than a destination – it is a site, a setting, a stage where connection and community were forged, and would be again.

At heart, Kevin's story is a story about community and where it's situated. His life and work were dedicated to using spaces – online, offline, literary – to bring people together and cultivate a sense of belonging among them. *Among us*. This devotion to community-building distinguishes him from the other artists and writers we have encountered in this book, whose relationship to the spaces they occupied was more of a personal, individual matter.

I get the urge to pull off my sweatshirt and jeans, and stand naked in front of Kevin's niche, channelling a part of the irreverence of his rituals, but it doesn't seem quite right. As a lapsed Catholic, I know a lot about ritual, and one of the most important things is that it must have a beginning, a middle and an end. The impulsive act of stripping off just doesn't pass muster: what would I do once I was naked? How would it end?

All at once it dawns on me that a different ritual, a more meaningful one, has already been under way – and for quite a while. This book is that ritual.

The efforts I've made over many pages to connect the present with the past. The pilgrimages I've undertaken that have led me far from home in search of forgotten queer spaces. The fellow pilgrims I've met along the way – the quick and the dead, and those who would join us in the future (including you, dear reader). All of it is my tribute. This book is my offering to Kevin and Spicer and their tradition, *in their tradition* – driven by the same impulse to preserve the traces of forgotten places and people in writing; to use the space of writing to join people together and create a shared experience. To attest to the fact that we are not alone. I stretch up to reach Spicer's niche, letting my fingers linger, tracing the letters embossed in brass, then down to touch Kevin's. Things fit together . . . it is the principle of magic.

From one end of the twentieth century to the other, through cities and across oceans, you and I have pursued a new history of queer culture, one attuned to a sense of place. We have found it in the quiet stone cloisters of Cambridge and the smoky jazz clubs of Paris; on the beach at St Brelade's Bay, on the battlements of Saint-Paul-de-Vence; on the gay streets of New York and San Francisco too. We have seen, in poetry and prose, photography and performance, the distinctive ways that queer people have responded to the places around them – individually or communally, with resigned acceptance or antagonism, in similitude or sympathy. When I started out, a part of me was looking for proof that queerness has a place in this world. In Dungeness, in Paris, in this columbarium in San Francisco, in all the other locations described in this book, was all the proof I needed.

My thoughts finally turn to home. Rising, I give the room one last look, and head back to the illuminated atrium and out through the big iron door into the dazzling California sun.

Derek Jarman canonized, arrayed in gold, Dungeness, 1991,
by Howard Sooley.

Epilogue: Sanctuary

*As the Establishment always writes the history,
I wonder how I'll come out.*

— Derek Jarman[1]

The sky over Prospect Cottage is blue. The kind of blue we imagine when we imagine blue. The blue of imagination. The blue of the ocean. The blue of abstraction. As it curves towards the horizon, this blue takes on deeper shades of ultramarine and indigo, shot through with vermilion and dashes of purple. All around, a pandemonium of deep, vibrant colours touches down on the desolate terrain of Dungeness. The nuclear power station's silhouette squats in the background, loitering ominously. The cottage itself is cast in an irreal phosphorescent glow. It appears to be deserted.

I walk across the shimmering band of tarmac, onto the shingle at the garden's edge. The pebbles make no sound at all, even though I feel them crunch and shift beneath my feet. All I can hear is the sea, which is nowhere to be seen but seems very close by. Waves pound and fizz loudly in my ears, the sound of a memory that has found its way here via some obscure neural pathway.

A foghorn booms as I step closer to the front of the cottage. Bushy heads of cotton lavender congregate here and there, and stones have been arranged in bulbous circles and spirals of bluish grey. Flint the size of big potatoes stand upright and tumescent on the borders. As I watch them, they begin to throb obscenely. They like the attention. So, too, does the valerian, tipped with tiny explosions in magenta, that seems to grow ever more erect under my gaze. 'Valerian is a sexy plant for me.'[2] The shy poppies flush scarlet and turn their heads aside. Fennel sways on the breeze, in its own world, as if nobody's watching.

On the side of the house, emblazoned in bright pink neon, is a poem by John Donne. A version of 'The Sunne Rising', abbreviated but still in antique seventeenth-century English, it reads:

> Busie old foole, unruly Sunne,
> Why dost thou thus,
> Through windowes, and through curtaines call on us?
> Must to thy motions lovers' seasons run?
> Sawcy pedantique wretch, goe chide
> Late schoole boyes and sowre prentices,
> Goe tell Court-huntsmen, that the King will ride,
> Call countrey ants to harvest offices;
> Love, all alike, no season knowes, nor clyme,
> Nor houres, dayes, monthes, which are the rags of time.
> Thou sunne art halfe as happy as wee,
> In that the world's contracted thus.
> Thine age askes ease, and since thy duties bee
> To warme the world, that's done in warming us.
> Shine here to us, and thou art every where;
> This bed thy centre is, these walls, thy spheare.

The poem's two lovers are lying in bed together with the morning sun streaming through the curtains, ushering in a new day. But their love isn't subject to time – to the rising and setting of the sun, to the passing of hours or days or months that so circumscribes the lives of everyone else. In their timeless love, they don't obey the sun. It obeys them. Their bed and the walls of their home are the centre around which it moves. Time is immaterial and this place, their bed, is the centre of the universe. The neon letters buzz and blink in agreement.

Slowly the sound of waves dissembles into a dissonant chorus of voices. A threnody. 'In the roaring waters, I hear the voices of dead friends.'[3] I'm drawn towards the back of the house, skirting rusted iron hoops and cones and discs deposited seemingly at random on the ground. The deliberate formality of the front gives way to a riot in the rear. Colour, shape and texture are all intermingled. The resonant chime of a singing bowl sounds out, and suddenly I'm standing in front of a massive wooden pillar. Cracked and weather-beaten, it has a curious square hole cut out of the middle of it. I bend down slightly and peer through. A Prospect Cottage peep show.

The film starts up, the images running in reverse from the present into past. As indicated by the pronounced grain of 35mm, the blue of the sky has turned into the blue of Jarman's *Blue* (1993). International Yves Klein blue. The projector whirs audibly in the background as a narrator speaks:

Ages and eons quit the room, exploding into timelessness. No entrances or exits now. No need for obituaries or final judgements. We knew that time would end tomorrow, after sunrise.[4]

The blue is then the blue of a mischievous boy's protruding tongue. *Wittgenstein* (1993). He's sitting in the front row of a cinema wearing big 3D glasses – the old rectangular kind with one red lens and one green. Retracting his wet, stained tongue, he sticks a vivid blue ice pop in his mouth. A click, and the boy is now seated at a desk, behind a manual sewing machine. He turns the hand crank slowly anticlockwise, removing stitches from the folds of red velvet that tumbles generously about. The white-powdered heads of his elders surround him, babbling instructions. Their cacophony swells to a crescendo.

Then it's Jarman himself who is seated and surrounded – by a host of gay men dressed as nuns. It's September 1991, and the radical drag troupe the Sisters of Perpetual Indulgence have come to Dungeness in dark habits and trendy sunglasses to make him a saint.

> The process of being canonized by the Sisters involves being nominated by the Sisters ... We have a long discussion – a Nunquisition – where we ask questions about the people and look at what they've done over a number of years for the gay community and for the promulgation of universal joy. That was the process we used to canonize Derek Jarman, the filmmaker, who we called Saint Derek of Dungeness of the Order of Celluloid Knights.[5]

Jarman is laughing, looking radiant in a shiny golden robe. He opens his eyes and the Sisters remove their outstretched hands from his glittering costume.

Sparkling flashes of yellow, orange and red. Fairground lights gleam and oscillate, gaudy and exciting. They recede to reveal two young men stretched out on the shingle in daylight – 'haircut boys', from Jarman's *The Garden* (1990), 'with shaved necks, looking like seals'.[6] They kiss and fondle one another slowly and surreptitiously, hidden behind a fishing boat. Withdrawing their hands from each other's bare chests, their shirts re-buttoned, they're standing together on the beach. Pebbles launch themselves from the sea into their waiting palms.

Tilda Swinton as the Madonna, arrayed in green and gold, with an enormous dazzling crown upon her head, sits on the shingle, bouncing a screaming baby on her knee. Over her shoulder, striped in bands of black and white, is a Dungeness lighthouse. Her crimped hair defies gravity, whipping that way and this. 'Blue is the universal love in which man bathes,' her voiceover intones. 'It is the terrestrial paradise. Blue.'[7] A flare, held aloft by an outstretched arm, burns incandescent, and here she is again. In *The Last of England* (1987). In a torn wedding dress. In the amber light of a blazing bonfire, twirling manically, desperately, endlessly.

She spins faster. The film speeds up, faces whizzing past too quickly to make any of them out clearly. Then, just as abruptly, it slows, and two boys are lying together in a sun-dappled, daydream garden in Hampshire.

It was here that I brought him, sworn to secrecy, and then watched him slip out of his grey flannel suit and lie naked in the spring sunlight. Here our hands first touched; then I pulled down my trousers and lay beside him. Bliss that he turned and lay naked on his stomach, laughing as my hand ran down his back, and disappeared into the warm darkness between his thighs. He called it the 'lovely

feeling' and returned the next day, inviting me into his
bed that night.

Obsessive violets drawing the evening shadows to
themselves, our fingers touching in the purple.[8]

I step away from the viewing slot to discover that evening has descended on the Ness. 'When the light faded, I went
in search of myself.'[9] Shuffling around to the other side of
the wooden pillar, I peer again through the square hole, looking this time back towards the cottage. In the twilight, the
clumps of cotton lavender flowers gathered by the back door
are luminous, as are the window and door frames of the cottage, glowing yellow.

A lamp goes on inside the house. Suddenly I can hear the
sound of talking, laughing, glasses clinking. Someone puts on a
record. The blues. Through the windows I can make out a half-
dozen or so people moving around – 'a flummox of friends'.[10] I
recognize their faces but they're too far away to be certain. The
door opens, an explosion of light in the gloom, and a familiar
voice says: 'You're not going to stay out there all night are you?
Come and join us, baby.'

Rear view of Prospect Cottage, Dungeness, 1990, by Howard Sooley.

Notes

INTRODUCTION

1 John Ashbery, 'Self-Portrait in a Convex Mirror', *Poetry* (August 1974), p. 248.

2 Derek Jarman, *Modern Nature: The Journals of Derek Jarman, 1989–1990* (London: Vintage Classics, 2018), p. 10.

3 Ben Campkin and Laura Marshall, *LGBTQ+ Cultural Infrastructure in London: Night Venues, 2006–2017* (London: UCL Urban Laboratory, 2017), p. 6, https://ucl.ac.uk/urbanlab.

4 Ibid., pp. 43–4.

5 Ibid., p. 17.

6 Wendy Moffat, *A Great Unrecorded History: A New Life of E. M. Forster* (New York: Farrar, Straus and Giroux, 2010), p. 162.

7 Japonica Brown-Saracino, *How Places Make Us: Novel LBQ Identities in Four Small Cities* (Chicago: Chicago University Press, 2017), p. 8.

8 John Donne, 'The Good-Morrow', in *The Complete English Poems of John Donne*, ed. C. A. Patrides (London: Everyman's Library, 1985), p. 48.

9 Sam D'Allesandro, 'Nothing Ever Just Disappears', in *Writers Who Love Too Much: New Narrative Writing, 1977–1997*, ed. Dodie Bellamy and Kevin Killian (New York: Nightboat, 2017), p. 156.

10 Marc Augé, *Non-Places: Introduction to an Anthropology of Supermodernity*, trans. John Howe (London: Verso, 1995).

11 Jarman, *Modern Nature*, p. 20.

1. EGRESS:
E. M. FORSTER IN CAMBRIDGE

1 Aristotle, *The Physics*, trans. Philip H. Wicksteed and Francis M. Cornford (Cambridge, MA: Harvard University Press, 1963), p. 277, my italics.

2 Roger Ebert, '*Maurice* Movie Review', RogerEbert.com (9 October 1987), https://www.rogerebert.com/reviews/maurice-1987.

3 Lytton Strachey, 'Letter to E. M. Forster, 12 March 1915', in *E. M. Forster: The Critical Heritage*, ed. Philip Gardner (New York: Routledge, 1973), p. 430.

4 E. M. Forster, 'Terminal Note', in *Maurice* (London: Penguin Classics, 2005), p. 220.

5 Forster to George Barger, 27 July 1899, in *Selected Letters of E. M. Forster: Volume One 1879–1920*, ed. Mary Lago and P. N. Furbank (Cambridge, MA: Harvard University Press, 1985), p. 31.

6 Quoted in Peter Parker, *Ackerley: The Life of J. R. Ackerley* (New York: Farrar, Straus and Giroux, 1989), p. 338.

7 Unsigned review, 'A Chalice for Youth [*Times Literary Supplement*, 8 October 1971]', in *E. M. Forster: The Critical Heritage*, ed. Philip Gardner (New York: Routledge, 1973), p. 490.

8 Cynthia Ozick, 'Morgan and Maurice: A Fairy Tale', in *Art and Ardor: Essays* (New York: Knopf, 1983), p. 64.

9 E. M. Forster, 'The Other Side of the Hedge', in *The Machine Stops, The Celestial Omnibus, and Other Stories* (New York: FKM Books, 2013), p. 90.

10 Ibid., pp. 91–2.

11 Forster, 'Terminal Note', p. 224.

12 E. M. Forster, *Maurice* (London: Penguin Classics, 2005), p. 119.

13 Forster, 'Terminal Note', p. 219.

14 Edward Carpenter, *My Days and Dreams, Being Autobiographical Fragments* (London: George Allen & Unwin, 1916), p. 13.

15 Ibid., p. 65.

16 Forster, 'Terminal Note', p. 219.

17 Moffat, *A Great Unrecorded History*, p. 114.

18 Forster, 'Terminal Note', p. 224.

19 David Leavitt, 'Introduction', in Forster, *Maurice*, p. xxii.

20 Moffat, *A Great Unrecorded History*, p. 43.

21 H. Montgomery Hyde, *The Trials of Oscar Wilde* (New York: Dover, 1962), p. 201.

22 Oscar Wilde, *De Profundis* (London: Methuen & Co., 1905), p. 14.

23 Alan Sinfield, *The Wilde Century: Effeminacy, Oscar Wilde and the Queer Moment* (New York: Columbia University Press, 1994), p. 125.

24 Moffat, *A Great Unrecorded History*, p. 11.

25 Forster, *Maurice*, p. 42.

26 Charles Kingsley, 'Thoughts on Byron and Shelley', *Fraser's Magazine* 48 (November 1853), p. 571.

27 John Addington Symonds, *A Problem in Greek Ethics* (London: publisher unknown, 1901), p. 1.

28 Ibid., p. 8.

29 Ibid., p. 36.

30 Ibid., p. 64.

31 Forster, *Maurice*, p. 216.

32 Ibid., p. 218.

33 E. M. Forster, *The Longest Journey* (London: Penguin Classics, 2006), p. 4.

34 E. M. Forster, 'Albergo Empedocle', in *The Life to Come and Other Stories* (New York: W. W. Norton & Company, 1987), p. 22.

35 Ibid., p. 25.

36 Ibid., p. 19.

37 Ibid., p. 35.

38 Forster, *Maurice*, p. 224.

2. INVERT:
LONDON'S QUEER SUFFRAGETTES

1 Michel Foucault, 'Of Other Spaces', trans. Jay Miskowiec, *Diacritics* 16:1 (Spring 1986), p. 22.

2 English novelist Margaret Irwin, who described 'Gloomsbury' as a circle 'composed of a few squares where all the couples are triangles', is a more likely source. See Stuart N. Clarke, 'Squares Where All the Circles are Triangles', *Virginia Woolf Miscellany* 92 (Fall 2017/Winter 2018), p. 40.

3 Emily Hamer, *Britannia's Glory: A History of Twentieth-Century Lesbians* (London: Cassell, 1996), p. 22.

4 Sarah Waters, *Tipping the Velvet* (London: Virago, 2014), p. 14.

5 Ibid., p. 105.

6 Ibid., p. 194.

7 Deborah Cohler, *Citizen, Invert, Queer: Lesbianism and War in Early Twentieth-Century Britain* (Minneapolis: University of Minnesota Press, 2010), p. xiii.

8 Jeffrey Weeks, *Coming Out: The Emergence of LGBT Identities in Britain from the Nineteenth Century to the Present* (London: Quartet, 2016), p. 88.

9 E. Sylvia Pankhurst, *The Suffragette Movement: An Intimate Account of Persons and Ideals* (London: Longmans, Green & Co., 1931), p. 225.

10 Naomi Paxton, 'Actresses' Franchise League', in *Oxford Dictionary of National Biography* (online edition) (14 June 2018), https://www.oxforddnb.com/view/10.1093/odnb/9780198614128.001.0001/odnb-9780198614128-e-109648.

11 Diane Atkinson, *Rise Up, Women! The Remarkable Lives of the Suffragettes* (London: Bloomsbury, 2018), p. 145.

12 Katherine Roberts, *Pages from the Diary of a Militant Suffragette* (Letchworth and London: Garden City Press, 1910), p. 52.

13 Atkinson, *Rise Up, Women!*, p. 230.

14 E. Sylvia Pankhurst, *The Suffragette: The History of the Women's Militant Suffrage Movement, 1905–1910* (New York: Sturgis & Walton, 1911), p. 384.

15 Martha Vicinus, *Independent Women: Work and Community for Single Women, 1850–1920* (Oxford: Oxford University Press, 1985), pp. 264–5.

16 Cicely Hamilton, *A Pageant of Great Women* (London: Suffrage Shop, 1910), p. 27.

17 Ibid., p. 45.

18 Cicely Hamilton, *Life Errant* (London: J. M. Dent & Sons, 1935), p. 65.

19 Cicely Hamilton, 'Triumphant Woman', in *Edy: Recollections of Edith Craig*, ed. Eleanor Adlard (London: Frederick Muller, 1949), p. 41.

20 Virginia Woolf, *Between the Acts*, ed. Stella McNichol (London: Penguin Classics, 2019), p. 40.

21 Victoria Glendinning, *Vita: The Life of V. Sackville-West* (New York: Quill, 1983), p. 271.

22 Vita Sackville-West, 'Triptych', in *Edy*, ed. Adlard, p. 122.

23 Christopher St John, 'Close-Up', in *Edy*, ed. Adlard, p. 19.

24 Christopher St John, *Hungerheart: The Story of a Soul* (London: Methuen & Co., 1915), p. 219.

25 Ann Rachin, *Edy was a Lady* (Leicester: Matador, 2011), p. 159.

26 Quoted in Katharine Cockin, *Edith Craig (1869–1947): Dramatic Lives* (London: Cassell, 1998), p. 86.

27 Ibid., p. 82.

28 Cicely Hamilton and Christopher St John, 'How the Vote Was Won', in *The Methuen Drama Book of Suffrage Plays*, ed. Naomi Paxton (London: Bloomsbury, 2013), p. 7.

29 Ibid., p. 16.

30 Ibid., p. 27.

31 Pankhurst, *The Suffragette Movement*, p. 278.

32 Hamilton and St John, 'How the Vote Was Won', p. 26.

33 Florence Locke, 'An American Rehearses with Edy', in *Edy*, ed. Adlard, p. 97.

34 Irene Cooper Willis, 'The Squares', in *Edy*, ed. Adlard, p. 108.

35 Cockin, *Edith Craig*, p. 88.

36 Quoted in Hamilton, 'Triumphant Woman', p. 38.

37 Sackville-West, 'Triptych', p. 123.

38 St John, 'Close-Up', p. 32.

39 Ibid., p. 32.

40 Violet Pym, 'A Great Treat', in *Edy*, ed. Adlard, p. 112.

41 Sackville-West, 'Triptych', p. 119.

42 Quoted in Michael Baker, *Our Three Selves: The Life of Radclyffe Hall* (New York: Morrow, 1985), p. 271.

43 Havelock Ellis, *Studies in the Psychology of Sex: Volume II: Sexual Inversion* (Philadelphia: F. A. Davis Company, 1908), p. 164.

44 Michel de Certeau, *The Practice of Everyday Life*, trans. Steven Rendall (Berkeley, CA: University of California Press, 1988), p. 96.

45 Ibid., p. 117.

46 Ibid., p. 93.

3. EXCESS:
JOSEPHINE BAKER AND PARIS

1 Quoted in Phyllis Rose, *Jazz Cleopatra: Josephine Baker in Her Time* (London: Chatto & Windus, 1990), p. 105.

2 John Maxtone-Graham, *The Only Way to Cross* (New York: Collier Books, 1972), p. 281.

3 Josephine Baker and Marcel Sauvage, *Les Mémoires de Joséphine Baker* (Paris: Éditions Dilecta, 2006), p. 39.

4 Josephine Baker and Jo Bouillon, *Josephine*, trans. Mariana Fitzpatrick (New York: Harper & Row, 1977), p. 21.

5 Booth Marshall, quoted in Jean-Claude Baker and Chris Chase, *Josephine: The Hungry Heart* (New York: Cooper Square Press, 2001), p. 38.

6 Ibid., p. 39.

7 Ibid., p. 63.

8 Maude Russell, quoted in ibid., p. 64.

9 Lynn Haney, *Naked at the Feast: A Biography of Josephine Baker* (London: Robson Books, 1981), p. 197.

10 Baker and Bouillon, *Josephine*, p. 42.

11 Baker and Sauvage, *Les Mémoires de Joséphine Baker*, p. 56.

12 A. E. Hotchner, *Papa Hemingway: A Personal Memoir* (New York: Carroll & Graf, 1999), p. 53.

13 Gertrude Stein, *Paris France: Personal Recollections* (London: Peter Owen, 1971), p. 11.

14 Rose, *Jazz Cleopatra*, p. 75.

15 Langston Hughes, 'Jazz Band in a Parisian Cabaret', in *The Collected Poems of Langston Hughes*, ed. Arnold Rampersad and David Roessel (New York: Vintage, 1995), p. 60.

16 Foucault, 'Of Other Spaces', p. 24.

17 Petrine Archer-Straw, *Negrophilia: Avant-Garde Paris and Black Culture in the 1920s* (London: Thames & Hudson, 2000).

18 Pierre de Régnier, quoted in Baker and Sauvage, *Les Mémoires de Joséphine Baker*, p. 10.

19 Haney, *Naked at the Feast*, p. 60.

20 Rose, *Jazz Cleopatra*, p. 81.

21 Baker and Sauvage, *Les Mémoires de Joséphine Baker*, p. 62.

22 Quoted in Pierre Assouline, *Simenon: A Biography* (New York: Alfred A. Knopf, 1997), p. 74.

23 Quoted in Baker and Chase, *Josephine*, p. 6.

24 Janet Flanner, *Paris Was Yesterday: 1925–1939*, ed. Irving Drutman (New York: Penguin Books, 1979), p. xxi.

25 Rose, *Jazz Cleopatra*, p. 40.

26 Haney, *Naked at the Feast*, p. 114.

27 Rose, *Jazz Cleopatra*, p. 107.

28 Baker and Sauvage, *Les Mémoires de Joséphine Baker*, p. 63.

29 Baker and Bouillon, *Josephine*, p. 58.

30 Haney, *Naked at the Feast*, p. 72.

31 Baker and Bouillon, *Josephine*, p. 54.

32 Unnamed Austrian vaudeville actor, quoted in Haney, *Naked at the Feast*, p. 87.

33 Baker and Bouillon, *Josephine*, p. 56.

34 Sarah Gutsche-Miller, *Parisian Music-Hall Ballet, 1871–1913* (Rochester, NY: University of Rochester Press, 2015), p. 295.

35 Baker and Bouillon, *Josephine*, p. 63.

36 bell hooks, *Black Looks: Race and Representation* (London: Turnaround, 1992), p. 141.

37 Baker and Bouillon, *Josephine*, p. 56.

38 Haney, *Naked at the Feast*, p. 99.

39 Ibid., p. 67.

40 Judith Thurman, *Secrets of the Flesh: A Life of Colette* (London: Bloomsbury, 1999), p. 170.

41 Baker and Bouillon, *Josephine*, p. 72.

42 Suzanne Rodriguez, *Wild Heart, a Life: Natalie Clifford Barney's Journey from Victorian America to Belle Epoque Paris* (New York: Ecco, 2002), p. 130.

43 Sylvia Beach, *Shakespeare and Company* (New York: Harcourt Brace, 1959), pp. 114–15.

44 Radclyffe Hall, *The Well of Loneliness* (London: Virago, 1982), p. 246.

45 Diana Souhami, *The Trials of Radclyffe Hall* (London: Weidenfeld & Nicolson, 1998), p. 146.

46 Hall, *The Well of Loneliness*, p. 152.

47 Ibid., p. 447.

48 James Douglas, 'A Book That Must Be Suppressed', in *Palatable Poison: Critical Perspectives on The Well of Loneliness*, ed. Laura

Doan and Jay Prosser (New York: Columbia University Press, 2001), p. 38.

49 Charlotte Wolff, *Love Between Women* (New York: Harper & Row, 1971), p. 224.

50 Quoted in Haney, *Naked at the Feast*, p. 174.

51 Bennetta Jules-Rosette, *Josephine Baker in Art and Life: The Icon and the Image* (Chicago: University of Illinois Press, 2007), p. 80.

52 Rose, *Jazz Cleopatra*, p. 161.

53 Marjorie Garber, *Vice Versa: Bisexuality and the Eroticism of Everyday Life* (New York: Simon & Schuster, 1995), p. 65.

54 Haney, *Naked at the Feast*, p. 201.

55 Ibid., p. 202.

56 Baker and Bouillon, *Josephine*, p. 103.

57 Baker and Chase, *Josephine*, p. 204.

58 Donald Wyatt, quoted in ibid., p. 203.

59 'Panthéonisation de Joséphine Baker', Élysée (website of the President of France) (23 August 2021), https://www.elysee.fr/emmanuel-macron/2021/08/23/pantheonisation-de-josephine-baker.

4. NEITHER:
CLAUDE CAHUN'S JERSEY

1 Hal Foster, 'L'Amour faux', *Art in America* (January 1986), p. 118.

2 Terry Castle, 'Husbands and Wives', *London Review of Books* 29:4 (13 December 2007), https://www.lrb.co.uk/the-paper/v29/n24/terry-castle/husbands-and-wives.

3 Claude Cahun, *Disavowals*, trans. Susan de Muth (Cambridge, MA: MIT Press, 2007), pp. 151–2.

4 Kate Bornstein, *Gender Outlaw: On Men, Women, and the Rest of Us* (New York: Vintage Books, 1995), pp. 4, 104–5.

5 Cahun, *Disavowals*, p. 183.

6 T. S. Eliot, 'The Love Song of J. Alfred Prufrock', in *Prufrock and Other Observations* (Project Gutenberg, 1998), https://www.gutenberg.org/ebooks/1459.

7 Cahun, *Disavowals*, p. 13.

8 Alfred Douglas, 'Two Loves', in *'Two Loves' and Other Poems: A Selection* (East Lansing, MI: Bennett & Kitchel, 1990), p. 1.

9 François Leperlier, *Claude Cahun: L'Exotisme intérieur* (Paris: Éditions Fayard, 2006), pp. 30–31. Unless otherwise indicated, all translations from the French, here and in later notes, are my own.

10 Rupert Thomson, *Never Anyone But You* (London: Corsair, 2018), p. 202.

11 Gertrude Stein, *The Autobiography of Alice B. Toklas* (New York: Vintage Books, 1933), p. 202.

12 Shari Benstock, *Women of the Left Bank: Paris, 1900–1940* (Austin, TX: University of Texas Press, 1986), p. 219.

13 Cahun, *Disavowals*, p. 1.

14 Ibid., p. 9.

15 Ibid., p. 14.

16 Ibid., p. 9.

17 Jennifer L. Shaw, *Exist Otherwise: The Life and Works of Claude Cahun* (London: Reaktion Press, 2017), p. 100.

18 Cahun, *Disavowals*, p. 200.

19 André Breton, 'Second Manifesto of Surrealism', in *Manifestoes of Surrealism*, trans. Richard Seaver and Helen R. Lane (Ann Arbor, MI: University of Michigan Press, 1972), p. 128.

20 José Pierre (ed.), *Investigating Sex: Surrealist Research 1928–1932*, trans. Malcolm Imrie (London: Verso, 2011), p. 5.

21 Claude Cahun, 'Réponse à la revue *Inversions*', in *Écrits*, ed. François Leperlier (Paris: Jean Michel Place, 2002), pp. 481–2.

22 Leperlier, *Claude Cahun*, p. 240.

23 Cahun, *Disavowals*, p. 12.

24 Jean (Hans) Arp, 'Notes from a Dada Diary', in *The Dada Painters and Poets: An Anthology*, ed. Robert Motherwell (Cambridge, MA: Harvard University Press, 1981), p. 223.

25 Jack (Judith) Halberstam, *In a Queer Time and Place: Transgender Bodies, Subcultural Lives* (New York: New York University Press, 2005), pp. 36–7.

26 Claude Cahun, 'Lettre à Gaston Ferdière', in *Écrits*, ed. Leperlier, p. 666.

27 Ibid., p. 667.

28 Ibid., p. 700.

29 Cahun, *Disavowals*, p. 152.

30 Walt Whitman, 'On the Beach at Night Alone', in *Leaves of Grass* (London: David Bogue, 1881), p. 207.

31 Cahun, 'Lettre à Gaston Ferdière', p. 668.

32 Ibid., p. 668.

33 Ibid., p. 673.

34 Claude Cahun, 'Confidences au miroir', in *Écrits*, ed. Leperlier, p. 581.

35 Cahun, 'Lettre à Gaston Ferdière', p. 678.

36 Ibid., p. 679.

37 Ibid., p. 682.

38 Ibid., p. 694.

39 Cahun, 'Confidences au miroir', p. 609.

40 Claude Cahun, 'Lettre à Paul Levy', in *Écrits*, ed. Leperlier, p. 748.

41 Shaw, *Exist Otherwise*, p. 236.

42 Cahun, 'Lettre à Paul Levy', p. 721.

43 Marcel Moore, 'Correspondence between Marcel Moore and Claude Cahun', 1944, Claude Cahun Collection, Jersey Heritage, JHT/1995M/00045/22.

5. EXILE:
JAMES BALDWIN BETWEEN AMERICA
AND FRANCE

1 James Baldwin, *The Cross of Redemption: Uncollected Writings*, ed. Randall Kenan (New York: Pantheon Books, 2010), p. 195.

2 David Leeming, *James Baldwin: A Biography* (London: Viking Press, 1994), p. 197.

3 James Baldwin, 'No Name in the Street', in *The Price of the Ticket: Collected Non-fiction, 1948–1985* (London: Michael Joseph, 1985), p. 453.

4 Eldridge Cleaver, *Soul on Ice* (London: Jonathan Cape, 1968), p. 110.

5 Randall Kenan, *James Baldwin* (New York: Chelsea House, 1994), p. 123.

6 Katherine McKittrick, 'On Plantations, Prisons, and a Black Sense of Place', *Social and Cultural Geography* 12:8 (December 2011), p. 948.

7 Magdalena J. Zaborowska, 'House as Archive: James Baldwin's Provençal Home', *032c* (11 April 2019), https://032c.com/magazine/house-as-archive-james-baldwins-home.

8 Thomas Chatterton Williams, 'Breaking into James Baldwin's House', *New Yorker* (28 October 2015), https://www.newyorker.com/news/news-desk/breaking-into-james-baldwins-house.

9 Heather Love, *Feeling Backward: Loss and the Politics of Queer History* (Cambridge, MA: Harvard University Press, 2007), p. 105.

10 James Baldwin, *Go Tell It on the Mountain* (London: Penguin Classics, 2001), p. 20.

11 Ibid., p. 34.

12 Ibid., p. 60.

13 Ibid., p. 61.

14 Ibid., p. 223.

15 Ibid., p. 255.

16 Kenneth B. Clark, *Dark Ghetto: Dilemmas of Social Power* (Middletown, CT: Wesleyan University Press, 1989), p. 22.

17 James Baldwin, 'The Harlem Ghetto', in *The Price of the Ticket*, p. 1.

18 Baldwin, *Go Tell It on the Mountain*, p. 24.

19 Baldwin, 'The Harlem Ghetto', p. 1.

20 James Baldwin, 'Notes of a Native Son', in *The Price of the Ticket*, p. 128.

21 Ibid., p. 130.

22 Baldwin, *Go Tell It on the Mountain*, p. 106.

23 Ibid., p. 254.

24 James Baldwin, *Giovanni's Room* (London: Penguin Classics, 2007), p. 82.

25 Alain Locke (ed.), *The New Negro* (New York: Atheneum, 1992), p. xxvii.

26 Eric Garber, 'A Spectacle in Color: The Lesbian and Gay Subculture of Jazz Age Harlem', in *Hidden from History: Reclaiming the Gay and Lesbian Past*, ed. Martin B. Duberman, Martha Vicinus and George Chauncey (New York: NAL Books, 1989), p. 318.

27 Langston Hughes, *The Big Sea: An Autobiography* (New York: Hill and Wang, 1996), p. 273.

28 'Hamilton Lodge, No. 710 in Annual Masquerade and Civic Ball', *New York Age* (5 March 1927).

29 Richard Goldstein, 'Go the Way Your Blood Beats: An Interview with James Baldwin', *Village Voice* (16 June 1984), https://www.villagevoice.com/2018/06/22/james-baldwin-on-being-gay-in-america/.

30 James Baldwin, 'Notes for a Hypothetical Novel', in *The Price of the Ticket*, p. 238.

31 Baldwin, *The Price of the Ticket*, pp. ix–x.

32 Ibid., p. xi.

33 Ibid., p. xii.

34 Leeming, *James Baldwin: A Biography*, p. 53.

35 James Baldwin, 'Encounter on the Seine: Black Meets Brown', in *The Price of the Ticket*, p. 35.

36 Quoted in Jordan Elgrably, 'The Art of Fiction No. 78: James Baldwin', *Paris Review* (Spring 1984), https://www.theparisreview.org/interviews/2994/the-art-of-fiction-no-78-james-baldwin.

37 Quoted in Karen Thorsen, *James Baldwin: The Price of the Ticket* (biographical film), 1989.

38 Baldwin, 'No Name in the Street', p. 460.

39 Quoted in Thorsen, *James Baldwin: The Price of the Ticket*.

40 Leeming, *James Baldwin: A Biography*, p. 76.

41 Quentin Crisp, *The Naked Civil Servant; How to Become a Virgin; Resident Alien* (New York: Quality Paperback Book Club, 2000), p. 56.

42 Baldwin, *Giovanni's Room*, pp. 7–8.

43 Ibid., pp. 23–4.

44 Ibid., p. 24.

45 Ibid., p. 27.

46 Ibid., p. 25.

47 Ibid., p. 56.

48 Ibid., p. 78.

49 Ibid.

50 Ibid., p. 114.

51 Quoted in Thorsen, *James Baldwin: The Price of the Ticket*.

52 Goldstein, 'Go the Way Your Blood Beats: An Interview with James Baldwin'.

53 James Baldwin, 'Preservation of Innocence', in *Collected Essays*, ed. Toni Morrison (New York: Literary Classics of the United States, 1998), p. 600.

54 Baldwin, 'No Name in the Street', p. 549.

55 Quoted in Fred L. Standley and Louis H. Pratt (eds), *Conversations with James Baldwin* (Jackson and London: University Press of Mississippi, 1989), p. 197.

56 Baldwin, 'No Name in the Street', pp. 539–40.

57 Baldwin, *Go Tell It on the Mountain*, p. 34.

58 Baldwin, *Giovanni's Room*, p. 76.

59 Williams, 'Breaking into James Baldwin's House'.

6. UTOPIA:
JACK SMITH AND NEW YORK

1   Frank O'Hara, 'Song', in *Lunch Poems* (San Francisco: City Lights Books, 1964), p. 59.

2   George Chauncey, *Gay New York: Gender, Urban Culture, and the Making of the Gay Male World, 1890–1940* (New York: Basic Books, 1994), p. 355.

3   'Laws of New York 1923', § 642 (1923).

4   John D'Emilio, *Sexual Politics, Sexual Communities: The Making of a Homosexual Minority in the United States, 1940–1970* (Chicago: University of Chicago Press, 1983), p. 43.

5   Edmund White, *States of Desire: Travels in Gay America* (New York: Dutton, 1980), p. 233.

6   David Ehrenstein, 'An Interview with Andy Warhol', in *I'll Be Your Mirror: The Selected Andy Warhol Interviews*, ed. Kenneth Goldsmith (New York: Carroll & Graf, 2004), pp. 66–7.

7   Oscar Wilde, *The Soul of Man Under Socialism* (London: Arthur L. Humphreys, 1900), p. 40, https://www.gutenberg.org/files/1017/1017-h/1017-h.htm.

8   Quoted in Mary Jordan, *Jack Smith and the Destruction of Atlantis* (documentary film), 2007.

9   Quoted in Jerry Tartaglia, 'The Perfect Queer Appositeness of Jack Smith', *Quarterly Review of Film and Video* 18:1 (2001), p. 39.

10 Mario Montez, quoted in Jerry Tartaglia, *Escape from Rented Island: The Lost Paradise of Jack Smith* (documentary film), 2017.

11 Jack Smith, 'The Perfect Filmic Appositeness of Maria Montez', in *Wait for Me at the Bottom of the Pool: The Writings of Jack Smith*,

ed. J. Hoberman and Edward Leffingwell (New York and London: Serpent's Tail, 1997), p. 35.

12 Quoted in Jordan, *Jack Smith and the Destruction of Atlantis*.

13 David M. Halperin, *How To Be Gay* (Cambridge, MA: Harvard University Press, 2012), p. 152.

14 Ibid., p. 183.

15 Smith, 'The Perfect Filmic Appositeness of Maria Montez', p. 25.

16 Ibid., p. 26.

17 Quoted in Jordan, *Jack Smith and the Destruction of Atlantis*.

18 Ibid.

19 Smith, 'The Perfect Filmic Appositeness of Maria Montez', p. 26.

20 Ibid., p. 28.

21 Richard Foreman, quoted in Jordan, *Jack Smith and the Destruction of Atlantis*; Amos Vogel, quoted in Constantine Verevis, *Flaming Creatures* (New York: Columbia University Press, 2019), p. 40.

22 Jordan, *Jack Smith and the Destruction of Atlantis*.

23 Susan Sontag, 'Jack Smith's *Flaming Creatures*', in *Against Interpretation and Other Essays* (New York: Octagon Books, 1982), p. 230.

24 Ibid., pp. 230–31.

25 Ibid., p. 227.

26 Verevis, *Flaming Creatures*, p. 34.

27 *Jacobs et al. v. New York* (United States Supreme Court, 12 June 1967).

28 Sylvère Lotringer, 'Uncle Fishook and the Sacred Baby Poo Poo of Art', in *Wait for Me at the Bottom of the Pool*, ed. Hoberman and Leffingwell, p. 107.

29 Ibid., p. 121.

30 Ibid., p. 107.

31 Dominic Johnson, *Glorious Catastrophe: Jack Smith, Performance and Visual Culture* (Manchester: Manchester University Press, 2012), p. 26.

32 Chauncey, *Gay New York*, p. 18.

33 Jack Smith, 'The Astrology of a Movie Scorpio', in *Wait for Me at the Bottom of the Pool*, ed. Hoberman and Leffingwell, p. 55.

34 Jack Smith, 'Belated Appreciation of V.S.', in *Wait for Me at the Bottom of the Pool*, ed. Hoberman and Leffingwell, p. 42.

35 Jack Smith, 'Jack Smith Film Enterprises, Inc.', in *Wait for Me at the Bottom of the Pool*, ed. Hoberman and Leffingwell, p. 149.

36 Ibid.

37 Ehrenstein, 'An Interview with Andy Warhol', p. 66.

38 Ronald Tavel, 'The Banana Diary', in *Andy Warhol: Film Factory*, ed. Michael O'Pray (London: British Film Institute, 1989), p. 84.

39 Robert C. Doty, 'Growth of Overt Homosexuality in City Provokes Wide Concern', *New York Times* (17 December 1963), p. 1.

40 Ibid., p. 33.

41 Gavin Butt, *Between You and Me: Queer Disclosures in the New York Art World, 1948–1963* (Durham, NC, and London: Duke University Press, 2005), pp. 113, 115.

42 D'Emilio, *Sexual Politics, Sexual Communities*, p. 84.

43 Doty, 'Growth of Overt Homosexuality in City', p. 33.

44 Jordan, *Jack Smith and the Destruction of* Atlantis (DVD bonus materials).

45 Lotringer, 'Uncle Fishook and the Sacred Baby Poo Poo of Art', p. 113.

46 Quoted in Jordan, *Jack Smith and the Destruction of Atlantis*.

47 J. Hoberman, 'The Theatre of Jack Smith', *The Drama Review* 23:1 (March 1979), p. 6.

48 Tartaglia, *Escape from Rented Island*.

49 Quoted in Hoberman, 'The Theatre of Jack Smith', p. 7.

50 Ibid., p. 8.

51 Lacey Fosburgh, 'Thousands of Homosexuals Hold a Protest Rally in Central Park', *New York Times* (29 June 1970), p. 1.

52 Gay Liberation Front, 'Christopher Street Liberation Day', 1970.

53 'Editorial', *Come Out!* (14 November 1969).

54 Jack Smith, 'Statements, "Ravings," and Epigrams', in *Wait for Me at the Bottom of the Pool*, ed. Hoberman and Leffingwell, p. 154.

55 José Esteban Muñoz, *Cruising Utopia: The Then and There of Queer Theory* (New York: New York University Press, 2009), p. 172.

56 Lotringer, 'Uncle Fishook and the Sacred Baby Poo Poo of Art', p. 112.

57 Chris Kraus, 'Posthumous Lives', in *Video Green: Los Angeles Art and the Triumph of Nothingness* (Los Angeles: Semiotext(e), 2004), p. 68.

58 Cynthia Carr, 'Flaming Intrigue', *Village Voice* (2 March 2004), https://www.villagevoice.com/2004/03/02/flaming.

59 Ibid.

60 Emma Allen, 'Ephemeral', *New Yorker* (31 August 2015), https://www.newyorker.com/magazine/2015/08/31/ephemeral.

61 Jack Smith, 'What's Underground About Marshmallows?', in *Wait for Me at the Bottom of the Pool*, ed. Hoberman and Leffingwell, p. 137.

62 Jack Smith, Mario Montez and Tony Conrad, 'Jack, Mario, and Tony' (mp3), 1964, https://ubu.com/media/sound/smith_jack/cinemaroc/Smith-Cinemaroc_08-Jack-Mario-And-Tony.mp3.

7. NICHE: KEVIN KILLIAN'S SAN FRANCISCO

1 Quoted in Diarmuid Hester and Kasia Boddy, 'New Narrative Now: A Collective Interview', *Textual Practice* 35:8 (2001), p. 1361.

2 Quoted in Chelsea Hodson, 'The Novel is Dead, Celebrity is a Disease, and More! Jarett Kobek Really Does Hate the Internet', *Literary Hub* (4 February 2016), https://lithub.com/the-novel-is-dead-celebrity-is-a-disease-and-more/.

3 Quoted in 'Kevin Killian, 1952–2019', Bookforum.com (17 June 2019), https://www.bookforum.com/papertrail/kevin-killian-1952-2019-23539.

4 Ibid.

5 Robert Glück, 'Epilogue: Remembering Kevin Killian', *KGB Bar Lit* (1 April 2020), https://kgbbarlit.com/content/epilogue-remembering-kevin-killian.

6 Kevin Killian, *Selected Amazon Reviews: Volume 3* (Athens, OH: Essay Press, 2017), pp. 7, 10, 16, 90.

7 Dia Felix, 'Introduction', in ibid., p. ix.

8 Dodie Bellamy and Kevin Killian, 'Introduction: New Narrative Beginnings 1977–1997', in *Writers Who Love Too Much*, ed. Bellamy and Killian, p. xix.

9 Armistead Maupin, 'A Pleasing Shock of Recognition: On Writing Tales', in *Tales of the City* (New York: Harper Perennial, 2007), p. 376.

10 Armistead Maupin, *Tales of the City*, p. 1.

11 Ibid., p. 262.

12 Ibid., p. 315.

13 Ibid., p. 313.

14 Ibid., p. 13.

15 Kevin Killian, *Bedrooms Have Windows* (New York: Amethyst Press, 1989), p. 105.

16 Ibid., p. 3.

17 Ibid., p. 5.

18 Ibid., p. 11.

19 Kevin Killian, *3841-B 24th Street, The Original Small Press Traffic* (recording), 2017, https://soundcloud.com/john-moore-williams/kevin-killian-3841-b-24th-street-the-original-small-press-traffic.

20 Ibid.

21 Ibid.

22 Carl Wittman, *Refugees from Amerika: A Gay Manifesto, with Notes* (New York: Red Butterfly, 1970), pp. 6–7.

23 Ibid., p. 7.

24 Bruce Boone, 'My Walk with Bob', in *My Walk with Bob* (San Francisco: Ithuriel's Spear, 2006), p. 21.

25 Ibid., p. 31.

26 Ibid., p. 35.

27 Quoted in Earl Jackson Jr, 'Bruce Boone', in *Contemporary Gay Male Novelists: A Bio-Bibliographical Sourcebook*, ed. Emmanuel S. Nealon (Westport, CT: Greenwood Press, 1993), p. 26.

28 Dodie Bellamy and Kevin Killian, 'Introduction', in *Writers Who Love Too Much*, ed. Bellamy and Killian, p. vi.

29 Kevin Killian, *Shy* (Freedom, CA: Crossing Press, 1989), pp. 209, 14.

30 Ibid., p. 4.

31 Ibid., p. 232.

32 Killian, *The Original Small Press Traffic*.

33 Dodie Bellamy, 'My Mixed Marriage', *Village Voice* (20 June 2000).

34 Ibid.

35 Megan Milks, 'Dodie Bellamy's Crude Genius', in *Dodie Bellamy Is on Our Mind*, ed. Jeanne Gerrity and Anthony Huberman (South Pasadena, CA: Semiotext(e), 2019), pp. 26–7.

36 Bellamy, 'My Mixed Marriage'.

37 Dodie Bellamy and Kevin Killian, 'Kevin and Dodie', in *Dodie Bellamy Is on Our Mind*, ed. Gerrity and Huberman, p. 134.

38 Bellamy, 'My Mixed Marriage'.

39 Dodie Bellamy, *The Letters of Mina Harker* (Madison, WI: University of Wisconsin Press, 2004), p. 14.

40 Andrew Durbin, '"A Common Misadventure in Queer Bohemia":
   Kevin Killian (1952–2019)', *Frieze* (18 June 2019), https://www.
   frieze.com/article/common-misadventure-queer-bohemia-
   kevin-killian-1952-2019.

41 Milks, 'Dodie Bellamy's Crude Genius', p. 33.

42 'Activism, Gay Poetry, AIDS in the 1980s', National Poetry Foundation Keynote Address, 29 June 2012 (video), 2012, https://
   www.youtube.com/watch?v=_d6AiUt7R8A.

43 Ibid.

44 Ibid.

45 Bellamy and Killian, 'Introduction', in *Writers Who Love Too
   Much*, ed. Bellamy and Killian, p. xviii.

46 Kevin Killian, *Spreadeagle* (Portland: Publication Studio, 2012),
   p. 56.

47 Eileen Myles, 'A Premature Attempt at the 21st Century Literary Canon', *Vulture* (17 September 2018), https://www.vulture.
   com/article/best-books-21st-century-so-far.html.

48 Kevin Killian, 'SF Stories', *San Francisco Bay Guardian* (16
   October 2012), http://sfbgarchive.48hills.org/sfbgarchive/
   2012/10/16/sf-stories-kevin-killian/.

49 Kevin Killian, 'Jack Spicer's Grave', Poetry Foundation (1 May
   2014),https://www.poetryfoundation.org/harriet/2014/05/jack-
   spicers-grave.

50 Jack Spicer, *My Vocabulary Did This to Me: The Collected Poetry of
   Jack Spicer*, ed. Peter Gizzi and Kevin Killian (Middletown, CT:
   Wesleyan University Press, 2008), p. 164.

51 Jack Gilbert, quoted in Lewis Ellingham and Kevin Killian,
   Poet Be Like God: Jack Spicer and the San Francisco Renaissance
   (Hanover, NH: University Press of New England, 1998),
   p. 84.

EPILOGUE:
SANCTUARY

1 Derek Jarman, *Smiling in Slow Motion: The Journals of Derek Jarman, 1991–1994* (London: Vintage Classics, 2018), p. 43.

2 Derek Jarman, *Derek Jarman's Garden* (London: Thames & Hudson, 1995), p. 53.

3 Derek Jarman, *Blue* (film), 1993.

4 Ibid.

5 Tom Stephan, *21st Century Nuns* (documentary film), 1994.

6 Jarman, *Smiling in Slow Motion*, p. 163.

7 Jarman, *Blue*.

8 Jarman, *Modern Nature*, p. 38.

9 Derek Jarman, *The Garden* (film), 1990.

10 Jarman, *Smiling in Slow Motion*, p. 7.

Acknowledgements

I'm deeply indebted to my agent and friend, Matthew Marland. I couldn't possibly list all he's done for me and the book over the past three years, but suffice it to say without his smarts and support I might not have got out of the starting blocks. I'm also hugely grateful to my editor, Maria Bedford, whose enthusiasm for the book from the very start was a constant source of strength and from whom I have learned so much. Thank you, Matthew and Maria; I hope I've repaid your confidence.

Thanks to the wonderful people at Penguin, who helped me to shape the book and ultimately find its readers: Noosha Alai-South, Matthew Hutchinson, Rebecca Lee, and Dahmicca Wright. Very special thanks to Jeremy Atherton Lin, Seán Hewitt, Chris Kraus, and Isabel Waidner for their kind words of early support. This book probably wouldn't exist without the previous one so I want say thank you again to Dennis Cooper, Daniel Kane, John Waters, and the readers and reviewers of *Wrong* for all they did to support it.

I wrote much of *Nothing Ever Just Disappears* in offices loaned to me by two friends and colleagues at the University of Cambridge: Rebecca Barr and Robert Macfarlane. There was always something strongly symbolic about writing the stories of precarious queer spaces in locations that were only provisionally mine. It also spoke to the necessity of solidarity with the progressive efforts of others: Rebecca is one of the hardest working feminists I know, whose research is anti-sexist and anti-colonial, and for decades Rob has been a passionate advocate for environmental rights. To write my book, a new cultural history of the marginalized and minoritized, in spaces provided by Rebecca and Rob felt absolutely fitting, and I'd like to thank them both for their generosity.

I'm also grateful to Rob for extending the hand of friendship to a very tattooed, initially rather out of place Irishman in Cambridge, for his effervescent words of praise for the book, and much more besides. Thanks to my other colleagues at the University of Cambridge who helped me to find my niche here, especially Kasia Boddy, Raphael Lyne, Geoffrey Maguire, Leo Mellor, Mathelinda Nabugodi, Corinna Russell, David Trotter, and of course David Hillman who agreed without hesitation to bring me into King's College and show me around E.M. Forster's rooms. I also want to thank my students at Cambridge from whom I have learned much – both about this project and about myself.

Many thanks to Alison Chomet at New York University's Fales Library and Special Collections for assisting me once again with archival queries and image reproduction, Louise Downie at the Jersey Heritage Trust for her help navigating the Claude Cahun archive and generously allowing me to reproduce Cahun's artworks, Nicci Obholzer and Susanna Mayor for opening the doors of Smallhythe Place to me on more than one occasion and sharing their expertise, and Daniel Payne at LSE Library for his help promptly acquiring images of Vera Holme, and the other queer suffragettes. I'm grateful to Howard Sooley for allowing me to use his beautiful photographs of Prospect Cottage, which stand at the beginning and end of my journey.

Acknowledgements

The origins of this book lie in *A Great Recorded History*, the queer audio trail of Cambridge I created in 2019 with David Bramwell. I'd like to thank David for making it with me, for his friendship, and his enthusiastic participation in all the hare-brained schemes we cook up together. Thanks to Cambridge residents, Paulina Palmer, Les Brookes, Phil Bales, Alison Hennegan, and Janie Buchanan, who shared their stories with me, and to Sarah Franklin and the LGBTQ+@cam project for supporting the trail at every turn.

Making the Cambridge trail opened up a path that led me to make more audio journeys and encounter new places and people who had a huge impact on me and my thinking. I'm grateful to Dzmitry Suslau and Jevgenija Ravcova of Climate Art, the Rye-curious Tim Redfern and Mel Cohen, and Peter Fillingham, David McAlmont, Brooke Palmieri, Pamela Thurschwell, and Jake Wood who joined me on a queer road trip that became the podcast, *Into That World Inverted*. Thank you to my friend and co-host of that podcast Holly James Johnston for wit, grace, and good humour – quite simply for being exactly who they are.

The Cambridge audio trail was something of a lament for lost queer spaces and also led me to Ema Boswood, Rosie Cooper, Ruth Dorber, Roeland Van Der Heiden, Hanna Wallis, and Celia Willoughby, with whom I set up a provisional queer space in the city. We called it Club Urania – a name steeped in queer history and utopian thinking, and I believe that creating it with my friends was the single most important influence on this book. Queer spaces aren't just found, they're also made; we make them, over and over if necessary until everyone has a place. I send my beloved Uranians and the immensely supportive LGBTQ+ community of Cambridge so much love and gratitude.

The opening notes of the Oscars play-off music have sounded, so I'll wrap up by expressing my heartfelt thanks, without measure or condition, to my family; my friends, Rebecca Groves, Jim Macairt, Sam Nesbit, and Josh Schneiderman; my partner and keeper of the knot, George Mind. *Go raibh míle maith agaibh*. This book is dedicated to Josh Schneiderman, another Nancy boy.

Nothing Ever Just Disappears was researched and written in part with the financial support of a Leverhulme Early Career Fellowship, and additional funding came from the University of Cambridge Faculty of English and the Isaac Newton Trust.

Selections from 'A Walk with Bob' are quoted with the permission of Bruce Boone (thanks Bruce) and selections from Kevin Killian's work are quoted with the permission of Dodie Bellamy (thanks Dodie). 'I can't stand a naked light bulb . . .' quoted in Chapter 1 is taken from Tennessee Williams's *A Streetcar Named Desire* (1947). 'Is it dirty . . .' quoted in Chapter 6 is from Frank O'Hara's 'Song' in *Lunch Poems* (1964). Poems by Vera Holme © Vera Holme, reprinted with permission of the family of Vera Holme; 'J'ai deux amours': Music by Vincent Baptiste Sotto, lyrics by Géo Koger and Henri Eugène Varna. © 1930 Éditions Salabert, a catalogue of Universal Music Publishing Classics & Screen. *International Copyright Secured. All Rights Reserved*. Reprinted by permission of Hal Leonard Europe BV (Italy); Kitty Wells, 'It Wasn't God Who Made Honky Tonk Angels' (Nashville: Castle Studios, 1952). © Lyrics by J. D. Miller; Judy Garland, 'San Francisco' (New York: Capitol, 1961). © Lyrics by Gus Kahn.

Index

Page references in *italics* indicate images.

Abatino, Pepito de 136–7, 140
Abbott, Berenice 120
Abbott, Steve 290–1, 298
Acker, Kathy 232, 272, 276, 295
activism
    AIDS 3, 232, 264, 272, 299, 301
    civil rights 187
    disability-rights 17
    queer 12, 20, 260, 283
Actresses' Franchise League (AFL)
    76, 86, 92
ACT UP (AIDS Coalition To
    Unleash Power) 299, 300–1
AIDS 21, 232
    D'Allesandro and 18, 19
    Jarman and 3, 4, 18–19
    Killian and 272–3, 276, 295–301
    San Francisco and 15, 272–3, 276,
        295–301
    Schulman and 264, 272
    Smith and 262, 264
Alex, Joe 119–20
Allan, Maud 74
Allégret, Marc 138
Allison, Bessie 110
Andy the Furniture Maker 6
Another Mask 152–3
Anthology Film Archives 245

apartments
    Bedford Street, Strand, suffrage
        movement and 87, 95–104
    Cahun and Moore, Notre-Dame-
        des-Champs apartment of,
        Paris 160–1
    Jack Smith, Ludlow St apartment
        of, New York 239, 240, 253, 266
    Jack Smith, Plaster Foundation of
        Atlantis apartment of, New
        York 256–8
    Jack Smith, 21 First Avenue
        apartment of, New York 262–4
    James Baldwin, Harlem family
        apartment of, East 131st Street,
        New York 197–201
    Josephine Baker, Bedford Hotel
        apartments of, East 40th
        Street, New York 140–1
    Josephine Baker, Hôtel Fournet
        apartments of, Montmartre,
        Paris 124–5
    Kevin Killian, San Francisco
        apartments of 288–9, 294–5
    lesbian scene, Left Bank, Paris,
        1920s and 130–2, 160–1
    Spreadeagle, Sam D'Allesandro's
        apartment in 298–9

Arcade, Penny 263–5
Archer-Straw, Petrine 117
Aristotle 21; *The Physics* 26–7
Arp, Hans 168
Artists Space 265
Ashbery, John 231; 'Self-Portrait in a
    Convex Mirror' 3
Asquith, Herbert 80
Association des Écrivains et Artistes
    Révolutionnaires (Association
    of Revolutionary Writers and
    Artists) 168
'At Home' meetings 94–5
Atkinson, Diane: *Rise Up Women!* 77
Atwood, Clare 'Tony' 13, 98–9,
    100–1, 131
Augé, Marc 22
Austen, Jane 85

Baker, Jean-Claude 110; *Josephine:
    The Hungry Heart* 122
Baker, Josephine 13–14, *106*, 107–42
    banana skirt 127–9
    Berlin, *La Revue négre* in 123,
        125–6
    Calder wire sculptures of 129
    Chez Josephine 130
    Colette and 129–30
    danse de sauvage 119–20, 121, 128
    death 142
    excess, committed to idea of
        138–9
    fame 124–5, 129, 140, 142
    Hôtel Fournet, Montmartre,
        rooms in 124–5, 127
    'J'ai deux amours' 137, 142
    'La Baker' 118, 139
    La Folie du jour 126–9
    La Revue négre 111–13, 117–22, 123,
        124, 125–6, 128

Le Beau Chêne 136
    menagerie 125
    Panthéon, remains transferred
        to 142
    Paris and 111–42
    Picasso, models for 129
    Plantation Days 110
    Shuffle Along 110, 141
    US, returns to 108–12, 140–2
    Ziegfeld Follies 106, 111–12, 141–2
    Zouzou 138
Bakhtin, Mikhail 116
Balanchine, George 111
Baldwin, James 14, *186*, 187–224
    alcoholism 212
    Another Country 202
    birth 197
    Chez Baldwin 187–94
    childhood 188, 197–201, 203
    civil rights movement and 188, 220
    depression 212
    Eugene Worth/'Eugene Worth
        syndrome' and 210, 214
    fame 188
    gay and lesbian movement,
        cynicism about 220
    Giovanni's Room 33, 188, 193, 204,
        215–20, 222
    Go Tell It on the Mountain 187–8,
        195–204, 213, 216
    Greenwich Village, move to
        207–9
    Happersberger and 213–14
    Harlem Renaissance and 204–5,
        207
    home, search for somewhere to
        call 204
    homosexuality, struggles with
        188, 194, 195–6, 197, 201, 203, 207,
        208, 209, 210, 214–16, 218–21

Ignorant Armies 209
Just Above My Head 202
labels, critical of 219–20, 222
Left Bank and 212
Loèche-les-Bains and 213–14
misogyny 193–4, 201, 215, 219
nervous breakdown 188
'No Name in the Street' 220
'Notes of a Native Son' 200–1
Paris and 187, 188, 193, 211–18, 220
place, out of 222
rootlessness 188, 191–2, 213, 222
Saint-Paul-de-Vence and 186,
    188–93, 214, 215, 223–4
school 199
'Season in Hell' period 209
'selectively affirmative history-
    making' and 195
self-isolation 221–2
'Stranger in the Village' 213–14,
    221
'a stranger everywhere' 188, 221
suicide attempt 213
women, relationships with 209
Ballets Russes 117
Barnes, Djuna 114, 131; *Ladies
    Almanack* 135
Barney, Natalie 131–3, 135, 136, 161
Barn Theatre 102
Bataille, Georges 161
Batterie Lothringen, Jersey 180
Beach, Sylvia 130, 132–3, 161–2
Beats 250–1, 302
Beauvoir, Simone de 212, 220
Bechet, Sidney 115
Bedford Street, Strand 87, 95–6, 97,
    104
Bellamy, Dodie 290–5, 294, 298, 303,
    304; *The Letters of Mina Harker*
    292, 294

Bell, Clive 66
Belle Époque 155
Bell, Vanessa 65, 66
Bentley, Gladys 205
Berlin 123, 125–6, 182
Beyoncé 128, 129
Birrell, Augustine 77, 78
bisexuality 12
    Baker and 13, 14, 110, 111, 116, 118–24,
        129–30, 135–6, 137, 138–40
    Bentley and 205
    Colette and 129–30
    Craig and 91
    excess and 123–4, 138–40
    sexual orientation categories and
        139–40
Black Power 20, 259
Blaser, Robin 302
Bloomsbury, London 30, 64–7, 95
Bloomsbury Group 13
Bonheur, Rosa 85
Boone, Bruce 283, 284, 292; 'My
        Walk with Bob' 285–7, 288
'borderline life' 153
Bornstein, Kate 153
Boy George 147
Brandt, Bill 57
Breton, André 161, 163–4, 166–7, 169
Brice, Fanny 111, 142
Bricktop 115, 136
Brighton 11, 28, 36, 40–1, 55, 156
Browning, Todd: *Freaks* 247–8

Cahun, Claude 14, 131, 144, 145–84,
    222
    Baker and 154, 160, 175
    birth (Lucy Renée Mathilde
        Schwob) 155
    Breton and 163–4, 166–7, 169
    childhood 155

Cahun, Claude – *cont'd.*
  Disavowals 152–3, 154, 162–4, 165,
    173
  fame 151–2
  family background 155
  gender identity 152–4
  homosexuality and homosexuals,
    opinion on 164
  Jersey Archive and 157–8, 160,
    165–6, 172, 183–4
  Jersey, arrival in 149, 171
  Jersey, love of 150, 175
  Je tends les bras 166, 167, 168, 172
  La Rocquaise and 171–5, 176, 181,
    183
  Left Bank lesbians and 161–2
  Les Jeux uraniens (Uranian
    Games) 156
  masks/mask-wearing and 154–5,
    157, 158, 160, 162–3
  Moore and 149, 151, 153, 154, 156–7,
    160–1, 165–6, 170, 171, 172, 175,
    176, 177–8, 180, 181, 182–4
  nature, fascination with/desire to
    connect body with 166, 167,
    168–9, 172–3
  Paris apartment 160–1
  Paris, flees to 149, 160
  prison 181–4
  queer artworks 169–70
  Second World War and 149,
    175–83
  Self-portrait (with leopard skin) 169
  self-portraits, photographic 144,
    151–2, 158, 159, 160, 166, 172
  surrealism and 148, 149, 151, 163–4,
    166–9, 172, 178, 182
  transgender icon 152–3
Calder, Alexander 129
Cale, John 239
Calypso, Greenwich Village 209
Cam, River 27, 41, 47
Cambridge
  author and 8–10, 11–13, 16–17, 40–2
  constraints of space in 11–12, 40–2
  Forster and 9, 10, 13, 24, 27–30,
    40–8, 52–9, 66, 83, 104, 116, 192,
    290
  place responsiveness and 11–13
Cambridge University
  Girton College 46–7
  Hellenism and 13, 27–8, 29, 47–56,
    91, 156, 257, 280
  King's College *see* King's College,
    Cambridge
  liberal, questioning atmosphere
    within 46
  Newnham College 46–7
  religious tolerance in 46
  tutorial at 48
  women at/misogyny and 46–7
camp 15, 287, 289
Campbell, Bobbi 296
Capote, Truman: *Other Voices, Other
    Rooms* 33
carnivalesque 116
Carpenter, Edward 9, 36–7, 38, 40,
    101, 102, 203; *My Days and
    Dreams* 36–7
Carr, Cynthia 264
Castle, Terry 152
Cat and Mouse Act (1913) 97
CBGB's, Bowery, New York 232
Cedar Tavern, Greenwich Village,
    New York 231
Certeau, Michel de 104
Chamberlain, Wynn 250
Charles, Jacques 121
Charleston House, Sussex 66
Chateau, Camberwell 8

Chauncey, George 229, 248
Chez Josephine, Montmartre 129, 130
Churchill, Lady Randolph 88
Churchill, Winston 88
Clam House, 133rd Street, New York
    205
Clark, Kenneth 198
Cleaver, Eldridge 188, 221
Clinton, Bill 299, 301
Clinton, Hilary 299
Club Hot Cha, 134th Street, New
    York 205
Cockin, Katharine 92
Cocteau, Jean 127
Cohler, Deborah 73
Cold War (1946–91) 230
Colette 129–30, 132, 155
Colin, Paul 124–5
Collins, Keith 6
Colma, California 271, 301–3
Colman Smith, Pamela 87, 96, 102
Colston Hall, Bristol 77
Conrad, Tony 239, 249, 266
Cooper, Dennis 271–2, 295
Covid-19 16–18, 262–3
Craig, Edith 'Edy' 13
    acting career 87–8
    Actresses' Franchise League
        and 76
    A Pageant of Great Women,
        producer of 83, 88
    Atwood and 98–100, 101, 102
    Bedford Street home 87, 95–8
    family background 87, 91–2, 97
    How the Vote Was Won, director
        and producer of 92–3, 95
    photograph of 84
    sexuality 75, 91
    Smallhythe Place and 99, 100,
        101, 102

St John and 87, 90–2
    subversion of domesticity 64, 87,
        95–8, 99, 100, 101, 102
    suffrage movement, becomes
        involved in 91–2
    Woolf and 88
Creative Folkestone 7
Crenshaw, Kimberlé 194
Crisp, Quentin: *The Naked Civil
    Servant* 215, 217
Cullen, Countee 199, 204, 205, 207
'Cult of the Clitoris' 74
Cummings, E. E. 129
Curie, Marie 85
Curzon, George 49

D'Allesandro, Sam 290–1, 297, 299;
        'Nothing Ever Just Disappears'
        18–20
dadaism 149, 160, 168, 178
Dance Magazine 110
danse de sauvage 119–20, 121, 128
Daven, André 120, 122
Davies, Christian 85
Davison, Emily 76
Dean, Tacita 6
Debord, Guy 228
De Carlo, Yvonne 235
Dehn, Mura 120
Delaney, Beauford 207–10
D'Emilio, John: *Sexual Politics,
    Sexual Communities* 230
D'Oyly Carte Opera Company 62, 75
Derval, Paul 126
Diaghilev, Sergei: *His Rite of Spring*
    117
Dickens, Charles 199, 288
Donne, John
    'The Good-Morrow' 16–17
    'The Sunne Rising' 310–11

'double identification' 236

Douglas, Lord Alfred 'Bosie' 43, 44, 45, 74, 161
   'Two Loves' 156

Douglas, James 134

Downie, Louise 165, 183–4

drag 8, 148, 206, 247, 288, 296, 312

Duncan, Robert 302

Durbin, Andrew 294

Ebert, Roger 30

Eliot, T. S.: 'Love Song of J. Alfred Prufrock' 155

Ellis, Havelock 134; *Studies in the Psychology of Sex* 73–4, 103

Emery ('Embry') Jones, Florence 115

Evers, Medgar 188

Factory, New York 231–2, 252–3, 255, 256, 262

fandom, gay 235–8

Fauré, Jeanne 188–9

Feinstein, Dianne 296–7

Felix, Dia 275

feminism 13, 81–2, 83, 86, 97, 98, 104, 163, 194, 232, 260

Fiacre, Paris 212, 216

First World War (1914–18) 13, 28, 58, 66, 98, 100, 103, 113, 134

Fitzgerald, F. Scott 114, 116

Fitzwilliam Museum 55–6

Flanner, Janet 120–1

Flatiron district, San Francisco 231

Folies Bergère, Paris 126–9, 130, 160

Forster, E. M. 20, 24, 24, 25–59, 118, 222
   A Room with a View 27, 32
   'Albergo Empedocle' 54
   Cambridge and 9, 10, 13, 24, 27–30, 40–8, 52–9, 66, 83, 104, 116, 192, 290
   closeted, mousy character 46, 83, 104–5
   gives up writing novels 58
   'a great unrecorded history', on queer past as 9, 59, 194–5
   Greenwood and 35–40, 42
   Hellenism and 13, 27–8, 47–55
   'Howards End' 27, 32
   King's College, Cambridge, accepted to study classics at 43
   King's College, Cambridge, rooms at 27–8, 42, 56–8, 66, 192, 290
   Maurice 25–7, 28–33, 34–6, 38–40, 42–3, 45–8, 50, 51–2, 55, 56
   'psychic landscape' for, Cambridge's geography as 41–2
   The Longest Journey 53
   'The Other Side of the Hedge' 34–5
   Wilde and 43–6

Foster, Hal 148

Foucault, Michel 63, 116

Francine, Francis 241, 250, 253

Gabin, Jean 138

Garber, Eric 205

Garber, Marjorie 139–40

gay
   conservatism 20–1
   economy 260–1
   fandom 236–8
   fixed position of 222
   liberation 14, 15, 32, 215, 230–1, 258–61, 283
   marriage 22
   metropolitan 169

shame 195, 200, 216, 220–2
word 206
Gay Liberation Front (GLF) 32,
    259–60
gender
    gendered spheres 63–4
    learned behaviour of 148
    'outlaw' 153
    pronouns 153–4
    stereotypes 14, 215
    studies 152
gentrification 8, 40
    Manhattan 246
    of the mind 300–1
    San Francisco 15, 276, 295, 300–1
George V, King 76
Gershwin, George 140
Gide, André 155, 156
    The Counterfeiters 161
    The Immoralist 31
Gielgud, John 99
Gilbert and Sullivan 62, 75
Gilbert, W. S. 62, 75
Gilmore, Buddy 115
Ginsberg, Allen 302
Girton College, Cambridge 46–7
Gladstone, Barbara 265
Gladstone Gallery 265
Glück, Robert 274, 283, 284, 285–6,
    287, 288–9, 291, 292
Gordon Square, London 65–6, 95
Grant, Beverly 249, 253
Grant, Duncan 66
Great Depression 171, 198
Greece, ancient 13, 27, 28, 29, 47–56,
    91, 156, 257, 280
    love in (*paiderastia*) 27, 50–1, 54,
    156, 280
Greenwich Village, New York 32,
    202, 207–11, 229, 231–2, 258, 262

Greenwood, The 35–6, 38–40, 42
Grindr 7

habitus 116
Halberstam, Jack 169
Hall, Radclyffe 72–3, 102, 131–5, 162;
    The Well of Loneliness 31, 33, 72,
    82, 103, 133, 135, 162
Halperin, David M. 236
Hamilton, Cicely 13, 64, 76, 84, 85–8,
    97–8, 102
    A Pageant of Great Women 83, 85,
    88, 92
    Diana of Dobson's 85–6
    How the Vote Was Won 92–4, 95
    Life Errant 86
    'The March of the Women' 87
Hamilton Lodge 'masquerade' 206
Happersberger, Lucien 213–14
Haring, Keith 238
Harlem, New York 14, 112, 115, 119,
    140, 188, 193, 195, 197, 198–9,
    200, 202, 204–5, 206–9, 211, 212,
    217, 221, 222
Harlem Renaissance 110, 204–5, 207
Hart, Lorenz 140
Haverfield, Lady Evelina 78, 79, 134
Hegel, G. W. F.: *Phenomenology of
    Spirit* 220
Hellenism 13, 27–8, 29, 47–56, 91, 156,
    257, 280
Hell, Richard 232
Hemingway, Ernest 114, 212
Her Upstairs and Them
    Downstairs, Camden 8
heterosexism 32, 37, 42, 202, 204,
    248, 260–1, 284
heterotopia 116
Hillman, David 56–9
Himes, Chester 212

Hirschfeld, Magnus 73
Hitler, Adolf 86, 175, 176, 179, 182–3
Hoberman, Jim 257–8, 264, 265
'Hohlgangsanlage', Jersey 180
Holme, Vera 'Jack' 13, 60, 61–3, 64,
 68–73, 75–80, 82–3, 87, 89, 90, 91,
 97, 102, 134
 actress and singer 69–70, 75, 83,
  111
 A Pageant of Great Women and 83,
  85–6
 appearance 63, 72
 birth 68
 Bedford Street ménage and 102–4
 chauffeur to Emmeline
  Pankhurst 61–3, 68, 80
 childhood 68–9
 Christopher St John, photograph
  of 89, 90
 Craig and 91
 Haverfield and 78–80
 mannish lesbian stereotype and
  72–3
 men's clothing, wears 72–3, 78
 mounted suffragette 79–81
 Radclyffe Hall and 131
 Tipping the Velvet and 70–2
 transgression and 82–3
 women's suffrage movement,
  becomes involved in 75–8
'homosexual' 49
Homosexual League of New York
 230
homosocial space 47
hooks, bell 127
hook-up apps 7
Hope, Bob 111
Hopper, Dennis 252
Hôtel Fournet, Montmartre, Paris
 124–5, 127

House of Commons 80, 92
houses
 Chez Baldwin 187–94
 Le Beau Chene (Baker) 136
 La Rocquaise (Cahun) 171–5, 176,
  181, 183
 Prospect Cottage (Jarman) 1, 3–7,
  23, 173–4, 309–14, 316
 Smallhythe Place (Atwood, Craig
  and St John) 89, 99–103
 20 rue Jacob (Barney) 131–2
 28 Barbary Lane (*Tales of the City*)
  278–9
Howey, Elsie 77
Hughes, Langston 204, 205, 207
 'Jazz Band in a Parisian Cabaret'
  115
 The Big Sea 205
Hypatia 85
Hyperbole Photo Studios 240

icons 72, 85, 132, 134, 152, 160, 235–6,
 274
immigration 10–11, 234, 279–80
International Yves Klein blue 311–12
intersectionality 194
invert 254
 'congenital' 134
 female sexual 103–5, 134, 135
 homosexual 31
'invisible women' 74
Ireland 10–11, 33, 40, 202, 203, 228,
 278, 279–80
Isherwood, Christopher 32

Jacobs, Ken 234, 240
James, C. L. R. 209
Jarman, Derek 298, *308*
 Andy the Furniture Maker and 6
 Blue 4, 311

Index

Caravaggio 4
death 4, 6, 23
Modern Nature 4–5
Prospect Cottage, Dungeness
  and 1, 3–7, 23, 173–4, 309–14, 316
Sebastiane 4
Sisters of Perpetual Indulgence
  and 312–13
Smiling in Slow Motion 5
The Garden 4, 313
The Last of England 313–14
Wittgenstein 312–13
Jazz Age 13–14, 116–17
Jersey 15, 145–84
  Cahun arrives in 149, 171–2
  Cahun's love of 150, 175
  Crown Dependency 150
  French and English identities
    150–1
  La Rocquaise, St Brelade's Bay
    170–5, 176, 178, 181, 183, 306
  Second World War and 175–83
  St Helier 145, 149, 150–1, 154, 157,
    176, 177, 179, 183
Jersey Archive 157–64, 165, 172, 183–4
Jersey Heritage Trust 183
Joan of Arc 85
Johnson, Marsha P. 260
Jones, LeRoi (Amiri Baraka) 231
Jules-Rosette, Bennetta 138
Julien, Isaac 6

Kessler, Count Harry 125
Keynes, John Maynard 46, 66
Killian, Kevin 18, 268, 269–307
  AIDS and 15, 272–3, 276, 295–301
  Amazon reviews 274–5, 276
  Argento Series 298
  autographed head-shots 269

Bedrooms Have Windows 280–1,
    287
  Bellamy and 290–2, 293, 294
  birth and childhood 279–81
  death 271–4, 298
  Internet and 275–6
  'Loveland' 280–1
  Minna Street apartment 294, 295,
    299
  New Narrative and 272–3, 274,
    283–5, 287, 289, 290–1, 297–8
  Poet Be Like God 302
  San Francisco and 15, 269–79,
    281–307
  Shy 287–8, 294
  Small Press Traffic 281–3, 287–8,
    289, 290–1
  Spicer and 272, 302
  Spreadeagle 277, 298–301
  Tagged 273, 304
King Jr, Martin Luther 188, 220
King, Nan 70–2
King's College, Cambridge 24, 29,
    41, 42, 43
  Forster accepted to study classics
    at 43
  Forster's rooms at 27–8, 42, 56–8,
    66, 192, 290
  Hellenism at 47
  homosocial space 47
  liberal, questioning atmosphere
    among students 46
  Maurice and 29, 42, 46, 56
  religious tolerance in 46
  The Longest Journey and 53
  women at/misogyny and 46–7
Kingsley, Charles 49, 50
Kingsway Theatre, London 86
kitsch 233, 287, 304
Kobek, Jarett 274, 276

Krafft-Ebing, Richard von 134
Kraus, Chris 263; *I Love Dick* 272

Lacan, Jacques 161
La Folie du jour 126–9
La Maison des Amis des Livres,
 Paris 130–1, 161
Landshoff, Ruth 125
La Revue nègre 111–13, 117–21, 122, 123,
 124, 125, 126, 128
La Rocquaise, St Brelade's Bay,
 Jersey 171–5, 176, 181, 183
Lavender Scare 254
Leavitt, David 39
Le Beau Chêne, Le Vésinet 136
Leeming, David 210, 214
Left Bank, Paris 130–5, 161, 212
Le Grand Duc, Paris 115
Le Jardin des Arts, Saint-Paul-de-
 Vence 188–9, 191, 222
Leperlier, François 151
lesbianism 9, 20, 31, 33, 67
 Baker and *see* Baker, Josephine
 Bellamy and 291, 292
 'butch' 32, 72
 Cahun and *see* Cahun, Claude
 Harlem Renaissance and 205
 Holme and 72
 Left Bank lesbian subculture
  130–5, 161
 Radclyffe Hall *see* Hall, Radclyffe
 Radicalesbians 260
 Stonewall riots and 231, 259
 suffrage movement and 61–105
 'Trial of the Century' and 74
Les Deux Magots, Saint-Germain-
 des-Prés 212
l'esprit nouveau 114
liberalism 301
Liberation Day (1970) 258–9

Lillie, Beatrice 140, 141
Locke, Alain: *The New Negro* 204–5
Locke, Florence 96
London
 gentrification in 8, 300
 queer spaces disappear in 7–8, 22
 queer suffragettes in 13, 17, 20, 60,
  61–105, 111, 116, 222, 233
London School of Economics 69
Lopokova, Lydia 66
'Lost Generation' 114–15, 212
Love, Heather 194–5
Lulu Belle's, Lenox Avenue, New
 York 205
Lyceum Theatre 62, 87

Mackenzie, Compton: *Extraordinary
 Women* 135
Macron, Emmanuel 142
Malcolm X 188
Malherbe, Suzanne. *See* Moore,
 Marcel
Manet, Edouard: *Un Bar aux Folies
 Bergère* 126
Manhattan, New York 15, 140, 141,
 205
 Jack Smith and 229, 232–3, 242,
  246–7, 258, 261–4
Manhattan Casino, New York 205
Markman, Joel 241, 253
Martin, Agnes 269
masculinity
 aggressive, straight 146–8
 Baldwin and 213, 215, 217–18, 219
 Cahun and 152–3
 Greece, ancient and 27, 49, 50,
  147–8
 lesbians and 73, 78, 86, 103, 131
 masks/mask-wearing 127, 154–7, 158,
  160, 162–3

'master-slave' dialectic 220

Mattachine Society 230, 254

Maupin, Armistead: *Tales of the City*
  277–9, 298

Maurice (film) 25–6, 28–30, 39, 47–8,
  56

Maurice (Forster) 27, 30–3, 34–6,
  38–40, 42–3, 45–6, 50, 51–2, 55

McCarthy, Joseph 230

McKay, Claude 209

McKittrick, Katherine 192

Mekas, Jonas 234, 244, 245, 257, 258,
  267

ménage à trois 95–104

Meredith, Hugh Owen 46

Merrill, George 36, 37–8

Metrograph 239, 265

metronormativity 169–70

metropolitan gay 169

Michelangelo 44

Midsummer Common 41

migration, rural to urban 10, 39,
  169–70

Milks, Megan 294–5

Miller, Henry 209

Millthorpe 36, 37

Milner, Alfred 49

Minnelli, Vincente 111

Miró, Joan 160–1

misogyny 46–7, 48, 50–1, 64, 104,
  193–4, 201, 215, 219

Missy de Mornay 130

Modern Nature 4–5

modernism 65, 130, 131–2, 154, 161

Moffat, Wendy 38, 41, 45–6

Monnier, Adrienne 130–1, 132, 161–2

monogamy 75

monosexual mindset 123–4, 139–40

Montez, Maria 233–8, 240, 241–2,
  249, 253, 254, 260, 263, 266

Moore, Marcel (Suzanne Malherbe)
  131, 149, 151, 153, 154, 156–7,
  160–1, 165–6, 170, 171, 172, 175,
  176, 177–8, 180, 181, 182–4

Motion Picture Production Code
  (Hays Code) (1934) 230, 237

Moulin Rouge, Paris 130

Muñoz, José Esteban 260

Myles, Eileen 232, 274, 289–90

National Union of Women's
  Suffrage Societies (NUWSS)
  75–6

natural spaces, Cahun and 166–7,
  172

Nazism 177, 255

negrophilia 117, 121

New English Art Club 98

New Narrative 272–3, 274, 283–5,
  287, 289, 290–1, 297–8

New Woman 52, 67

New York, US 32, 108–12, 140–2
  author and 227–32
  Baker and 110, *106*, 108–11, *112*, 113,
    115, *119*, 120–1, 140–2
  Baldwin and 14, 187, 188, 193,
    195–6, 197–9, 200, 202, 204–9,
    211, 212, 215–16, 217, 221, 222
  Covid-19 and 262–3
  gentrification 246
  queer scene 229–31
  Smith and 15, 232–67
  Stonewall riots/gay liberation in
    22, 32, 229, 230–1, 258–9
  TV shows and 227–8
  Warhol and 231–2
  See also individual area and place
    name

New York Dolls 232

New Yorker 120–1, 224

New York Times 141, 253, 254, 258
Newnham College, Cambridge 46–7
Nightingale, Florence 85
'non-place' 22
Normandie, SS 108, 112, 140, 142

Obholzer, Nicci 100, 102, 103
O'Hara, Frank 229, 231
Oldenburg, Claes 250
Oppenheim, Méret: *Objet (Déjeuner en fourrure)* 168
Orlando (drag king) 8
Orloff, Chana 161

Pageant of Great Women, A 83–4, 85–6, 88, 92
Pankhurst, Christabel 75
Pankhurst, Emmeline 63, 67, 68, 75, 80, 86, 98
Pankhurst, Sylvia 76, 79–80
Paris, France
    Baker and 13, 14, 111–42, 175
    Baldwin and 187, 188, 193, 211–17, 220
    Cahun and 149, 155–6, 158, 160, 162, 168, 171, 175
    Left Bank 130–5, 161, 212
    See also individual place name
Parker, Dorothy 66
Peace Cottage, Exmoor National Park, Devon 79
Pemberton-Billing, Noel 74
Pettibon, Raymond 273, 295, 304–5
Picasso 129
place
    making of 104–5
    non-place 22, 191
    placelessness 22, 192
    place responsiveness 11–12, 104–5

queer, importance of 7
queered 7, 87
significance of 22
space and 21, 104
symbiotic relationship between person and 116
term 21–3
Plantation Days 110
Plato 27, 44, 47, 52, 91; *Symposium* 48
Poiret, Paul 125, 127
Pollock, Jackson 231
Porter, Cole 115
Pound, Ezra 114
Prima, Diane di 250, *251*, 252
primitivism 121, 128
Prohibition 114, 206–7
pronouns, gendered 153–4
Prospect Cottage, Dungeness 1, 3–7, 23, 173–4, 309–14, *316*
P.S.1 Contemporary Art Center: *Jack Smith: Flaming Creature* 264

Queensberry, Marquess of 43–4
'queer'
    etymology and definition of 3, 7, 20–1
    history, unrecorded 9, 59, 194–5
    modern queer identity, Wilde and 45
    queered places 7
Queercore 300–1
Queer Nation 20–1

Radicalesbians 260
Reagan, Ronald 297
Rechy, John: *City of Night* 33
Reine Blanche, Paris 212, 213
Renault, Mary: *The Charioteer* 33, 218
Rhodes, Cecil 49

Rimbaud, Arthur: 'Season in Hell' 209
Rivera, Sylvia 260
Robeson, Paul 209
Rockland Palace, West 155th Street, New York 205
rooms
    dressing 99, 109–10, 111, 124
    Forster's rooms at King's College, Cambridge 27–8, 42, 56–8, 66, 192, 290
    Giovanni's Room and 193, 217–19, 222
    Holme, boarding room of 71–2
    King, boarding room of 70–1
Rose, Phyllis 121, 138
Roy, Camille 290–1
Royal Academy 98
Royal Army Clothing Depot 99
Royalty Theatre, London 92

Sackville-West, Vita 66, 88, 90, 99, 101–2, 135
Salinger, J. D.: *Catcher in the Rye* 195–6
San Francisco, US 15, 18, 20, *268*, 269–307
    AIDS crisis and 15, 272–3, 276, 295–301
    Club Baths 278
    Cypress Lawn Memorial Park, Colma 271, 301–7
    EndUp 278
    'free territory' 284
    gay ghetto 283–4, 295
    gentrification 15, 276, 295, 300–1
    homelessness in 269–70
    Killian and 15, 269–79, 281–307
    Maupin's *Tales of the City* and 277–9, 298
    Minna Street 294, 295, 299

    New Narrative and 272–3, 274, 283–5, 287, 289, 290–1, 297–8
    Pacific Heights 298–9, 301
    Tenderloin 301
Sappho 85, 132
Sartre, Jean-Paul 212, 220
Savoy Theatre, London 62, 75, 76
Scala Theatre, London 83–4
Schulman, Sarah 264, 272, 300
Schütz, Alfred 221
Schuyler, James 231
Schwob, Marcel 155–6, 161
Schwob, Victorine Mary-Antoinette 155
Scottish Women's Hospital unit, Serbia 72, 134
Scotto, Vincent: J'ai deux amours' 137
screen goddesses, flawed 236–41
Second World War (1939–45) 14, 142, 149, 175–83, 196, 211, 230, 238
separate spheres 80–3, 89
Serra, M. M. 263
sexology 73, 103, 134, 162
sex workers 32, 115
Shakespeare and Company 130–1, 161
Shakespeare, William 44, 56
shame
    Baker and 127, 139
    Baldwin and 15, 195–9, 199, 200, 203, 209, 210, 215, 216, 217, 219, 221
    De Profundis and 45
    Maurice and 33
    queer label and 21
    The Well of Loneliness and 134
Shaw, George Bernard 87–8
Shaw, Jennifer 163
Shaw, Martin 91
Sheppard, Evelyn 110
Shuffle Along 110, 141

Simenon, Georges 120
Simpson, Minna Rae 294
sin 195–7, 200, 201, 203
Sinfield, Alan: *The Wilde Century* 45
Siodmak, Robert 235
Sisters of Perpetual Indulgence 296, 312
Situationism 228
Slade School of Art 98
Slater, Mary Sue 239
slave trade 179, 192
Smallhythe Place, Kent 89, 99–103
Small Press Traffic, San Francisco 282–3, 287, 289, 290–1
Smallwood, Mildred 110
Smith, Ada 115
Smith, Clara 109, 110
Smith, Crickett 115
Smith, Jack 15, 226, 227, 232–67
    anti-capitalism 255–6, 259, 260, 261
    apartments 232–3, 235–6, 239, 253, 256, 262, 264
    Artists Space exhibition 265–6
    childhood 234
    Cinemaroc Studios 252–3, 255
    commercial photographer 240
    death 233, 262, 263, 264
    father's death and 234
    Flaming Creatures 15, 239, 240–6, 243, 247, 248, 249, 252, 267
    gay movement and 254, 260–1
    Jack Smith: Flaming Creature 264
    Jack Smith's Apartment 263
    legacy 263–7
    lexicon 247–8
    'Live Film' events 250, 266
    monologues 265–6
    Montez/Montez-land and 233–8, 240, 241–2, 249, 253, 254, 260, 263, 266

New York, arrival in 233, 239
    Normal Love 248–52, 250n, 251, 254
    performance art and independent film, influence on 232
    Plaster Foundation of Atlantis 256–7
    Sinbad in the Rented World 234, 263
    'superstars' 253
    'The Perfect Filmic Appositeness of Maria Montez' 236
    utopia 233
    Warhol and 252–6
    Waters and 247
    Withdrawal from Orchid Lagoon 257–8
Smith, Pamela Colman 87, 96, 102
Smith, Patti 232
Smyth, Dame Ethel 87, 90, 102
Snell, Hannah 83, 85
social media 7, 269, 273, 274, 275, 276, 300
'society of the spectacle' 228
Somerville College, Oxford 88
Somerville, Jimmy 203–4
Sontag, Susan 244
space
    Aristotelian concept of 27–8
    Baldwin and significance of 193, 204, 205, 208–9, 217–18
    de Certeau definition of 101
    digital 275–6
    domestic 10, 16–17, 19, 87, 94–5, 217–18
    epoch of 63–4
    heterotopia and 116
    homosocial 47
    Lebensraum, or 'living space' 175
    need for/disappearance of queer 7–12, 18–19
    private 13, 17, 63–4, 94, 160

public 10, 17, 41, 52, 94–5
term 21
utopian 39–40
women's enfranchisement and
63–9, 73, 80–3, 98
Spicer, Jack 272, 302–3, 304–5, 306
St Brelade's Bay, Jersey 170–1, 172,
173, 178, 306
Stein, Gertrude 114, 130, 132, 161
Sternberg, Josef von 248
St Helier, Jersey 145, 149, 150–1, 154,
157, 176, 177, 179, 183
St John, Christopher (Christabel
Marshall) 13, 76, 87, 88–101, 89,
102, 131
Bedford Street ménage and 95–104
How the Vote Was Won 92–5
Hungerheart: The Story of a Soul 90,
91
Smallhythe Place and 89, 99, 100–1
The Crimson Weed 90
Stoker, Bram 87, 294
Stonewall Inn riots (1969) 22, 32,
229, 230–1, 258, 259
Strachey, Lytton 30, 31, 32, 66
'stranger' 221
Streetcar Named Desire (film) 57
streets
Cahun's dissident tracts on
streets of Jersey 180, 196
suffragettes and the 63, 64, 67, 72,
76, 80–2, 87, 92, 94, 104
Street Transvestite Action
Revolutionaries 260
Suffrage Atelier 87
suffragette movement 13, 17, 20, 60,
61–105, 84, 89, 116, 118, 131, 163,
222, 233
'Suffragette's Home, A' 95
Sullivan, Arthur 62, 75

Sunday Express 134
surrealism 14, 148, 149, 151, 163–4,
166–9, 172, 178, 182, 212, 287
Swinton, Tilda 4, 6, 313
symbolism 153, 155
Symonds, John Addington 49–51,
54, 91, 156, 280–1; *A Problem in
Greek Ethics* 50

Tatchell, Peter 32
Tavel, Ronald 253, 256
Tavistock Square, Bloomsbury 64–5
Tea, Michelle 272, 274
Terry, Dame Ellen 87–8, 90, 99, 100,
102
Théâtre de l'Étoile, Paris 124
Théâtre des Champs-Élysées, Paris
13–14, 112–13, 117, 121, 124
theatres
Baker and 13–14, 109, 110–11,
112–13, 117, 120, 121, 124, 126, 141
Smith and 256, 261
suffragettes and 13, 69, 75–6, 83,
85–6, 87–8, 90, 92, 99, 102, 163
Third World Gay Revolution 260
Thomson, Rupert: *Never Anyone But
You* 160
Tillman, Lynne 262
Time 141
Times Literary Supplement, The 32
Toklas, Alice B. 130, 132, 161
Tolliver, Michael 277
Tomlin, Stephen 65
topos 27
transgender 32, 152–3, 232, 242–3,
277, 279
Troubridge, Una, Lady 102–3, 131
'trouser role' 69, 83
'twilight men' 74
Tzara, Tristan 161

United Procession of Women 75–6
University College London: Urban
    Lab 7, 8
Uranian poets 156
utopias 15, 33
    Jack Smith and 233, 260
    Greenwood as a 35–6, 38–40, 42
    Millthorpe as a 36–8
    Smallhythe place as a queer
        utopia 89, 99–103

Velvet Underground 232, 239, 252
venues, queer 7–12, 17–18, 22, 205,
    278. *See also individual venue
    name*
Vicinus, Martha 81–2
Vidal, Gore: *The City and the Pillar*
    33, 218
virginity 75, 147
'Votes for Women' campaign 62,
    77–8, 81, 83, 93, 95, 97
Votes for Women 77–8, 80, 92

Waite-Smith tarot deck 87
Warhol, Andy 15, 231–2, 242–3, 250n,
    251, 252–6, 275
    Factory and 231–2, 252–3, 255, 256,
        262
    Mario Banana 253
    Normal Love and 250n, 251, 252
    Screen Tests 255
    Smith and 15, 231–2, 242–3, 250n,
        251, 252–6, 275
    The Chelsea Girls 253
Warren, Chief Justice Earl 244
Waters, John 15, 232
    Pink Flamingos 247
    Role Models 246–7
Waters, Sarah: *Tipping the Velvet*
    70–2

Weeks, Jeffrey 74
Wells, Willie 110
White, Edmund
    A Boy's Own Story 39
    *States of Desire: Travels in Gay
        America* 231
Whitman, Walt 37, 38; 'On the
    Beach at Night Alone' 174–5
Wilde, Oscar 27, 29, 43–6, 47, 50, 73,
    74, 135, 155–6, 161, 233; *De
    Profundis* 45
William the Conqueror 150
Williams, Thomas Chatterton 193,
    194, 224
Wittman, Carl 283–4
Wojnarowicz, David 232, 298
Women's Caucus of GLF-NY 260
Women's Exhibition (1909) 67
Woman's Franchise Movement 76
Women's Freedom League 92, 97
Women's Social and Political Union
    (WSPU) 75–81, 86, 92, 94, 97,
    98
Women Writers' Suffrage League
    (WWSL) 86–7, 92
Woodlawn, Holly 242–3, 245
Woolf, Virginia 102
    Between the Acts 88
    Bloomsbury Group and 65–6
    Mrs Dalloway 299
    Orlando 8, 135
workspaces 17
Worth, Eugene 210, 214
Wright, Richard 212

Zaborowska, Magdalena J. 193
Zedd, Nick 236
Ziegfeld Follies 106, 111–12, 141–2
Zola, Émile 126
Zouzou 138